THE
COLLECTOR'S
BOOK OF
BOOKS

Eric Quayle

Photographs by Gabriel Monro

Clarkson N. Potter, Inc./Publisher NEW YORK

DISTRIBUTED BY CROWN PUBLISHERS, INC.

Published in the United States of America in 1971 by Clarkson N. Potter Inc./
Publisher.

© 1971, in Great Britain, by Eric Quayle and November Books Limited,
London, England.

Library of Congress Catalog Card Number: 71-141776

Printed in Great Britain

Produced by November Books Limited

Contents

An Aubrey Beardsley drawing for the first issue of *The Savoy*, 1896.

Size at outside line:
21cm × 16.2cm.

Coloured Plates

Introduction

I am a bibliophile; an otherwise rational member of the community consumed by a love of books. It gives me pleasure to handle any printed work that has something important to say; but most of all I cherish rare editions, finely printed texts, beautifully illustrated books, and volumes scarce and unprocurable except by knowledgeable means.

The mute but articulate ranks of old leather bindings and time-mellowed spines, that climb in order of size from floor to ceiling in the study where I am now writing, exude a sense of ageless serenity and unruffled calm. Looking at the close-packed rows of octavos and duodecimos that top the polished oak shelves, the 18th-century quartos in their blind-stamped russia immediately below them, then down at the ponderous folios, secure behind their bevelled wooden-boards and coats of sprinkled calf, I am reminded of the decades that have merged into centuries since their original owners unpacked the parcels that brought them home. Now they are here with me, collected in years past from the dispersal of libraries that once knew them as freshly printed books, uncut and unopened (and sometimes for generations unread), waiting their first visit to the binder before the family embrace of book-plate and shelf-mark. They have stood unperturbed through war and disaster, peace and calm, quietly awaiting their next reading. A sense of security pervades old books. George Crabbe called them 'The lasting mansions of the dead'. They have become my faithful and trusted friends and the intimate companions of my everyday life. To part with any one of them disturbs me: to lose them all would translate me to a barren existence and a life lacking its chief intellectual comfort and most relaxing pleasure.

Book-collecting absorbs your interest to an extent that relegates many of the other balms of human existence to second place. Before long you find yourself snatching the illicit half-hour from more mundane concerns, business and domestic, to indulge a passion that the uninitiated deride. For the book lover, once he surrenders to the fascination his hobby exerts over him, begins to resent every leisure hour not devoted to its demands. It becomes an *affaire de coeur* that deepens with each passing year.

The gradual acquisition of a well-chosen library of first and other important editions of English literature, or in the fields of science or the arts, gives a satisfaction that is difficult to equal in any other sphere. The books offered on the shelves and in the catalogues of antiquarian booksellers assume a personality of their own. You begin to look on certain (long-dead) authors as close friends, and on the binding styles of favourite publishing houses with affection. You gradually become the victim of the least vicious of hobbies, and of a pastime that is financially most rewarding.

Book-collecting need not be only a rich man's diversion, or a lucrative investment for those in the six-figure bracket. Everyone, no matter what his income, can have at least a shelf or two of personal favourites in the style of binding in which their original writers would themselves have handled the volumes they created. Not everyone can afford to possess a fine library of several thousand books, but there are still many authors whose first editions can be picked up for small sums, and many subjects in which the pioneer collector can acquire all the key volumes before his rivals pick up the trail.

There is no quicker way to be transported through time than by a half-remembered scent or odour. I know all my best-loved books by their smell, that exciting aroma of old paper, book-binder's glue, and printer's ink. I have

Although a collector usually prefers a copy without inscriptions, the exception is made for an author's presentation inscription or notes of ownership by well known names of the past or present. This copy of the first edition of Oliver Goldsmith's *The Life of Richard Nash*, 1762, was once in the library of George Augustus Sala, who has noted the fact on the title-page.
Size of title-page:
20.3cm × 12cm.

Nash Esq.[r]
ainted by M.[r] Hoare, and
ation of the City of Bath.

THE

LIFE

OF

RICHARD NASH,

Of *BATH*, Efq;

Extracted principally from

His ORIGINAL PAPERS.
By Oliver Goldsmith

―――――*Non ego paucis*
Offendar Maculis.―――― Hor.

The First Edition

LONDON:
Printed for J. Newbery, in St. Paul's Church-yard;
and W. Frederick, at Bath.

MDCCLXII.

only to nose between their leaves for memories to come tumbling back of their discovery in a favourite old bookshop. The attic of a dead uncle, filled with cobwebs, tea-chests, and parcelled three-deckers; a damp cellar in Ireland with Dickens in parts; the red-winey polish of mahogany shelves in a manor-house library that I saved from the auctioneer's hammer to establish the background to a specialist part of my present collection; the locations of my first meeting with strange books are remembered as soon as I open any one of them. Dozens were purchased with money that should have been thriftily squandered on the mundane necessities of our 20th-century existence. Some had to be smuggled into my study (one particularly bulky consignment even disappearing for a time through a trap-door let for inspection purposes into the floor-boards). But my only regret is for those I failed to buy – the volumes I was offered and which I turned down because of price or for fear of the amount of books I was accumulating in a period of high activity. Many of these I am unlikely ever to see again. But the rest are with me here and form the fabric with which *The Collector's Book of Books* is woven.

Once you have started to form your own private library you will find that the pace will quicken. If my own experience as a collector is anything to judge by, or that of many friends absorbed in the same pursuit, you will discover that the more you learn about the hobby the greater your interest in books in general and first or early editions in particular. One never tires of collecting books. The practice is habit-forming. In fact, during the many years since I first admitted to being a bibliophile I can remember no case of a fellow collector giving up and turning his attention to lesser things. The reason why this is so will perhaps become apparent when you have finished reading this present work, which may also help you to avoid having your fingers badly burnt in the school of trial and error.

The intrinsic value of any collection of books entirely depends on the taste and skill of the person who compiled it. The appreciation and understanding of what is of importance in literature, and the specialised knowledge that comes from the intelligent use of works of reference and bibliographies covering the fields you wish to explore, are both augmented by reading books for pleasure.

There are many other aids besides reference books and bibliographies to assist the beginner, the greatest being his constantly increasing contact with the world of rare and important books and texts that have withstood the test of time. By handling and examining books in the fields most interesting to him, whether these are poetry or prose, science or the arts, early children's books or philosophy, or any of the other hundred or so differing aspects of bibliography, he enriches his experience and stores facts and appreciations that will one day be used in assessing a volume's worth. As a private collector he will have a number of advantages over a bookseller who makes a living at the trade. An antiquarian bookseller, dealing with all types of books and every aspect of literature, needs an all-embracing knowledge that spans the entire field in which he deals. A private collector, specialising as most people do, can concentrate his attention on one or more small segments of the entire circle the dealer has to view. Almost inevitably, with the passage of time, he becomes an expert, in some cases a world expert, against whom the professional bookseller stands little chance of winning. For one of the most heart-warming excitements in any sphere of collecting is the 'snapping up of unconsidered trifles', unrecognised by the trade, that your knowledge of the subject has unearthed in a market where you might well have had to pay twice, treble, or ten times the amount asked if the dealer had known as much as you. This is the bonus knowledge and experience brings, both of which may have cost more pounds and man hours than you care to recall.

Those who have the critical ability and foresight to plough a fresh bibliographical furrow, or tread new paths in book-collecting rather than walk the well-trodden ways, are the pioneers who reap the richest financial benefits and the well-deserved plaudits of the followers of the trend they set. Of those books which posterity has condemned unfairly, and which for many generations were thought to have sunk without trace, there is always the hope – rather, the absolute certainty – that some future collector will recognise their worth. Fashion, in the sense of literary appreciation, may have discarded them, but, with the passage of time, they may well depict the age in which the author allowed us a glimpse of his hopes and fears, and the people around him, that would otherwise have gone unrecorded. As such they are of value and demand to be preserved. The works of some long-dead poet or all-but-forgotten author can be rescued by a collector from undeserved oblivion and be brought to the attention of modern scholarship many years sooner than would normally have been the case. The late Michael Sadleir did this with the novelist Anthony Trollope, to an extent that has put the rarer of Trollope's three-decker works into the three-figure bracket as first editions. To a lesser extent he did much the same for many other Victorian writers following the publication of his *XIXth Century Fiction*, issued in 1951. Collectors must not be content to stalk only the majestic giants of literature, or the 'high-spots' and rare ephemera so lovingly clothed in effusive adjectives in the catalogues they receive. By his discoveries in forgotten or unexplored territory he may add something worth while to our knowledge of the past and by doing so he will also add to the sum total of human research and endeavour.

This is one of the several ways in which the book-collector and/or bibliophile can influence literary taste. His library reflects his own individual personality. What one man will seek avidly in every bookshop in the land, crouching over hastily opened catalogues while his breakfast cools on the plate, will leave another completely unmoved. Show a collector of 18th-century poetry an almost complete set of the first editions of Charles Dickens in the original cloth, or Ernest Hemingway, or W. H. Ainsworth, or Benjamin Franklin, or any literary figure, great or small, whose work lies outside the magic and esoteric circle of poets from the reign of Queen Anne (give or take a few years) to that of the turn of the century, and he will have difficulty in evincing any but polite interest. It is rather like displaying to a collector of early motoring books a library devoted solely to the works of the restoration dramatists.

This is one of the many aspects that have attracted me to the hobby of book-collecting: the field is so wide and there are so many facets to examine and by-ways to explore that you never have a chance to lose interest. As one door closes another opens. When an author you have been quietly collecting for many years is re-discovered by the critics, you can sit back and relax, fighting any tendency to say 'I told you so!' Your perception will pay handsome financial dividends as your fellow bibliophiles seek out what you left and then pester you for crumbs. But once your one-time favourite is promoted to a literary high-spot, with all that means in hard cash, then it is time to move on. Either by collecting in a later century – as I did with early children's books when

Engraved title-page and portrait-frontispiece from John Murray's *Johnsoniana; or, Supplement to Boswell,* 1836, a delightful book, containing 45 fine quality full-page plates, and originally issued in boards at 24/- ($2.80). Copies now fetch £75 ($180).

Size of title-page:
22.5cm × 13.5cm.

Pa

This First B
Man's diso
in he was
the Serp
from God
was by th
his Crew
the Poem
with his A
the Center
not made
ter darkn
Angels ly
astonish'd
calls up h
center of
who lay til
their Num
according
Countries
sets them
them. Lastly
orated, an
ven; he
too, was
that the rus
on, he rep
attempt
both ma
Council

the Georgian era was priced out of my market – or by seeking another unknown name of intrinsic worth.

There are two points which I should mention here. I have used as illustrations only books from the shelves of my own library. Choosing a representative cross-section of some 10,000 volumes dating in time from the days of William Caxton to those of Dylan Thomas, and attempting to cover the entire spectrum of English literature within the compass of a single volume, has proved an exacting task in which I have only partly succeeded. I have been forced to ignore too many important titles. Nevertheless, here is at last a work the layman and novice collector can turn to for guidance; with the ground-rules learned, and perhaps his appetite whetted he can later consult the specialised bibliographies that match his taste in books.

The other matter concerns the prices I have quoted for the various works itemised in the text. I debated whether or not to value books subject to such constant upward fluctuations in price that the figures given would certainly be out of date almost before the first edition of this work is sold out.* But the fascination old book-catalogues exert is derived almost wholly from the figures at which the coveted volumes were then offered. 'If only I could have one week to tour the bookshops of the early 1930s!' This present work will tantalise the collectors of the 21st century gifted with the same hindsight I use myself. It was this knowledge that prompted me to place present-day values on good copies of the works I describe. The cautions to be observed when reading the figures I have given are contained in the body of the text, and I do not propose to repeat them here.

Good books are pleasurable things, whatever they cost. But much of the enjoyment in book-collecting is derived from steering one's own course. For then you pit your taste and knowledge against the rest of the world, and your library will mirror your own identity, not that of the professional bookseller who made it for you.

* From the sales of the last few years, a leading auctioneers have estimated that prices of books at auction rise about 10 per cent a year; this can be a guide to future readers wishing to update prices mentioned in the text. American prices correspond almost exactly to English prices in the book market, and I have estimated dollar equivalents by taking 2.4 dollars to the pound sterling.

'Cain and Abel'. One of the woodcut engravings for *Dalziel's Bible Gallery*, 1881, made from a drawing by Sir Frederick Leighton.

Size of engraved portion of plate: 18cm × 15.8cm.

Left
One of the dramatic copperplate engravings from the 1695 edition of John Milton's *Paradise Lost*, published by Jacob Tonson.

Size of engraved surface of plate: 28.5cm × 18.5cm.

Points and Pitfalls

Without being too pedantic, for there are occasions when crusty old bibliophiles can advance abstruse arguments to confound us all, the term *first edition** means the first appearance in print of the work we are examining, independently, and between its own covers, be these of paper, board, vellum, leather, plastic, or what you will. How to recognise the quarry, be it a first or other sought-after edition, is the concern of this chapter. And how to make sure that the book you seek to acquire is complete and in its original pristine condition, or otherwise, is another lesson to be learned.

To the uninitiated it will appear unbelievable that a collector, gifted with the eye of experience, can recognise a first edition at a distance of several feet and be proved wrong on surprisingly few occasions. Having made that observation

* For terms commonly used in the catalogues of booksellers and auctioneers, see Glossary.

Enlargements of portions of the engraved titles of the first edition of *Pickwick Papers,* 1837. On the left is shown the original copper-plate engraving with the mis-spelt 'Veller' title over the doorway. In the re-engraved plate shown on the right, this has been corrected to 'Weller' and the whole plate has been altered and almost completely re-drawn. The first issues of the first edition have the earlier 'Veller' title.

Size of original por-
tion of engraving:
8cm × 5.5cm.

I have to hedge it with a number of qualifications, for by no means all categories of books submit to this test of bibliographical skill and expertise without the most minute examination. Nevertheless, a glance at the drab paper-labelled spine of a boarded book, or the gilded magnificence of fine-ribbed cloth, or the muted splendour of contemporary calf, each in its own way radiating dates and time-scales, is enough to set the trained bibliophile on the scent by evaluating the chances of the text inside matching the promise of the binding. If it does, and the title-page confirms in finer detail the assessment he made when inspecting the exterior appearance of the volume, he can make his first quick collation. If the date on the title-page is correct as being the year to which the book was dated (although in some cases it may actually have been issued earlier or later), he will concentrate on collating the preliminary leaves, the plates – if plates there should be – and the rear-guard of tipped-in advertisements that perhaps constitute an issue point and thus alter the accepted market value of the book. These are generalisations, for the advertisements (if any) can as soon be at the front of the volume as at the end; the plates (if any) may be printed on the text-paper; half-titles and other prelims may not be called for; with several only too obvious faults, the work may be of such absolute rarity that any sort of a copy may be acceptable providing the price asked allows for the state of the lot.

Any collector who wishes to be accorded the respect of his like-minded fellows in the world of books must be able not only to recognise almost immediately, in catalogues and on the shelves, the editions he is seeking for his library (and this pre-supposes a degree of bibliographical know-how), but also to assess their approximate market value. The condition of the book he wishes

to add to his collection is an all important factor in arriving at its financial value, both as regards the state of its binding and in its internal make-up. Let me give an example that I have purposely made extreme. A first edition of, say, Charles Dickens' *The Posthumous Papers of the Pickwick Club,* 1837, re-bound in half-roan about the turn of the century, well-read and marked by generations of page-turning fingers, the binding cracked at the hinges and scuffed, lacking one plate and with the rest foxed, is less than a bargain at £5 ($12), even though it may boast the 'Veller' title (a sign of an early issue). The description I have just given conjures up a horrible vision that will cause a shudder of revulsion in every book-collector who takes pride in the condition of the books on his library shelves. Some take less pride than others; but to a man who insists on his books being in as near original state as possible and seeks them in the form in which the author of the works would himself have first handled them, the copy described above would be anathema. Had it been bound in half-calf or morocco at a date contemporaneous with the book's first appearance, and was collated as being complete with all its plates, it would have been quite acceptable, especially as it was almost surely bound up from the leaves of the original part issue, as most copies with the 'Veller' title are. But the date at which this cheap re-bind was carried out destroys the feel of the age in which the book was first read. The missing plate damns it almost completely, as in even greater measure would a missing page of text. *Never* buy a work that is incomplete. With but few qualifications that rule is always to be kept in mind. The fact that I have given any sort of a price to the *Pickwick* is that it can still be read in the form in which it was originally printed. It may also be of service in making complete another copy of the same issue of the same edition that perhaps lacks a plate, but is otherwise clean and presentable. The foxing on its copperplate engravings can be removed by a method I will describe later in this chapter.

In complete contrast, another copy of the first edition of *Pickwick Papers,* but this time in the publisher's blind-stamped purple cloth, clean and complete, the leaf edges only lightly trimmed as issued, the text firm and unsprung, the plates unfoxed (though with the re-etched 'Weller' title), a very good or nearly fine copy, could be a most desirable purchase at anything less than £100 ($240). The work is one of the great literary achievements of all time, a Rabelaisian fairy-tale of over 300 characters (and over 20 different inns), all created by a young man only 24 years old. With the exception of Shakespeare, English literature can boast of no finer example of a truly creative genius than Charles Dickens, and that this, his first major work should be so comparatively lowly priced, as, in my opinion, are all his first editions, is a transient state of affairs that collectors in a later age will view with envy. Between these quoted figures, £5 and £100, lies a wealth of bibliographical experience, and the poor copy could reduce to £3 ($7.20) and the fine increase to £150 ($360) without the knowledgeable collector having to ask why. Like a driver who has been on the road for many years, and now handles a car almost automatically, so the book-collector of many years' standing almost instantly gets the 'feel' of a volume. In money terms, he can assess its financial worth with an efficiency that auction prices will later confirm, for dealers in books are well aware of the demand amongst private collectors and literary institutions for books in fine original state.

Half a loaf is better than no bread, and it is sometimes necessary to place a copy of a work on your shelves that is below the standard you have set yourself. I always view a book in poor or indifferent condition as merely holding the fort until a replacement can be obtained. Until I can find a better copy there it must stay, supplying a text that can be read but acting as a constant bibliographical irritant. I hope that what I have written above will emphasise to the beginner an aspect of book-collecting that might otherwise result in his having his fingers burnt. The lesson to remember is that the same issue of the same edition of the same title can command a range of prices so wide as to be unbelievable to those not versed in the art. A glance at *Book Auction Records* will reveal this fact in full measure, and this well known guide to the market price of sought-after books must be interpreted with the bibliographical skill that the bibliophile will gradually acquire and then have at his finger-tips for the rest of his collecting days.

A most valuable asset to a book-collector is his own knowledge of literature derived from reading the works he now wishes to acquire in the form of first or other important editions. Coupled with the use of the bibliographical tools that past and present collectors and literary historians have prepared for him, this knowledge enables him to seek out titles that he knows to be worthwhile, rather than to rely on the literary fashions set by others. There are a number of guide-lines that I can lay down to assist the novice collector who is hoping to build up a library of first or early editions of works in the English language, but the titles he selects are a matter of personal choice. I cannot state a set of hard-and-fast rules by which the game can be played, much less give a rule-of-thumb by which a first edition can be recognised with complete certainty. Book-collecting is a satisfying hobby; but membership of the club is of necessity confined to students of literature who possess enquiring minds. For there is a lot to learn and many problems to solve by critical analysis of the facts.

A working acquaintance with the binding styles of the period, and some knowledge of the social and literary cultures of the age in which the books that attract your interest were written, are both of importance. After the 18th century, the external appearance of a book can reveal a great deal about the probable composition of its interior. This rule applies to some extent to books of any age, but with the appearance of publishers' binding styles it takes on a real significance. By studying the dates of the works illustrated in this present volume, and applying that knowledge to the bindings shown, you will realise how quickly binding styles changed, thus enabling the experienced book-collector to approximately date a title-page without having to open the book. The actual date at which any particular book first appeared can only be learned by bibliographical research, and this means turning to the general and specialist bibliographies. In the case of the lesser known author, ignored by bibliographers, one has to do the detective work oneself, visiting the larger reference libraries likely to have copies of his or her works. It is a time-consuming task, but intensely interesting, the title-pages and the advertisements all lending clues to the facts you are seeking. But for the great and not-so-great, and all those who the compilers believe deserve in some measure to be remembered, the *C.B.E.L.* will be the work you will turn to. It is now being re-issued as *The New Cambridge Bibliography of English Literature*; Volume 3, covering the period from 1800–1900, having been published in 1969, with the other volumes in the series to follow later. This most excellent piece of literary scholarship will prove invaluable, giving first edition dates and those of other important or significant editions, and also an indication of the format in which the works were originally issued. This gives the collector such information as the number of volumes in which any particular work first appeared, or details as to part issues, but of course in a work of so wide a scope no collations can be given. For full descriptions of internal and external make-up the specialist bibliographies must be consulted. These cover much narrower fields, many being limited to individual authors, or to some particular aspect of literature, science or the arts. No matter where your interest lies, in drama, poetry, modern first editions, novels, children's books, natural history, Africana, detective fiction, early motoring, the circus, the ballet, pick where you will, there are bibliographies to match the subject. Each with a strictly limited appeal they are sometimes expensive to purchase, many extremely so, especially if they have been out of print for many years. But the larger reference libraries have most bibliographies on their shelves, although there are occasions when a visit to one of the national libraries or university libraries may be necessary.

Let me enumerate some of the points which will enable you to identify a book as a first edition. These points are given in general terms for there are the inevitable exceptions that need not detain us here.

It is essential that you learn the first edition dates of the author, or group of works, that you aim to collect. These dates you discover by consulting bibliographies, biographies, encyclopedias, and other reference works. Personal research will have to be undertaken if the writer you collect has not excited the attention of literary historians and bibliographers. The British Museum catalogue, and that of the Library of Congress, U.S.A., are two fruitful sources of unhoped for facts, as are the university libraries. The advertisements of new and forthcoming books, appearing at or about the time when you suspect your subject first appeared in print, give clues that narrow the field.

The engraved title of the first issue of the first edition of *Martin Chuzzlewit*, 1844, can be identified by the reward notice on the sign-post having the reversed figures '100£', a mistake that was later corrected.

Size of engraved title:
22cm × 13.5cm.

The writer's published works usually carry advertisements of his previously issued books, and once you have discovered his or her publisher you have a most valuable lead. Literary research often means hard work and painstaking enquiries, but the satisfaction of having at last established previously unrecorded bibliographical dates and data repays one handsomely for the efforts involved. You also have a head start in a field unoccupied by the general ruck of book-collectors.

If you are satisfied that the work you are examining was first issued in, say, 1850, and the bibliography you consulted states that it was so dated, then any other printed date of issue later than 1850 appearing in the volume shows it to be of a later edition than the first. This statement must be qualified by the rider that the volume may be of the first edition in the uncommon (but not unknown) circumstance of a late issue of the same setting of type appearing with a date subsequent to 1850. Should our supposed book have the date '1867' on the title-page, on the verso thereof, in the colophon at the end, or elsewhere, as an

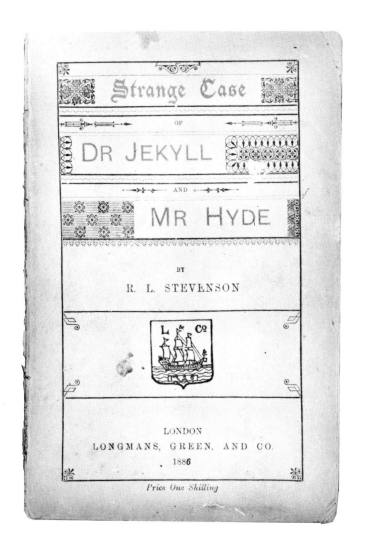

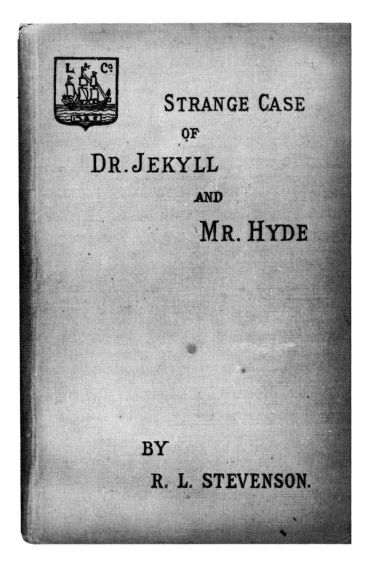

The first and second issues of the first edition of one of Stevenson's most famous works. The first issue, on the left of the picture, was published in printed paper-wrappers. The date upon the front cover was originally 1885, but the last figure was altered by the publishers in ink to '6'. It had been intended to publish the novel in December 1885, but publication was postponed to January 1886, when it was discovered that the bookstalls were already full of Christmas numbers of other works. The second issue, on the right of the picture, was published in a cloth binding, but internally is identical with its neighbour. The New York edition appeared five days earlier than the English edition.

indication of its date of issue, then it obviously cannot be a first edition if the bibliographical information that gave you the date of 1850 is correct. This is all very elementary and perhaps self-evident; but the number of times experienced book-collectors are consulted about books that the hopeful owners believe to be 'firsts' because the words 'second edition' or 'nineteenth edition' do not appear on their title-pages, while a date of some kind does appear, makes me stress the obvious.

The fact that a work was issued in our supposed year of 1850 does not necessarily mean that it will be so dated. If the date in the work of reference consulted is given parentheses '(1850)', this bibliographical device indicates that it was issued without a date on its title-page (and I have followed this when mentioning titles in this work). Broadly speaking most first editions do bear a date; but it is equally true to say that many do not. Certain publishers have their own house rules, dating the first issue but not re-prints from the same type setting. Others, in the past, did not bother to date even the first issue of a work.

The preliminary leaves are usually the most important factors in deciding to which edition a work belongs. To read the words 'Preface to the First Edition' consigns the volume to a later edition, for in the first edition the word 'Preface' is sufficient. Some publishers and authors, especially in the 19th century, reprinted the prefaces that had originally appeared in as many as four previous editions. Other clues are found on the title-page. The words 'Author's edition', 'First published edition' (revealing that a privately printed edition has already appeared), 'Authorised edition', 'First illustrated edition' (or simply 'Illustrated edition'), 'First single-volume edition', or 'Octavo edition', all strongly indicate that a previous edition, or editions, have already appeared. If the plates in the book are dated, and this date precedes (possibly by several years) the date on the title-page, then one must view the volume with suspicion. A Dublin, or foreign, imprint on the title-page of a book that one would have expected to appear first in England, usually means that the book is not of the first edition: but not always, for one can think of a string of titles where the reverse is true and the foreign imprint in fact denotes the first edition. One has to learn these irregular verbs in schoolboy fashion, and the longer you collect the greater the store of miscellaneous facts and figures you have to draw on. The longer you collect the fewer mistakes you make.

In the United States of America a distinguishing mark of a first edition is the date of registration, usually found on the verso of the title-page. If the date on the front of the title-page is, say, 1836, then the legend of entry must carry the same date. In this imagined case it would read in the form of: 'Entered according to Act of Congress, in the year 1836'. If the date given here should be earlier than that on the title-page, then the volume is almost certainly not of the first American edition; and, if the book was first published in the U.S.A. this means it cannot be a first edition. Modern practice is simply to give the Library of Congress catalogue card number. Should the book have been first published in England it is usual to give the copyright date, probably followed by the words 'First American edition' with the date of this publication.

Renovation and repair without the most compelling of reasons is frowned on by the purists, unless the volume is in so tattered a condition that the only way to save the interior from disintegration is a complete re-bind. This must be trusted to experts and the volume sent to a professional binder together with clear instructions as to the manner in which it is to be re-bound. Whenever possible the original fabric of the book should be underlaid and retained. Often a spine has all but disappeared and must be completely renewed, but sometimes, if it is merely detached at one hinge, it can be laid down again by the use of a strip of cloth or leather. When completed by an expert, only the hinges betray that a repair has been carried out. The corners can be dealt with in much the same way. But if in fact the present binding is well on the way to disintegration the book will have to be completely re-bound. Try and choose a binding contemporaneous with the styles in fashion when that particular edition first appeared. In this the binder can usually be relied upon to offer sound practical advice. The services he offers must be paid for, and the work of a craftsman will not be purchased cheaply, especially taking into account the price of present-day fine quality leathers. You may order, in the case of a leather-bound book, a quarter-calf or half-calf (or morocco) binding, rather than a full-leather heavily tooled binding. The saving in cost will be considerable.

Amateur repairs, carried out on cloth or leather bindings, have caused the ruin of many a book. Apart from a few exceptional cases, any attempt to re-bind a volume at home results in a freakish, lop-sided, ill-fitted embarrassment that glares conspicuously from the shelves. Without proper training the task is impossible, and ends up like a home-made dress that always proclaims its short-comings. But there are a few permitted repairs that the owner can carry out. The leather labels that proclaim a book's title and author sometimes loosen and come adrift. A touch of paste and all is well. A cloth or leather binding that is starting to peel from its board can be re-seated by a little adhesive applied by the aid of a cocktail-stick or thin taper. Push the glue-covered stick through an aperture, applying pressure with the finger when it is withdrawn. Remember that a very little glue or paste goes a very long way, especially when replacing a loose plate. Tipped-in illustrations can often be saved from loss and destruction by a timely application of paste, but only a touch on the extreme inside margin. Make sure that all three outside edges are correctly positioned before closing the book.

I always de-fox my own plates, but there were many costly failures before I mastered the technique. Experiment on a worthless copy that would otherwise end in the dustbin until you are confident you know how to carry through the operation. The rules are simple and the satisfaction derived from having removed unsightly blemishes is worth the effort. The tipped-in plate is removed from the volume and placed in a flat dish such as photographers use. Add about one pint of cold or slightly warm water, making sure the whole of the paper is thoroughly wetted. Without pouring directly onto the illustration, add two tablespoons of liquid household bleach, rocking the dish to mix and cover the plate. Within a few minutes the stains will start to fade, but it is inadvisable to wait until all have completely disappeared. With a knife blade raise the plate and slide on to the hand, remembering that wetted paper has lost most of its strength *and must be handled with extreme care*. Rinse on both sides for several minutes under a not too fiercely running tap. In the meantime the cleaned and washed dish has been refilled with a like amount of cold water to which half a teaspoonful of powdered coffee has been added and mixed. Return the plate to the dish for about a minute, then remove and once again rinse thoroughly. Lay on a flat surface to dry, a metal meat-dish placed on a warm surface, or sheet of plate-glass similarly warmed, being ideal. Once dry any slight creases can be removed with a barely warm iron. The plate can then be glued back into place and the book placed under light pressure for several hours. Without the coffee-staining process the paper would appear far too white and glaring, but this treatment tones it down. Experience alone will teach you the exact amounts of bleach to use for the various weights of paper, and the times to be allowed for washing all traces clear. Certain types of paper will need re-sizing, and to do this a little starch is added to the final water used. These instructions have let you into the secret of removing the brown fox marks so often found on plates of early and mid-19th century books. Despite having written this, I most strongly advise any book-collector who values his literary possessions to think twice before embarking on the experiment. Professional book-binders can be trusted to do the job properly and safely, but are likely to charge fairly heavily even for an average octavo size illustration. Coloured plates of any type must never, under any circumstances, be washed or bleached.

Taste and technique in book-collecting are moulded by the activities of eminent collectors and by those of the wealthy university libraries and national institutions, both in Great Britain and in the United States of America. The collector of moderate financial means relies on his own judgement and ability to ferret out, often from the most unpromising places, the books he is after. I would not derive any real pleasure from commissioning an antiquarian bookseller to supply me with a complete set of first editions of an available author (in the sense that Dickens is available – while an all but forgotten writer like R. M. Ballantyne is not) by presenting him with a blank cheque and a time limit of a year or more. Given *carte blanche,* he would do his job and the books would flow to you by the boxful, with occasional pauses while he obtained *Great Expectations*, 3 vols. 1861, in the original cloth, or coveted ephemera that would force an extended time limit. These are the commissions executed on behalf of some of the wealthier American libraries, although the increasing difficulty in obtaining the sought after high-spots, despite almost unlimited funds, has caused horizons to be extended and sights to be lowered. Nowadays the instructions are more likely to read 'All early books on natural history' or 'Minor poets of the 19th century'. The time is rapidly approaching when any early text of a writer who had something individual to say will be appreciated as a volume to grace a library's shelves. Already, books that were once despised and ignored as being unworthy of the bargain box are avidly hunted at prices that would astound the booksellers of the 1930s. For a collector to invest his money in the books which give him pleasure to own, and that is the only valid reason for collecting, is the soundest possible investment for the future.

I started collecting books some 20 years ago, in the sense that about that time I first admitted to being a book-collector and bibliophile. I am constantly adding to my library, despite the fact that I now live in a remote country area. Catalogues keep flowing in, and I make frequent forays to the bookshops within motoring distance, and on my visits to London and the provinces. Occasionally I weed out part of the collection, discarding and selling works of which I have obtained better copies. Unless one has unlimited space and a pocket to match there is the necessity of keeping one's hobby within the bounds of the shelving you have room for. The pleasure is in the collecting. Once you have an author complete (and how rarely that happens) the zest is gone and the time has come to perhaps permit others to share your good fortune and to pass on that part of your collection to an institution where it will be preserved intact. By this means your hobby can be made self-supporting financially; but in my own case my taste is so wide-ranging that I can usually find an excuse for retaining an author collection by marrying it to others in the same *genre.* At the same time, it is comforting to know that you are unlikely to experience the extremes of want while you continue to indulge your passion for books of a quality that make them desirable possessions in the eyes of your fellow men.

The Earliest Printed Books

The Latin word *incunabula* translates literally into the old biblical term of 'swaddling-clothes'. The latter half of the 15th century witnessed the birth of printing, the infancy of the art, and the term 'incunabula' has come to be accepted by bibliographers as denoting books printed before the arbitrary but convenient date of 1500. 'Fifteeners' the Victorians called them, with a familiarity that has now been replaced by a respectful reverence. One no longer rubs shoulders with the distinguished folios and quartos our grandfathers and great-grandfathers seemed to know so well. An era came to an end during the years spanning the gap between World Wars I and II. Until then it had always been possible for a collector of modest means (and I realise this is a comparative term, capable of an infinite variety of interpretations), provided he avoided the 'high-spots' and was gifted with a modicum of good luck and a deal of patience, to gather together a small shelf or two of complete and not too heavily cropped incunabula. Not just the dry-as-dust black-letter Latin texts, but splendidly illustrated examples, complete with the detailed and elaborate woodcuts and the capital flourishes and chapter-headings that the 15th-century craftsmen produced with such meticulous care.

Those halcyon days remain only as a fast-fading memory; a memory that young and not-so-young collectors sometimes have tantalisingly conjured before them by the old-guard of book-collectors sighing over the volumes they failed to buy in the 1920s, or so foolishly sold in the early 1930s. Every age has its consolations. Remember that we, in our turn, have bibliographical opportunities, perhaps hidden in the catalogue that arrives by tomorrow morning's post, or on the shelves of our favourite and most visited antiquarian bookseller. If we only have the know-how and the foresight to perceive them there are bargains to be found today that will arouse the envy of generations of book-collectors still to come. That, in essence, is what this book is all about.

The development of printing in the western world owed comparatively little to the earlier methods employed for centuries in China. Ink of the type used later for printing is known to have been derived from a mixture of lamp-black in China about A.D. 400, and by the 11th century a form of movable type made from hard-baked tablets of clay was in use there. Paper-making had been invented long before this, and the oldest dated printed book extant, comprising the long string of aphorisms known as the *Diamond Sutra,* and dated A.D. 868, is now in the British Museum. It bears little resemblance to books as we know them today, having been printed from wooden blocks on to unsized sheets of mulberry-bark paper. These printed squares were then pasted together to make one long continuous roll, rather like the vellum scrolls used by heralds in the Middle Ages.

It is to a German, Johann Gensfleisch zum Gutenberg (*c.* 1400–68), that we now accord the laurels for the invention of printing by means of movable metal type. Leaving his native Strasbourg, where he had worked on the invention of the printing press for some 20 years, he settled in the city of Mainz. Here he borrowed the capital necessary to promote his enterprise from a local money-lender named Johann Fust. But as soon as the success of Gutenberg's new-fangled invention seemed assured Fust found an excuse to oust him, setting up his own printing workshop with the help of his son-in-law, Peter Schoeffer. It was in this workshop in Mainz, that Fust and Schoeffer supervised the printing of the first complete book known to the western world, the magnificent and noble masterpiece identified as the '42-line' Bible. It is a fitting

Right
A page of text from the earliest printed book in my collection, Thomas Aquinas's Latin version of *The Consolation of Philosophy,* by Boëthius. This edition was printed from movable metal type in 1476, by Anton Koberger, at Nuremberg, Germany. The initial letters were rubricated and added by hand after the book was printed. It is difficult to find incunabula in as clean and complete a condition as the one illustrated.

Total size of page: 37.5cm × 25.5cm.

¶ Sancti thome de aquino sup libris Boecij de consolatione philosophie comentum cum expositione feliciter incipit.

Philosophie seruias oportet vt tibi contingat vera libertas. Hec sunt verba. Senece octaua epistola ad Lucillum · quia vocari philosophiaz scientiam veritatis recte se habet ex secundo methaphisice & philosophia affert delectacones mirabiles firmitate & puritate ex decimo ethicorum. Et multis visa est phia res mirabilis & diuina ex de celo & mudo Aristotelis. Item q̃ nulla scientia similis est philosophie q̃ clarificat animam & facit delectari eam in hoc seculo in perfectione & rectitudine ex libro de pomo & morte. Et philosophia trabit hominé ab obscuritate ignorátie ad scientiam · a tenebris stultitie ad lucem sapientie & ad clantatem intellectus · ex eodem libro Aristotelis. Item q̃ philosophia a superstitione liberat metu mortis ñ oturbat fm Tullium in libro de finibus bonoz & maloz. Ideo Seneca has & consimiles conditiones & effectus laudabiles philosophie aduertens · hortat nos ad seruicuz philoso phie in ppositione pposita sic dicens · Philosophie finias oportet · Que quidem ppositio potest probari multis racombz. Primo sic. Illi oportet seruire p cuiusseruitutem homini cótingit vera libertas · sed philosophia est hmói · igitur · Maior nota · q̃ libertas est nobilissima conditio quá natura humana desiderat & affectat. Minor ptz p cundem Senecam · qui postq̃ premisit ppositoem istá · philosophie finias oportet · subiungit vt tibi cótingat vera libertas · & paucis interpositis dicit · hoc em scz ipm seruire phie libertas est · Probatur secundo sic · Illi oportet seruire quod aim perficit · vitam disponit · actones regit · agenda & obmittenda demó strat & sine quo nemo est securus · philoso phia est hmói · igitur &c · Maior nota · Naz

iste conditones sunt de pfectione hominis Minoz declaraf p Senecam · xvj · epistola ad lucillum loquens de philosophia dicit · Hec animum format & fabricat · vitam disponit · actiones regit & obmittenda demó strat · sed & ad gubernádum errátia · fluctuantiú dirigit cursum · sed sine hac nemo est securus · Probatur terció sic · Illi est seruiendum quod tradit cognitoem vltim finis magnum incrementum · philosophia est hmói · igitur &c · Maior nota · quia cognitio vltim finis magnum incrementum cófert ad vitam ex pmo ethicoz · Minor declaraf Nam vltimus finis vite humane est beatitudo cuius cognitoem philosophia tradit · Dicit em philosophia in tercó de consolatóe prosa secunda · q̃ beatitudo est status oim bonoz aggregatóne perfectus · Et in eodz tercó ostendit philosophia in quo sit vera beatitudo & quó ad eá peniat · Probaf quarto · Illi oportet seruire quod facit hominem parē deo · philosophia est hmói igit &c · Maior nota de se · Minor patet per Senecam · xlix · epistola ad lucillum qui dicit · Hoc em mihi philosophia promittit vt me parem deo reddit · Probatur qnto · Illi est seruiendu quod est magistra oim scietiaz · nutrix oim virtutú · summum solatiú lapsoz animoz · qd est premiú veri luminis & cuius exhortato est recta sui auctoritate digssima · philosophia é hmói · igit &c · Maior nota · q̃ rónabiliter pr has oditones laudabiles alicui seruire · Minor declaraf · Nam phia é magistra oim virtutú ex pmo de ósolatóne prosa tercia · Ipsa est nutrix oim virtutum secudo de consolatóne prosa quarta · Ipsa é summum solatium lapsoz animoz tercó de consolatione pfa pma · Ipsa est premia veri luminis quarto de consolattóne prosa pma · & cuiz exhortatio est recta sui auctoritate digmssima qnto de consolatione prosa pma Sic ergo patet ppositio declarata que dicit · Philosophie seruias oportet · Sed dices res · quid mihi prodest philosophia si fatus est · quid mihi prodest phia si deus rector est · quid mihi prodest phia si casus impat · Ad hoc respondet Seneca · xiij · epistola tribute to the inventor of the process that gave it birth that the work is known throughout the world as the 'Gutenberg Bible'.

Some conception of the task which Fust and Schoeffer set themselves is gained when one realises that no less than six hitherto untried printing presses were employed to print the thick and heavy folio, worked by men who trained themselves in the art by learning from the numerous mistakes they must have made. The task was completed before the late summer of 1456, a date never forgotten by those with a true love of books and the printed word. Peter Schoeffer went on to complete another masterpiece, the Mainz *Psalter,* finished in 1457. He had not been content merely to master the basic principles of the new medium he was employing, but was constantly experimenting with unknown techniques. The *Psalter* reveals a host of fresh innovations. It is the first book printed in colours (most pages having no less than four); the first to have the previously hand-drawn initial letters actually printed on the press; the first to have a distinctive printer's mark; and the first to display a dated colophon. In addition, Schoeffer made a not altogether unsuccessful attempt at printing musical notations.

Within a decade printing presses were to be found in many of the principal towns and cities throughout Europe, and in 1476, William Caxton (*c.* 1421–91), the first English printer, set up his own press in Westminster, London. From 1465 to 1469 Caxton had been governor of the English merchants trading in Bruges, and his interest in literature had led him to begin work on translating the *Recuyell of the Historyes of Troye,* a task he finally completed at Cologne in September 1471. The text of his book was in great demand, and (as he informs us in his 'Prologe') he became determined to master the newly invented art of printing in order to multiply the copies available. It seems certain that about this time he worked in a printing-house in Germany before returning to the Low Countries. But it was in Bruges that he erected his own press, printing on it his translation of the history of Troy (the first book to be printed in English), and also *The Game and Playe of the Chesse,* most probably in 1475.

Shortly afterwards he returned to England and set up a printing press, knowing he had no rival or competitor on that side of the English Channel. Altogether Caxton printed about 100 books in England, using eight different founts of type, the first of which he brought over with him from Bruges (as he may well also have done with the earliest press he used). The first dated book he printed in England was *The Dictes or Sayengis of the Philosophres,* 1477. His first illustrated book appeared *c.* 1480, about three years after his pupil and able assistant, Wynkyn de Worde, whose real name was Jan van Wynkyn, joined him in London. After Caxton's death in 1491, de Worde inherited the business and printed nearly 800 books, including *The Golden Legend,* 1493, *Morte D'Arthur,* 1498, and Chaucer's *Canterbury Tales,* 1498. Caxton is not only remembered as the first English printer, but also for the contribution he made to the formation of an English prose style, having an influence on the early 16th-century and Elizabethan writers who came after him.

The earliest printed book in my own collection dates from the same year that Caxton returned to his native England from the Low Countries. *De Consolatione Philosophiae* was written by a Roman statesman, Anicius Boëthius (*c.* 480–*c.* 524) while he was awaiting execution in a prison cell. Many consider this work to be one of the noblest manifestations of the human spirit, and in the Middle Ages it was one of the most widely read of all philosophical texts. Boëthius was condemned for treason by his Gothic masters, and, after years of imprisonment at Pavia he was executed for asserting the independence of Rome and its citizens. His 'Consolation of Philosophy' enjoyed immense popularity: it was translated into Anglo-Saxon by King Alfred the Great, and into English by Geoffrey Chaucer and by Queen Elizabeth I. Caxton was the first to print the work in English in 1478, but numerous editions have appeared since then. My copy was printed by Anton Koberger, at Nuremberg, Germany, in 1476. I have other early editions, not in Latin as were all incunabula except the Caxton, but in English. Boëthius also wrote a series of diverse and independent works that covered arithmetic, astronomy, geometry, logic, music and philosophical treatises. The most modern edition of his complete works appeared in Paris as long ago as 1860.

Of all the many incunabula that appeared in the short space of years between

Right
Two of the most difficult first editions to find in fine condition in their original cloth bindings. *The Book of Household Management,* 1861, by Mrs Isabella Beeton, and *On the Origin of Species,* 1859, by Charles Darwin.
Height of 'Mrs Beeton': 18.5cm.

Over page
Part of the author's library.

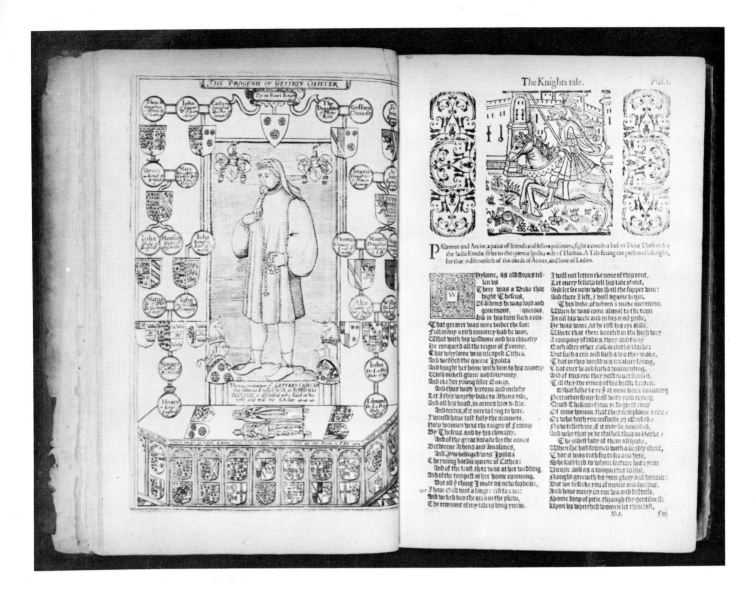

The progenie leaf and a page of text of Chaucer's *Workes*, 1602, edited by Thomas Speght. There are no page numbers, each separate leaf of text being numbered at top right with a folio number.

Size of right-hand page: 31.8cm × 20.5cm.

Left
Part of the author's collection of Victorian 'three-deckers'.

1456 and 1500 the book I would most like to possess is the *Hypnerotomachia* printed by Aldus Manutius; with the Gutenberg *Bible* of 1456, surely the two supreme masterpieces of the art of printing. Aldus finished the book in 1499, nearly the end of the period when an incunabula can boast of impeccable credentials. The *Hypnerotomachia,* a typically medieval story of a lover's sleeping vision, with its woodcuts and dream-pictures of a beauty which haunt the reader long after he has closed the book, is yet gloriously of the Italian Renaissance. The *Bible* of Fust and Schoeffer is sternly and uncompromisingly Teuton, almost Prussian, with the medieval Gothic of its black-letter type-face defying any tendency to the soft worldliness and gracious appreciation of aesthetic taste displayed so wantonly in Aldus's great work. The two books, bracketing the period, seem almost to mark the boundaries of 15th-century human endeavour.

Medieval illuminated manuscripts and the laboriously hand-written texts that preceded the invention of the art of printing with movable metal type are outside the province of this present work. Yet as the fore-runners of the book as we know it today, these fascinatingly beautiful examples of the art of illumination, the text and plates blending together with a harmony seldom equalled in the centuries that have rolled by since their original production, well repay a visit to the university libraries and national museums where most of the finest examples have found a permanent resting place. Those that still come on the market have long been embraced by the four- or five-figure price-brackets that remove them from the sphere of all but a handful of private collectors. Even a single initial letter, pictorially illuminated on emblazoned vellum, but cut from the leaf of text which once accompanied it, can now fetch large sums at auction. Complete works, or even those only partially deficient, are now, almost without exception, the preserve of the larger institutional libraries or else in the air-conditioned strong-rooms of literature's patronal millionaires.

A finely produced facsimile may not content the heart of the fastidious present-day collector, but its possession allows him a pictorial example of the glories of the medieval period and as such fills a gap on his library shelves. Some of the better modern collotype-reproductions themselves cost well over £100 ($240), or as little as £12 ($28.8), while hand-painted 19th-century books devoted to the subject are becoming increasingly difficult to obtain at any realistic price. I have been satisfied to obtain a copy of *Illuminated Illustrations of the Bible: Copied from select MSS of the Middle Ages,* 1846, by J. O. Westwood, a fine copy in heavily gilt publisher's morocco, with 40 plates in gold and colours. In 1866–8 Westwood also issued a large 2-volume folio, entitled *Facsimiles of Miniatures of Anglo-Saxon and Irish MSS,* which now fetches about £60 ($144) at auction. There are numerous other works to choose from, and those produced in gold and colours by the latest present-day printing techniques rival or surpass anything of a similar nature published in the past.

Modern scholarship has set a stricter time-limit to the term accorded to incunabula than did the 19th-century bibliographers. The short period of its genesis they allot to the decades from 1450 to 1480. It was then that the newly fledged printing technicians so assiduously copied the letter-forms used by the scribes and compilers of manuscripts. In the epilogue to his *Recuyell of the Historyes of Troye,* the first book he printed, Caxton was at pains to inform his readers that it was 'not wreton with penne and ynke as other bokes ben'. The birth pangs of printing we witness in the earliest of the incunabula account for their unfailing fascination through the five centuries and more since the first movable metal type was inked in Mainz by pioneers in a craft which now embraces every human endeavour.

Works of reference dealing with the subject are *Repertorium Bibliographicum* (1826–38), by Ludwig Hain; *Index to the early printed books in the British Museum . . . with notes on those in the Bodleian Library,* 1898, by Robert Proctor; *The printers and publishers of the XVth century,* 1902, by Konrad Burger; and the monumental (and as yet unfinished) nine volumes of the *Catalogue of books printed in the XV century,* 1908–62, issued by the British Museum. A reprint of the first eight volumes of this latter work, all of which had long been out of print, was made by the British Museum in 1964, the ninth volume still being available. There are still two further volumes to appear and these are in active preparation. As the holding of incunabula in the British Museum is incomparably greater than that of any other library in the world (a total of 9,349 different volumes have so far been listed) this catalogue is proving of immense value to historians, collectors, librarians and all students of the period. The importance of the British Museum Catalogue as an aid to scholarship is constantly increasing the nearer it comes to completion. It provides us with the only existing geographical survey of the leading presses of the 15th century, and of the books they so painstakingly produced.

William Caxton, the first English printer, in his workshop in Westminster Abbey, in 1480. A bas-relief from the entablature, Jerusalem Chamber, in the Abbey, reproduced in *The Pentateuch of Printing,* 1891, by William Blades.

Novels and Romances

The novel has a wider appeal to the general reading public than any other form of literature. Allowing for the vast difference in the quality of published writing in this art form, we may say that the novel appears to exert an equal fascination over those in the highest and lowest intellectual and social brackets.

In its original form the word 'novel' meant a new or freshly told story, thus distinguishing it from the legends and fables of previous days. It now denotes any fictional prose narrative, as opposed to a story told in verse, and the contents of the tale may be romantic, adventurous, or what you will. The novel still exhibits and mirrors life, both present, past, and future, and displays an unremitting vigour that shows little sign of flagging. Would-be novelists still jostle and clamour for recognition and the manuscripts of the hopeful lie piled in renewing heaps on the tables and desks of publishers the world over.

First and other important editions of those writers who actually made the grade have been sought by collectors for many years. The well-known names and titles that have become household words will be costly acquisitions if looked for in acceptable state in the original bindings. But, speaking in a general sense, they will do little to test the assiduity or book-hunting skill of the private collector. Providing he can afford to pay and is gifted with a certain amount of patience, then the sought-for volumes will eventually appear on his shelves in steadily increasing numbers. Barring a few non-starters, for not even an open cheque-book will corner *The Macdermotts of Ballycloran,* 1847, by Anthony Trollope, or *Wuthering Heights,* 1847, by Emily Brontë, plus a number of other titles that have all but disappeared. The test of a collector's ability comes when he attempts to make a complete collection of the first editions of some hitherto despised or forgotten author for whom no bibliographical catalogue of published titles exists. Even to find the text in any format is difficult enough with many of these unknown or dimly remembered names. No self-respecting bookseller of the past bothered to keep them, except for inclusion in his bargain box. He just had not the shelf-space or the inclination to gamble on them being sought after by generations of collectors as yet unborn. Most of the lesser fry fell early by the wayside, perhaps deservedly so in the majority of cases, with the result that the works their authors struggled so hard to produce were pulped during the paper-salvage drives in two world wars or finished on the garden bonfire. But some escaped, safely hidden in attics, or cared for by elderly owners who looked after the books they had inherited. These are the quarry the present day collector of early novels looks for and hunts down with a persistence that often brings results in an unexpected manner, and for a small expenditure. You need a modicum of luck and a good nose for the scent.

The first woman writer to make a living by her pen in England also contributed some of the earliest novels in much the same form that we recognise them today. Mrs Aphra Behn (1640–89) was a romantic in every sense of the word; lively, good-looking, intelligent and sophisticated, whose coarsely witty plays packed several London theatres in the hey-day of the Restoration dramatists. Her novels, of which the best known is *Oroonoko; or the Royal Slave,* 1688 (first separate printing 1690), are all extremely rare and seldom come on the market. Even the first collected edition of her novels, published in 1696, will now cost a collector well over £100 ($240), but this is only to be expected when the original texts of her individual publications are so difficult to acquire. First collected editions are the form we turn to when thwarted in our hunt for the first editions of an author's works. They are often

27

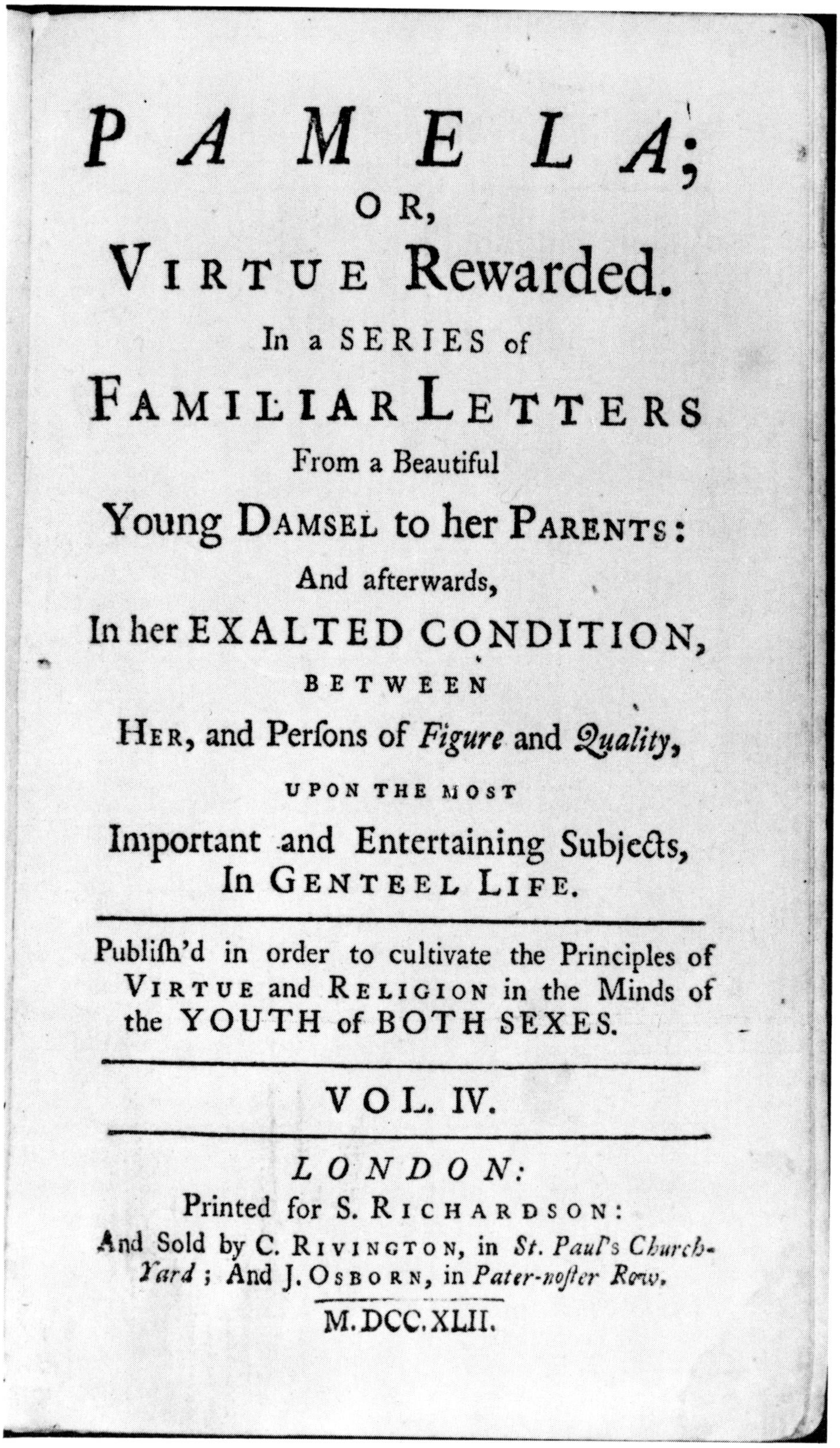

PAMELA;
OR,
VIRTUE Rewarded.
In a SERIES of
FAMILIAR LETTERS
From a Beautiful
Young DAMSEL to her PARENTS:
And afterwards,
In her EXALTED CONDITION,
BETWEEN
HER, and Perſons of *Figure* and *Quality*,
UPON THE MOST
Important and Entertaining Subjects,
In GENTEEL LIFE.

Publiſh'd in order to cultivate the Principles of
VIRTUE and RELIGION in the Minds of
the YOUTH of BOTH SEXES.

VOL. IV.

LONDON:
Printed for S. RICHARDSON:
And Sold by C. RIVINGTON, in *St. Paul's Church-Yard*; And J. OSBORN, in *Pater-noſter Row*.

M.DCC.XLII.

Pamela is described as the first 'true' novel written in English. Volumes 1 and 2 appeared in 1741; volumes 3 and 4 (shown here) in 1742. Size of title-page: 16.3cm × 9.5cm.

finely printed, take a great deal less shelf-space, usually include portrait frontispieces, and are sought in their own right for the historical, biographical and editorial matter they contain. With the earlier writers, poets, and dramatists, they constitute the only format in which a collector of moderate means can afford to purchase an early printing of the texts he requires.

Mention must be made of John Bunyan's *Pilgrim's Progress,* 1678, even though none of us is ever likely to see or hear of a first edition appearing for sale. It is a remarkable work in a number of respects, not the least of which is the impact its simplicity of prose and vivid story-telling made on generations of readers of nearly every nationality. It is a book that has been translated into well over a hundred languages, has appeared in hundreds of differing editions, and is still in print today. I keep my own early 19th-century reprint, with its hand-coloured copperplate engravings, amongst my early children's books, for it was a favourite in the 18th-century playroom long before books for the amusement and pleasure of young people first appeared. The first American edition appeared in Boston in 1681. I doubt if any copy of the 'excessively rare' (to use a phrase beloved by antiquarian booksellers) first edition remains in a privately owned library, and if any freshly discovered copy of the earliest edition does come to light at some future date the competition to acquire it by the largest national institutions on both sides of the Atlantic would be very fierce indeed.

The earliest novel in my own collection is the first 'true' novel written in English. By this I mean a modern novel of character, having the passionate interest that holds the attention of the reader in a way unequalled by fictional scenes of a less intimate nature: a story of human desires frustrated and achieved and telling of man's pursuit of the female. In other words – a love story. Samuel Richardson (1689–1761), set up a printing business in London, and it was here that he produced his first novel *Pamela; or, Virtue Rewarded*, 1741, later followed by a further two volumes dated 1742. This four-volume work constitutes the corner-stone of my collection of novels, but I have to confess that only Volumes III and IV are of the first edition, the first two being of the third edition although still dated 1741. This is commonly the case with this rare work, Volumes I and II being most difficult and costly to acquire in the earliest issues. All four volumes are in full contemporary calf bindings of the period, and in this condition would be worth about £80 ($192). The last copy of the complete set of four volumes, all of the first edition, was sold by auction in the U.S.A. in 1963 and fetched £750 ($1,800). Richardson's other novels are *Clarissa; or, The History of a Young Lady*, which appeared in seven volumes dated 1748; and *The History of Sir Charles Grandison*, 1754, also in seven volumes.

Henry Fielding (1707–54) was not at all impressed by Richardson's work, and is believed to be the anonymous author of a parody called *Shamela*. In 1742 appeared *The Adventures of Joseph Andrews*, but it was the publication of Fielding's great novel *Tom Jones* in 1749, in six volumes, that set the seal on his fame as a writer of prose fiction, as well as contributing so powerfully to the shaping of the character of the English novel. His last novel was *Amelia*, which appeared in four volumes in 1752. He represented the people of his day as warm-blooded human beings, and the characters in his books are alive with the earthy vulgarity of the people he saw around him. I have had all three first editions of his novels in my collection at one time or another. *Tom Jones*, boosted to some extent by the recent film of the same name which apparently introduced the title (if not the novelist) to a section of the public that had never heard of this or any other 18th-century novel (with the possible exception of Defoe's *Robinson Crusoe*, 1719), is now an expensive acquisition in its original six volume form. Copies in contemporary full-leather bindings now fetch about £300 ($720), but it is a delightful book to have and I regret greatly having parted with my own copy. Of Fielding's other works (and he wrote a number of plays, edited periodicals, and contributed largely to the political and social controversies of his day), I refuse ever to barter, swap or sell my copy of the first edition of *The Journal of a Voyage to Lisbon*, 1755, a delightful autobiographical account of a voyage he took when heavy with dropsy and light-hearted with wit. His unfortunate wife, suffering horribly with toothache, accompanied him to Portugal, and the slim little volume contains one of the most vivid accounts of a vain attempt to extract an aching tooth which the 18th century provides. Fielding never returned to England and died before the book was published.

T. G. Smollett (1721–71) was a contemporary of Fielding, and wrote in much the same spirit. His chief novels are *The Adventures of Roderick Random*, 2 vols. 1748, *The Adventures of Peregrine Pickle*, 4 vols. 1751, *The History and Adventures of an Atom*, 2 vols. 1769, and *The Expedition of Humphrey Clinker*, 3 vols. 1771 (with vol. I of the first edition misdated '1671'). The collector must expect to have to pay at least £100 ($240) for the first issue of any of these works.

It was the latter half of the 18th century before the inimitable Laurence Sterne (1713–68) produced his finely spun web of whimsical imaginings entitled *The Life and Opinions of Tristram Shandy*. Denounced for its immorality and capricious literary style by Dr Johnson, Horace Walpole, Oliver Goldsmith, and other established writers, it nevertheless achieved immense popularity. But poor Sterne eventually died penniless in a London lodging-house, leaving his wife and daughter destitute. *Tristram Shandy* presents a number of bibliographical difficulties, not the least of which being that the work appeared in a strung-out series of nine volumes over a period of eight years or more. In 1759 the first two volumes were issued in York, the other seven eventually appearing under London imprints. Volumes III and IV are dated 1761; V and VI 1762; VII and VIII 1765, and Volume IX 1767.

The other work by Sterne which I am pleased to have in my collection is not a novel and really has no place in this chapter. *A Sentimental Journey through France and Italy,* 1768, was written under the pseudonym of 'Mr. Yorick' and issued in only two volumes of the intended four. As an autobiographical tale of sentimental travel it holds its place against any rivals and can be dipped into and read with pleasure and amusement whenever the spines catch your eye. *Tristram Shandy* will now cost the collector of first editions as much as £300 ($720) to acquire. *A Sentimental Journey,* complete with its half-titles, list of subscribers, and with the misprint in Volume II, page 133, reading 'whho ave' (one of the first-issue 'points' made much of by the fastidious), now fetches in the region of £100 ($240). A scarce reprint of 1809 contains two hand-coloured plates in Rowlandson's racy style. It would have been interesting to see how this depicter of life in the flesh interpreted the final paragraphs of Sterne's sudden and intriguing ending.

But the *Fille de Chambre* hearing there were words between us, and fearing that hostilities would ensue in course, had crept silently out of her closet, and it being totally dark, had stolen so close to our beds, that she had got herself into the narrow passage which separated them, and had advanc'd so far up as to be in a line betwixt her mistress and me –

So that when I stretch'd out my hand, I caught hold of the *Fille de Chambre's*

The final full-stop is missing from this and all subsequent editions, so the reader can make his own assumptions.

I have space to mention only the more important works issued in the remaining years of the 18th century. In 1766 appeared Oliver Goldsmith's *Vicar of Wakefield.* It was issued in two volumes at Salisbury, and pirated editions appeared in both Dublin and Cork the same year. To enumerate all the first issue 'points' would take several paragraphs of technical prose, and to acquire the book in worthy state would leave you the richer by the possession of one of the classical works of English literature, and the poorer by some £500 ($1,200) in cash. Goldsmith's masterpiece has attracted the attention of the most accomplished artists and illustrators from the time of Rowlandson to the present day. There is no lack of choice for the collector who requires a finely printed copy, whether he prefers the 18th-, 19th-, or 20th-century format.

The first member of what we may term the romantic school of novelists was Horace Walpole, Earl of Orford (1717–97), whose Gothic story *The Castle of Otranto* was dated 1765. This work marked the tentative beginnings of the romantic revival, introducing a new vein of romance that had its influence on many of the literary pacemakers that followed. Next in line was Clara Reeve (1729–1807) with her book *The Champion of Virtue,* 1777, whose title was later changed to *The Old English Baron,* and which went through eight editions before the turn of the century. The copy I have of the first edition of Ann Radcliffe's *The Mysteries of Udolpho,* 1794, is a fine four-volume set, complete with all the half-titles so often missing in novels of the period that have been through the binder's hands. I bought the work in 1960 for £10 ($24); but the latest cataloguing by a leading London antiquarian bookseller offers it at £120 ($288).

The appearance of Maria Edgeworth's *Castle Rackrent,* 1800, marked the commencement of the 19th century, rich with the genius of writers who have deservedly established themselves amongst the immortals. Jane Austen (1775–1817), despite the fact that her literary work appeared during the seven years bounded by 1811–18, may almost be regarded more properly as belonging in literary style to the late 18th century. Her novels, quietly satirical, appear to look both ways in time. *Sense and Sensibility,* 3 vols. 1811, *Pride and Prejudice,* 3 vols. 1813, *Mansfield Park,* 3 vols. 1814, *Emma,* 3 vols. 1816, and the two separate tales in one issue, *Northanger Abbey and Persuasion,* 4 vols. 1818, will

Opposite page:
Top
Mrs Gaskell's *Life of Charlotte Brontë,* 1857, ranks with the greatest biographies written in the English language.
Size of title-page:
20cm × 12.5cm.

Bottom left
The first issue of the first edition of a book that hastened the outbreak of the American Civil War. Mrs Stowe's famous anti-slavery novel first appeared as a serial in the magazine *National Era* in 1851–2, before publication as a two-volume work.
Size of title-page:
19cm × 12cm.

Bottom right
The title-page of the first English edition of *Uncle Tom's Cabin,* 1852. Within 12 months of the work appearing in America, over 20 pirated editions were issued in Britain. The first into the bookshops bore the imprint of Clarke & Co., but there was no time to incorporate any illustrations (these came later). Notice that the sub-title is incorrect and reads differently from the Boston edition. Other British publishers used the text of Clarke & Co.'s edition for their own pirated versions (except H. G. Bohn & Co.) and therefore made the same mistake.
Size of title-page:
18.5cm × 12cm.

Sincerely yours, C Brontë

THE LIFE

OF

CHARLOTTE BRONTË,

AUTHOR OF

"JANE EYRE," "SHIRLEY," "VILLETTE," &c.

BY

E. C. GASKELL,

AUTHOR OF "MARY BARTON," "RUTH," &c.

> "Oh my God,
> —— Thou hast knowledge, only Thou,
> How dreary 'tis for women to sit still
> On winter nights by solitary fires
> And hear the nations praising them far off."
> AURORA LEIGH.

IN TWO VOLUMES.

VOL. I.

LONDON:
SMITH, ELDER & CO., 65, CORNHILL.
1857.

[*The right of Translation is reserved.*]

UNCLE TOM'S CABIN;

OR,

LIFE AMONG THE LOWLY.

BY

HARRIET BEECHER STOWE.

VOL. I.

BOSTON:
JOHN P. JEWETT & COMPANY.
CLEVELAND, OHIO:
JEWETT, PROCTOR & WORTHINGTON.
1852.

UNCLE TOM'S CABIN;

OR,

NEGRO LIFE

IN THE SLAVE STATES OF AMERICA.

BY

HARRIET BEECHER STOWE.

REPRINTED VERBATIM FROM THE TENTH AMERICAN EDITION.

LONDON:
CLARKE AND CO., 148, FLEET STREET.
MDCCCLII.

tax a collector's ingenuity to acquire in contemporary half-calf bindings, even though they originally appeared in the now almost unobtainable paper-covered boards and uncut edges. The first title mentioned is much the most difficult to find and may well cost as much as £400 ($960) in half-calf. Jane Austen's most famous work, *Pride and Prejudice,* first appeared in America with a Philadelphia imprint in 1832, under the title of *Elizabeth Bennet.*

Sir Walter Scott (1770?–1832) has never been a difficult author to collect in first edition form; he became famous early in his career with the result that most of his works had a first printing of several thousands of copies. Until a few years ago a complete set of his novels, all in the original boards with paper-labels, was by no means impossible. The only title to present any real difficulty was his first novel, *Waverley; or, 'Tis Sixty Years Since,* 3 vols. 1814. This small 12mo, the forerunner of forty or so 'Waverley Novels' that were to follow from his pen, is acknowledged as the archetype of the host of imitators cast in much the same mould. Without being aware of the fact, Scott had established a new literary form; he had brought forth the first historical novel. By setting the characters of the tale against a factual background of well recognised historical events he lent an authenticity to the plot that his readers found a refreshing change from the improbabilities they were expected to swallow in the pages of the Gothic novels of the period. The 20th-century novel, *Gone With the Wind,* 1936, by Margaret Mitchell, uses the same basic construction that Scott employed before the Battle of Waterloo had been fought. After falling from favour his first editions are once again being sought, and they can still be bought comparatively cheaply. Complete with their half-titles and all the etceteras required, but in half-calf rather than in original boards, his three-volume novels now command about £10 to £30 ($24 to $72) apiece, with a first of *Waverley* making in the region of £75 ($180). In the original boards, with uncut edges, I should consider the work a bargain at twice that figure.

To collect with confidence in your own ability to assess their relative worth, it is necessary to evaluate the historical and literary background of the books you wish to shelve with the rest of your library. Read the texts before you buy, for by doing so you allow your own taste to guide you and are not swept along by fashions or fads. To form an author-collection of a prolific writer, with perhaps as many as a hundred books to his credit, it is not necessary to plough your way through several thousand pages of closely printed text in order to come to a conclusion of his or her literary worth. But one must at least make an acquaintance with what the writer has to say, relating it strictly to the age in which the book was written. Literary pioneers in any field of writing were not always able to enrich our heritage with deathless prose, but at least they had something new to say. A Model 'T' Ford gives one a rougher ride than the latest production model, but it is a far more interesting vehicle, whether you are merely inspecting the bodywork or actually taking a journey. I have included this digression in order to illustrate the importance of books that have made an impact on literary style or have pointed the way for those writers who were to follow in later years. *Waverley,* by Sir Walter Scott, is a key book in this respect, and *Guy Mannering,* 1815, *Rob Roy,* 1818, *Ivanhoe,* 1820, *Kenilworth,* 1821, *The Fortunes of Nigel,* 1822, *Quentin Durward,* 1823, *Redgauntlet,* 1824, and *Woodstock,* 1826, are others that deserve a place beside it. All, except *The Fortunes of Nigel* (four volumes), first appeared in three volumes.

James Fennimore Cooper (1789–1851) has been called 'the American Scott', and in youth he listened to the tales of the Indian wars as told by his father Judge William Cooper, himself the author of *A Guide in the Wilderness,* 1810, with the same fervour that kept Walter Scott silent and attentive to the stories of '45. As Scott used his first-hand knowledge of the Highlands and the Borders, so Cooper was to add colour to his father's tales by his own expeditions into the backwoods. *The Pathfinder,* 1840, and *The Deerslayer,* 1841, continue the series of *Leather-Stocking Tales,* as they came to be known, that had commenced with *The Pioneers,* 1823, and continued through *The Last of the Mohicans,* 1826, and *The Prairie,* 1827. Their central character is the rough-and-ready homespun philosopher and backwoodsman Natty Bumppo. Cooper's first novel attempted to mirror domestic life in England and appeared under the title *Precaution,* 1820. *The Spy,* 1821, is a romance of the Revolution set in New York, and saw Cooper writing about the America he knew so well. By the mid-1830s he was internationally famous and his name a household

Right
One of the elegant 19th-century annuals of 1855. Printed in gold, with lithographed plates coloured by hand, the text was by F.W. Bayley. When published by Paul Jerrard, London, in quarto size, they cost '1½ guineas'.
Size of front cover:
37.5cm × 27cm.

THE HUMMING BIRD KEEPSAKE,

A BOOK OF BIRD BEAUTY.

London:
Paul Jerrard, 111, Fleet Street.

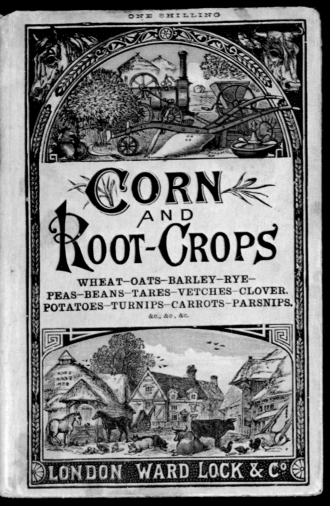

ONE SHILLING

CORN AND ROOT-CROPS

WHEAT—OATS—BARLEY—RYE—
PEAS—BEANS—TARES—VETCHES—CLOVER.
POTATOES—TURNIPS—CARROTS—PARSNIPS.
&c., &c., &c.

LONDON WARD LOCK & Cº

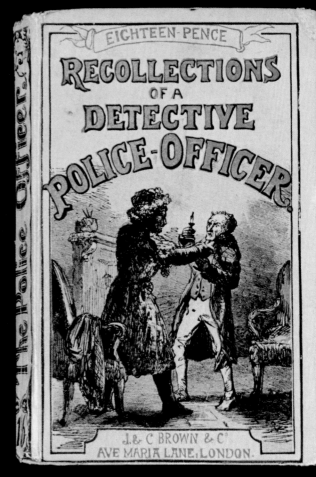

EIGHTEEN-PENCE

RECOLLECTIONS OF A DETECTIVE POLICE-OFFICER

J. & C. BROWN & Cº
AVE MARIA LANE. LONDON.

Pascarel
By Ouida

Chatto & Windus. Piccadilly

Mr POTTER OF TEXAS
BY
THE AUTHOR OF
"Mr BARNES OF NEW YORK"

GEORGE ROUTLEDGE AND SONS

word wherever books were read. He, more than any other writer, created the legend of the Redskin and the Paleface and the countless bow-stringed adventures that continue in Western novels and films to the present day.

Washington Irving (1783–1859) was born in New York but spent nearly a third of his life in Europe, visiting Scott at Abbotsford in 1817. His first essays were published in *Salmagundi*, 1807, a New York magazine that quickly expired. *A History of New York*, 1809, a satire on the city's manners and politics which has become an American classic, was written under the pseudonym of 'Diedrich Knickerbocker'. The work which brought him international fame, *The Sketch Book*, 2 vols. New York, 1819–20, is supposedly written by 'Geoffrey Crayon, Gent'. The first issue now fetches about £50 ($120); while the first English edition of 1820, also in two volumes, realises about half this amount. Most of the essays and stories in this once celebrated collection had only a contemporary value; but two exceptions are *Rip Van Winkle* and *The Legend of Sleepy Hollow*, both early examples of American folk-lore that have never lost their appeal. *Bracebridge Hall*, 1822, in which Irving recalls his visit to an English country house at Christmas time, was followed by *Tales of a Traveller*, 1824, *Legends of the Alhambra*, 1832, and, amongst many other titles that cannot properly find a place in this chapter, *The Life of George Washington*, 5 vols. 1855–9, perhaps his greatest work. Irving was the first American man of letters to be internationally celebrated, and well deserved his fame. Van Wyck Brook's meticulously detailed study, *The World of Washington Irving*, 1946, confirms him as the first 'mid-Atlantic' literary figure, followed by others who include Henry James, George Santayana and T. S. Eliot.

The delights and difficulties of collecting 19th-century fiction have been set out in detail by the late Michael Sadleir in *XIXth Century Fiction*, 1951. From W. H. Ainsworth (1805–82), who alphabetically heads my own collection, through the works of R. D. Blackmore, the Brontë sisters, Bulwer Lytton, William Carleton, Wilkie Collins, Charles Dickens, Conan Doyle, George Eliot, Mrs Gaskell, Thomas Hardy, Henry James, and so on to the end of the alphabet with Mrs Henry Wood, and Emile Zola, there is a field so wide that you need a keen sense of direction to guide your collecting. Unless you possess unlimited shelf-room and the resources to keep filling room after room, then certain disciplines must be observed. To try and collect the lot, even with the limitations imposed by insisting on good to fine copies in original bindings, is to become hemmed in with rising walls of unconsumable fiction. This type of all-embracing acquisition is better left to the British Museum or Library of Congress. The private collector can make his contribution to bibliographical studies by specialising in one or more aspects of novel collecting.

Early in my career as a book-collector I decided to aim at possessing a library of prose fiction that contained a representative selection of first editions of novels that had become household names by reason of their literary worth. These are designated as 'high-spots', and are the most sought after titles in the catalogues of auctioneers and booksellers. Even in the 1950s good copies were fast becoming scarce and expensive, but many I acquired easily enough although there are others that have so far eluded me. Charles Dickens (1812–70) was of course a primary target, but the monthly parts in which so many of his novels were originally issued did not attract me. They are exasperating things to try and read, and usually so flimsy one is afraid to handle them in anything approaching the manner of a book. On the shelves they sag sideways unless enclosed in a presentable cloth-bound box, and they are so bedevilled with points of order that a *Pickwick* in parts, complete and in first issue state, seems all but unique. I am content with firsts of Dickens, and other novelists of the period, in the publishers' original cloth bindings, which were issued as soon as the parts issue was completed. In Dickens' case I have also a set of his novels in contemporary half-calf, bound up from the parts and in which the stab-holes for the (now removed) paper-wrappers can still be seen. These volumes have the first issue points, such as the 'Veller' title for *Pickwick Papers*, 1837; the '100£' sign (instead of the later corrected '£100') on the engraved title of *Martin Chuzzlewit*, 1844; and other too-numerous-to-mention 'points' set out in the various bibliographies of the author. *Oliver Twist*, 1838, appeared first as a three-decker cloth-bound novel (the parts issue coming later) with 24 spirited engravings by George Cruikshank. The first issue of this work has 'Boz' on the

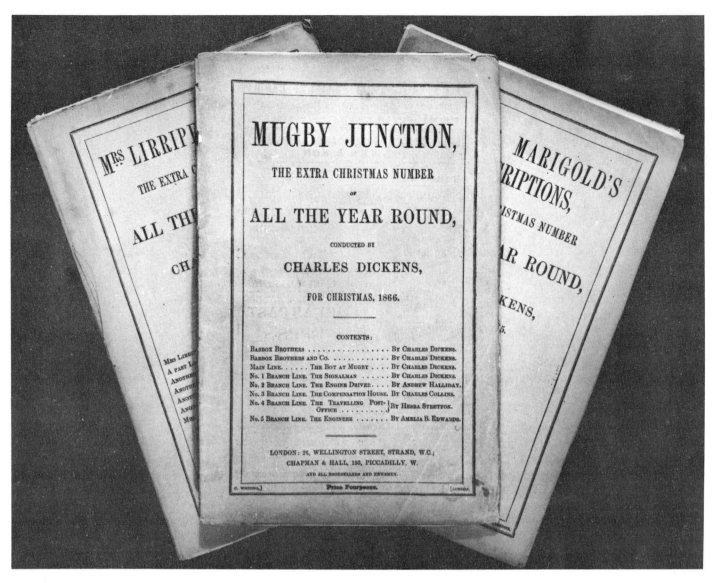

title-page (the pseudonym Dickens sometimes used) but later issues had this leaf cancelled and replaced by one bearing the author's name.

William Makepeace Thackeray (1811–63), who sometimes sheltered behind the pseudonym 'Michael Angelo Titmarsh', I have represented by first editions of *Vanity Fair*, 1848, *The History of Henry Esmond*, 3 vols. 1852, *The Newcomes*, 2 vols. 1854–5, *The Virginians*, 2 vols. 1858–9, and *The History of Pendennis*, 2 vols. 1849–50, amongst his major works and those by which he is remembered by the public at large. Equally enjoyable and harder to find in acceptable state are copies of *The Irish Sketch Book*, 2 vols. 1843, *Notes on a Journey from Cornhill to Grand Cairo*, 1846, *Mrs Perkin's Ball*, 1847, *The Kickleburys on the Rhine*, 1850, *The Four Georges*, 1860, New York (I have the London edition issued the following year), and one of the most difficult 'firsts', *The Paris Sketch Book*, 2 vols. 1840. All these I have in the original cloth, but *Vanity Fair*, *The Newcomes*, *The Virginians*, and *Pendennis*, first appeared in monthly paper-wrappered parts. *Vanity Fair* is a very difficult first edition to find in acceptable condition in the original publisher's cloth, for the tipped-in plates are nearly always badly foxed. Thackeray himself supplied the illustrations to most of his books. The first issue of *Vanity Fair* is now catalogued at over £100 ($240), and has the following points: the headline on page 1 is in 'rustic' type; the woodcut of the 'Marquis of Steyne' on page 336 (later cancelled as being too like a noble member of the British aristocracy); the reading 'Mr. Pitt' on line 31, page 453 (later changed to 'Sir Pitt'); and the full-page advertisement for 'The Great Hoggarty Diamond' on the leaf inserted before the frontispiece. As the book was first issued in 20 monthly parts, the first issue of the first edition can only be found in a volume made up from these parts and bound up by the purchaser (more often than not in half-calf or half-morocco). Copies in the publisher's cloth binding, issued at the end of the part-issue, although much harder to come by, are of the second issue

Three of the paper-wrappered extra Christmas numbers of *All the Year Round*, edited by Charles Dickens.

Size of front wrapper: 24.5cm × 17cm.

Right
Three first editions sought by collectors specialising in the field of early horror-stories: *Vikram and the Vampire*, 1870, the first issue (in black cloth), *Dracula*, 1897 (blood-red lettering on bright-yellow cloth), and *The Book of Were-Wolves*, 1865, by Sabine Baring-Gould.

Size of bottom book: 19.5cm × 13cm.

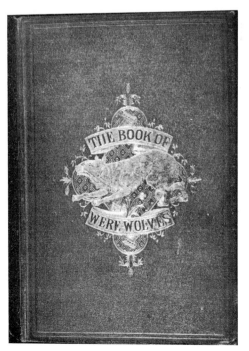

of the sheets, and you will find that the Marquis has disappeared from page 336. But the advertisement leaf before the frontispiece should certainly be present, and I believe that this leaf is more indicative of the second issue than of the first. The same observation applies to Dickens' *Pickwick Papers.* In the original cloth it is an extremely rare book, but you will not find the 'Veller' title as this plate was re-etched by the time the cloth-bound volume was issued.

Political and social novels, sometimes attacking the new industrialism with its too often accompanying poverty, came from the pens of Benjamin Disraeli (1804–81), Charles Kingsley (1819–75), Mrs Gaskell (1810–65), and George Eliot (1819–81). These were the most important figures in the field, with Disraeli setting the pace with his 'Young England' trilogy. *Coningsby, or The New Generation,* 3 vols. 1844, *Sybil, or The Two Nations,* 3 vols. 1845, and *Tancred: or The New Crusade,* 3 vols. 1847, presented the future Earl of Beaconsfield's solutions for the problems confronting the nation. His last two novels, *Lothair,* 3 vols. 1870, and *Endymion,* 3 vols. 1880, are set in the 19th-century corridors of power, but neither seeks to offer political solutions to the affairs of the day. No other writer approached Disraeli's brilliance in using politics as background material for his fictional tales until the advent of C. P. Snow in our own age.

Charles Kingsley is represented in my collection by *Yeast: a Problem,* 1851, *Hypatia: or, New Foes with an Old Face,* 2 vols. 1853, and, in the shelves reserved for children's books, *The Heroes,* 1856, together with the immortal classic by which he is best remembered, *The Water-Babies,* 1863. *Alton Locke,* 2 vols. 1850, published anonymously, as was *Yeast,* was unsuccessful as a novel, but is full of interest for the social picture it projects. *The Water-Babies,* with its refreshingly new plot now fetches anything up to £40 ($96). The first issue has a leaf known as 'envoi' from the wording of its text: this was later cancelled and is not present in later issues of the first edition. But the most successful of all Kingsley's novels was *Westward Ho!,* published under a Cambridge imprint in three volumes in 1855.

Thomas Hughes (1822–96) was the author of *Tom Brown's School Days,* 1857, also published at Cambridge, three editions appearing the same year. His *Tom Brown at Oxford,* 1861, was a three-volume work, but was much less purposive and direct in its impact. *The Scouring of the White Horse,* is the only other work of Hughes I have, with its delightful illustrations by Richard Doyle, always known as 'Dickie' Doyle, and this is a book that can still be picked up for a small amount. In Mrs Gaskell, the wife of a Unitarian minister of Manchester, we have the first novelist to centre her theme around the conflict between management and labour. *Mary Barton, a Tale of Manchester Life,* appeared anonymously in two volumes in 1848, followed by *The Moorland Cottage,* 1850, and *Ruth,* 3 vols. 1853. Elizabeth Cleghorn Gaskell, is best remembered for her *Cranford,* a prose idyll, in which she draws on her childhood memories of Knutsford, in Cheshire. The novel first appeared in 22 weekly parts in *Household Words,* between December and May 1853, appearing in book-form later the same year. It has become one of our minor prose classics, depicting, with a quiet blend of humour and pathos, life in a Cheshire village in the early 19th century. Mrs Gaskell is also to be thanked for writing the two-volume biography of Charlotte Brontë, published by Smith, Elder & Co., in 1857. It is a remarkable work, ranking amongst the best half-dozen biographies written in the English language. As a first edition it is still under-priced and will undoubtedly rise steeply in value.

I have space to touch only briefly on other works in my collection, but mention must be made of George Eliot, the pseudonym of Mary Ann Evans. *Scenes of Clerical Life,* 1858, published in two volumes, is much her rarest and most expensive novel to purchase in first edition form. Thackeray believed the author to be a man; but Charles Dickens had no difficulty in identifying the female hand behind the pen. The 'scenes' are composed of three separate short stories, *Amos Barton, Janet's Repentance,* and *Mr Gilfil's Love Story,* the latter being one of the best short stories ever written in English. In 1859, her *Adam Bede* appeared, this time in three volumes, and it fully lived up to the expectation aroused by her earlier works. The last copy to come under the hammer fetched £60 ($144), more than the £42 ($100.8) paid for *Scenes of Clerical Life,* despite what I said above. But this copy of *Adam Bede* had an interesting provenance, having once been in the library of Jerome Kern, and containing his bookplate. I also have copies of *The Mill on the Floss,* 3 vols., Edinburgh, 1860, *Silas Marner: The Weaver of Raveloe,* 1861 (no less than seven editions appearing the first year), *Romola,* 3 vols. 1863, and *Felix Holt the Radical,* 3 vols. Edinburgh, 1866, a novel based partly on the life of the Socialist poet Gerald Massey. *Middlemarch,* which was also published in Edinburgh, this time in four volumes, appeared during 1871-2 and is so dated. *Daniel Deronda,* 4 vols. 1876, was her last major work, but it disappointed her admirers.

The works of the Brontë sisters have always been difficult to find in anything approaching acceptable condition, and I confess that I have never seen a first of Emily Brontë's *Wuthering Heights,* 1847, perhaps the greatest of English novels. It was issued under the pseudonym 'Ellis Bell', in three volumes, the last being devoted to another novel, *Agnes Grey,* written by Emily Brontë's younger sister, Anne, under the name 'Acton Bell'. The second edition appeared in 1848 in New York in a single volume, and this is also a rarity. It was in 1846 that Charlotte (1816–55) who used the pseudonym 'Currer Bell', Emily (1818–48), and Anne (1820–49), sent off a collection of poems that were published by Aylott and Jones, Paternoster Row, London. 1,000 copies were printed, but, as Charlotte wrote to Hartley Coleridge on 16 June 1847, ' . . . our book is found to be a drug; no man needs it or heeds it; in the space of a year our publisher has disposed but of two copies and by what painful efforts he succeeded in getting rid of those two himself only knows.' Hardly a propitious beginning to a literary career, and *Poems,* by Currer, Ellis and Acton Bell, with the imprint of Aylott and Jones, is now a notorious rarity, the very few copies that appear for sale being catalogued at high prices. In November 1848, the balance of 961 unsold copies was transferred to Smith, Elder & Co., who reissued the book with a cancel title-page, still retaining the original date. This constitutes the first edition, second issue, and a good copy in the original cloth can possibly be obtained for £30 to £50 ($72 to $120). But it is the novels of the Brontë sisters that interest us here. *Jane Eyre,* which appeared in three volumes in 1847, is Charlotte Brontë's best known work and an expensive addition to any library. In the original cloth, with the 36-page catalogue dated June and October 1847 at the end of Volume 1, its half-titles, and with the (sometimes missing) leaf advertising the *Calcutta Review,* you would be lucky to obtain a copy for less than £300 ($720). Her other novels, *Shirley,* 3 vols. 1849, *Villette,* 3 vols. 1853, and *The Professor,* 2 vols. 1857, can still be obtained in reasonable condition for £50 ($120) or so, with the last of the three making about half that sum.

Anthony Trollope (1815–82) has always been a favourite author of mine. His *Barchester Towers,* published in three volumes in 1857, with its struggle between the hypocritical Mr Slope, the bishop's chaplain, and the towering figure of the formidable Mrs Proudie, the bishop's wife, for the control of the diocese, is a masterpiece of its kind. It is an extremely difficult three-decker to discover in anything approaching reasonable condition in the original cloth. Few copies, when new, escaped the lending libraries, and this ordeal tattered the covers and too often left the text sprung and loose. My own copy, in the pale-brown horizontally-grained cloth, displays traces, on the red-brown printed end-papers, of once having had a circulating library list tipped in. But I am pleased to be able to report having a copy of *Barchester Towers,* for I know of fellow collectors who have searched for years without success for any sort of a copy with the 1857 imprint. The story actually formed the second of the series of Barchester novels, *The Warden,* 1855, issued in a single volume, being the first. *The Macdermotts of Ballycloran,* 3 vols. 1847, and *The Kellys and the O'Kellys,* 3 vols. 1848, his first two books, are seldom offered for sale, but the rest of the Barchester series (in which these two works played no part) being *Doctor Thorne,* 3 vols. 1858, *Framley Parsonage,* 3 vols. 1861, *The Small House at Allington,* 2 vols. 1864, and *The Last Chronicle of Barset,* 2 vols. 1867, are sought as a set of six first editions. It's a lucky man who manages to find the complete half-dozen. I still lack *Doctor Thorne,* although perhaps make up for this by having a large percentage of other 'firsts' by this prolific writer. Of these I can only mention *La Vendée,* 3 vols. 1850, *The Three Clerks,* 3 vols. 1858, *The Bertrams,* 3 vols. 1859, *Castle Richmond,* 3 vols. 1860, *Orley Farm,* 2 vols. 1862, *North America,* 2 vols. 1862, *Can You Forgive Her?* 2 vols. 1864, *The Belton Estate,* 3 vols. 1866, *The Claverings,* 2 vols. 1864, and *Phineas Finn: the Irish Member,*

2 vols. 1869. Many of these works first appeared in weekly or monthly parts in magazines, but for a full bibliography of Trollope's works the collector will have to consult Michael Sadleir's *Trollope*, 1928, of which a reprint of the revised edition appeared in 1964. Frances Trollope, née Milton (1780–1863) mother of Anthony, when her family were reduced to near poverty, supported them to a large extent by writing novels. The best of these I think was *The Widow Barnaby*, published in three volumes in 1839. *The Vicar of Wrexhill*, published two years earlier, also in three volumes, seems to have started the family preoccupation with the doings of the clergy, continued with so much success by her son. Mrs Trollope's *Domestic Manners of the Americans*, 2 vols. 1832, her first published work, caused a great deal of anger amongst readers in the United States of America on a par with the buzz of irritation that followed Dickens' *Martin Chuzzlewit* some 12 years later.

Amongst the lesser novelists of the earlier part of the 19th century I have space only to mention those whose works form a part of my collection. Susan Ferrier (1782–1854) wrote *Marriage*, 3 vols. 1818, *The Inheritance*, 3 vols. 1824, and *Destiny: or The Chief's Daughter*, 3 vols. 1831. John Galt (1779–1839) who in 1830 wrote a much criticised *Life of Byron*, is perhaps best known for *The Ayrshire Legatees*, 1821, *Annals of the Parish*, 1821, *The Entail: or The Lairds of Grippy*, 3 vols. 1823, and *The Spaewife*, 3 vols. 1823, being a few titles of one we may designate as the founder of the 'Kailyard School' of fiction, dealing with everyday life in Scotland. Mary Wollstonecroft Shelley, the second wife of the poet, is remembered for her *Frankenstein: or The Modern Prometheus*, 3 vols. 1818, of which I have never been able to secure a copy. The text has now been translated into nearly every modern language, yet, in its own day, it was five years before a second edition (in two volumes) was called for. *Valperga*, 3 vols. 1823, and *The Last Man*, 3 vols. 1826, are others from her pen that a collector of

George Cruikshank's dramatic frontispiece to W. H. Ainsworth's *The Tower of London*, 1840, a work first issued in 13 monthly parts. To find the one-volume first edition in the original publisher's cloth is now extremely difficult.
Size of title-page: 23cm × 14.5cm.

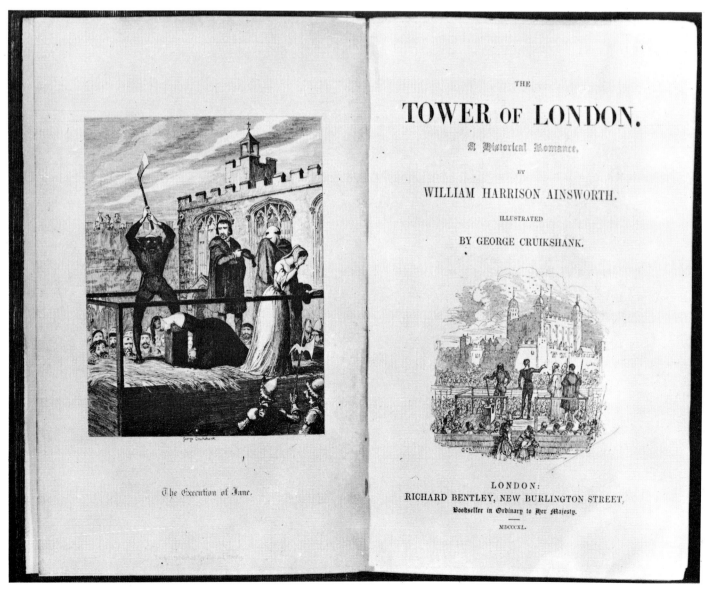

The Execution of Jane.

THE

TOWER OF LONDON.

A Historical Romance,

BY

WILLIAM HARRISON AINSWORTH.

ILLUSTRATED

BY GEORGE CRUIKSHANK.

LONDON:
RICHARD BENTLEY, NEW BURLINGTON STREET,
Bookseller in Ordinary to Her Majesty.

MDCCCXL.

the works of the 'horrific' novelists may seek for years before he adds them to his shelves.

G. P. R. James (1799–1860) who professed to be a follower of Scott, did much to stimulate in the young a desire to learn more of history. *Richelieu: a Tale of France*, 3 vols. 1829, *Darnley: or The Field of the Cloth of Gold*, 3 vols. 1830, and *Henry Masterton*, 3 vols. 1832, were perhaps amongst his best, and I also have a fine copy of *Russell: a Tale of the Reign of Charles II*, 3 vols. 1847. James seemed able to churn out at least one novel yearly, sometimes as many as three, during 30 or so years of writing, and his works cover well over two closely printed columns of the *C.B.E.L.*

William Harrison Ainsworth (1805–82) was just as prolific, but I have been able to put together a collection of his novels that is not far from complete. There are still several that have eluded me, and the price of his three-deckers is now at a level that makes one think twice before purchasing. Most are still eminently readable, and their spirited, and often blood-curdling illustrations by George Cruikshank, John Franklin and others, add much to the interest of many of his books. *Rookwood*, 3 vols. 1834, published anonymously, and, if we discount *Sir John Chiverton*, 1826, of which he was only part author, his first novel is also one of his best, containing the galloping excitement of Dick Turpin's ride to York on the never-to-be-equalled stayer Black Bess. *Jack Sheppard*, 3 vols. 1839, *The Tower of London*, 1840, *Guy Fawkes*, 3 vols. 1841, *Old Saint Paul's*, 3 vols. 1841, *The Miser's Daughter*, 3 vols. 1842, *Windsor Castle*, 3 vols. 1843, *The Lancashire Witches*, 1849 (privately printed), and *The Star Chamber*, 2 vols. 1854, read as well today as when they were first written, and seem to have lost nothing of their vivacity with the passage of time. Most of Ainsworth's novels were first published in magazines. He was still writing when well into his seventies, but his popularity had waned and his last book, *Stanley Brereton*, 3 vols. 1881, was reduced to a first appearance in an obscure provincial magazine called *The Bolton Weekly*.

R. D. Blackmore (1825–1900) has never been an easy man to collect, and his *Lorna Doone: a Romance of Exmoor*, 3 vols. 1869, is missing from my collection. Some of his other stories, such as *Springhaven*, 3 vols. 1887, and *Perlycross*, 3 vols. 1894, can still be read without boredom or the skipping of half-chapters of descriptive prose, and are by no means over-priced at, say, £10 to £15 ($24 to $36) apiece. But *Lorna Doone* is likely to cost well over £100 ($240). Edward George Earle Lytton Bulwer (1803–73) who took the additional name of Lytton on succeeding to the Knebworth estate, is represented by his historical novel *The Last Days of Pompeii*, 3 vols. 1834, which is more readable in an abridged or condensed version, as any schoolboy who has suffered the full text will confirm. Bulwer-Lytton's *Pelham*, 3 vols. 1828, *Eugene Aram*, 3 vols. 1832, and *Godolphin*, 3 vols. 1833, give me a holding of an author whose fault was verbosity without humour, yet who was gifted with an inventiveness that conjured plots from thin air. His son, the first Earl Lytton, wrote just as extensively, using the pseudonym 'Owen Meredith' for his verse-novels.

Charles Reade (1814–84) was a playwright as well as a novelist. *Peg Woffington*, 1853, appeared in the same year as *Christie Johnstone*, but there is then a gap on my shelves until the appearance of his *White Lies*, 3 vols. 1857. Then come his better known titles, *The Cloister and the Hearth*, 4 vols. 1861, *Hard Cash*, 3 vols. 1863, *The Double Marriage*, 1867, and *A Woman Hater*, 3 vols. 1877.

In America there had appeared literary works now remembered as classics of their kind. Nathaniel Hawthorne (1804–64), had published his *Scarlet Letter* at Boston in 1850, the scene of the story being this same town in Puritan New England in the 17th century. *The House of the Seven Gables* followed in 1851, published by that distinguished house responsible for so many best-sellers of the age, Ticknor, Reed & Fields, as were many another of Hawthorne's works. Herman Melville's *Moby Dick*, 1851, the first American edition of which, published in New York, is now priced at over £1,000 ($2,400), dealt with man's relationship to sin, as had Hawthorne's *Scarlet Letter*. Henry David Thoreau (1817–62), rebelled against the materialistic values of the modern society of his times and disappeared to a self-built cabin by Walden Pond. *Walden; or Life in the Woods*, 1854, was an account of his life there, displaying an independence of thought and acute observation of nature and the rural world around him. His other works include *A Week on the Concord and Merrimac Rivers*, 1854,

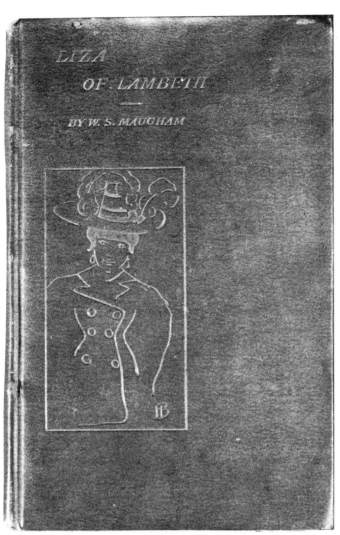

LIZA
OF LAMBETH
—
BY W. S. MAUGHAM

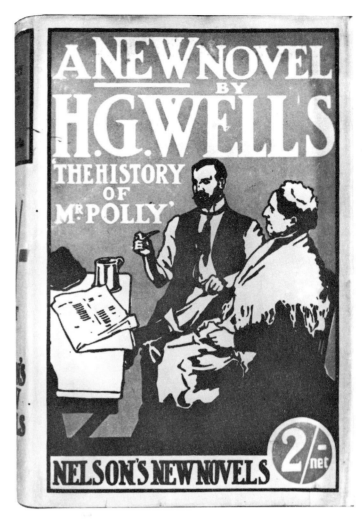

A NEW NOVEL
BY
H.G.WELLS
THE HISTORY
OF
Mr POLLY

NELSON'S NEW NOVELS 2/-net

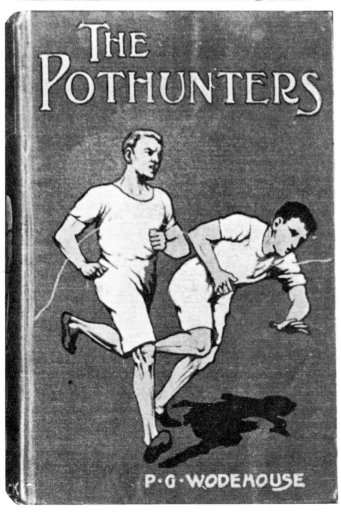

THE POTHUNTERS

P·G·WODEHOUSE

Tarzan of the Apes

Chicago
A. C. McClurg & Co.
1914

Edgar Rice Burroughs

A

Honeymoon in Space

By
George Griffith
Author of
" Valdar the Oft-Born," " The Virgin of the Sun,"
" The Rose of Judah," &c., &c.

ILLUSTRATED BY STANLEY WOOD AND
HAROLD PIFFARD

London
C. Arthur Pearson Ltd.
Henrietta Street
1901

ERICH MARIA REMARQUE

Im Westen nichts Neues

Remarques Buch ist das Denkmal
unseres unbekannten Soldaten
Von allen Toten geschrieben
Walter von Molo

The Maine Woods, 1864, and *Cape Cod*, 1865. Francis Bret Harte (1836–1902), startled magazine readers on the East coast with his tales of California. *The Luck of Roaring Camp*, 1870, Boston, is distinguished as a first issue by being without the name 'Brown of Calaveras', and now fetches about £30 ($72). The first issue of *Outcroppings*, 1866, has no tailpiece on page 102 among other points. Harte's *Queen of the Pirate Isle*, 1886, is now sought more for the Kate Greenaway illustrations than for the text.

In the meantime the irrepressible 'Mark Twain', the pseudonym of Samuel Langhorne Clemens (1835–1910), had come into prominence with his *Jim Smiley and his Jumping Frog*, 1865, and he shortly afterwards established himself as a popular lecturer. A cruise in the Mediterranean in 1867 resulted in the appearance of *The Innocents Abroad*, 1869, to be followed by *Roughing It*, 1872, the story of his life in Nevada. And it was his own childhood that provided the material for his greatest novels: *The Adventures of Tom Sawyer*, 1876, *Life on the Mississippi*, 1883, and *The Adventures of Huckleberry Finn*, the first edition appearing in England in 1884, to be followed by the first American edition, New York, 1885. Points regarding this issue are the word 'was' for 'saw' on page 57; pages 283–4 tipped in on a stub; the second '5' in page 155 is larger than the first; but even with all these desirable attributes fine copies only make about £50 ($120). An underpriced book. *Tom Sawyer*, 1876, is a much rarer work and seldom appears in the market at less than £300 ($720). The first issue has the verso of the half-title and preface left blank.

Mark Twain may have been the one great genius the West produced; but there was a remarkable cross-section of literary talent at work in the western and mid-western states during his lifetime. Ambrose Bierce (1842–1914?) is best known for his short stories, published in collected form in *Tales of Soldiers and Civilians*, 1891; while Jack London (1876–1916), who took part in the Klondike gold rush in 1897, made good use of his experiences in *The Son of the Wolf*, 1900, the first of his many collections of tales set in the Frozen North. *The Call of the Wild*, New York, 1903, is now priced at about £30 ($72), and *The Sea-Wolf*, 1904, and *White Fang*, 1906, are amongst the many titles of this prolific author that can be collected for a small outlay.

And there, in full flight as it were, I must leave the novel with a good nine-tenths of the volumes on my shelves unlisted and unexamined. One can, as I have said, endeavour to collect a favourite author in as comprehensive a first edition form as possible, hoping for eventual completeness. Always, if my own experience is anything to go by, a title or two eludes one's fingers.

Those stirred by the collecting instinct will know exactly the acquisitive nature of the feeling which pervades one's frame when the hunt is up. Hard indeed to replace the telephone receiver with a light heart knowing a rival

Above left
The works of early science-fiction writers are now eagerly sought by collectors on both sides of the Atlantic. One of the earliest in the field was George Griffith, a contemporary of H. G. Wells.

Size of title page: 19.5cm × 12cm.

Above centre
Undoubtedly the best book to come out of World War I was Remarque's *Im Westen nichts Neues*, 1929, translated into English by A. W. Wheen, under the title *All Quiet on the Western Front*, 1929. Remarque (b. 1898) whose real name is Kramer, now lives in the U.S.A. The first edition and the first English edition are shown here.

Size of right-hand front cover: 19.5cm × 13cm.

Above right
George Orwell's nightmare story of totalitarianism *Nineteen Eighty-Four*, 1949, and Aldous Huxley's equally chilling *Brave New World*, 1932, are both difficult first editions to acquire.

Size of right-hand cover: 19.5cm × 13cm.

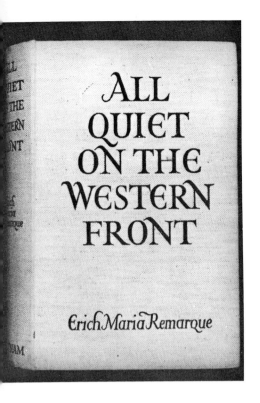

The first English edition of Georges Hènot's *The Poison Dealer*, (1905), an author who used the pseudonym 'Ohnet' as a scrambled version of his real name. The work contains one of the earliest fictional descriptions of a motor-car crash (p. 41).

Height of cover: 19cm.

collector has pipped you by minutes for a title you have sought for years. The gap remains unfilled until next time the quarry is sighted, and even then you may once more be unlucky. But exasperation whets the appetite and glints the eye, and is incitement to further effort that eventually brings success. And then is the time to look for fresh fields to conquer, for the excitement is in the hunting.

Poetry

Illustration by Thomas Woolner (1825–92) for the title-page of Francis Turner Palgrave's *The Golden Treasury*, one of the most famous 19th-century poetical miscellanies. Woolner was one of the original members of the pre-Raphaelite Brotherhood.

Size of title-page:
16cm × 10cm.

The 14th century witnessed the birth of English literature in the form we recognise today, although the country was still multi-lingual, as is proved by the fact that John Gower (*c.* 1330–1408) wrote his three most important works in three different languages – French, Latin and English. Geoffrey Chaucer (*c.* 1340–1400) always wrote in English, although many of his early poems follow French models. His work is of supreme importance in the annals of English literature, for his influence moulded the dialects and foreign strains to create the amalgam that was to produce our modern English tongue. In fact the first substantial book of poetry to be printed in the English language was William Caxton's edition of Chaucer's *Canterbury Tales,* printed at Westminster in 1478. Only two perfect copies are recorded as having survived, the British Museum copy and that at Merton College, Oxford. In 1532 appeared *The Workes of Geffray Chaucer newly printed,* his first collected works. As some 20 pieces in it are not in fact by Chaucer it could claim to be the first English poetical miscellany, although this title has been accorded to 'Tottell's Miscellany' in the publication called *Songes and Sonettes, 1557.*

Chaucer's *Workes* were continually re-printed, and a variety of editors saw the massive folios through the press. The 1532 edition was edited by W. Thynne and printed by T. Godfray. Ten years later saw the appearance of the third collected edition of 1542, again with Thynne as editor. There are two differing imprints on the title-pages as being by W. Bonham, or John Reynes. The folio of 1550 cannot be dated other than as being about that year, but again the name of Thynne appears as editor, this time with four printers as having had a part in its production. Any of four names, W. Bonham, R. Kele, T. Petit, or R. Toye, can appear, but except for the printer's name in the colophon each issue of this edition appears to be identical. John Stowe was responsible for the folio of 1561 of which there are two slightly differing issues, although each are printed by Ihon Kyngston for Ihon Wight. The folio of 1598 is edited by T. Speght, and is the first to contain substantial notes and a life of Chaucer. There are three differing imprints, but otherwise each issue is identical. Finally I must mention the folio of 1602, of which I have a copy as perfect as one could wish. It is again edited by T. Speght, and the imprint can have either the name of Adam Islip or that of George Bishop. An interesting point is the early use of a pasted slip to correct errata, and in *The Plowman's Tale,* on folio 88 verso, bottom line, column two, Islip printed in error the first word of the line as being the catchword for the following page, giving the word 'Han' (i.e. 'Have'). The line it came from was missed in the printing, so a printed slip with the missing words was pasted in place, covering the faulty catchword, giving us 'Han in this land as much lay fee', and making the stanza complete.

All these early folio editions command high prices and complete copies seldom come on the market. Most have been made up from leaves added from other copies, or have facsimile leaves inserted. The edition of 1561 now makes in the region of £500 ($1200) in a contemporary binding; the 1598 edition £200 ($480); and the Speght edition of 1602 about £100 ($240). Careful collation is needed, especially with the preliminary leaves; these were often unsigned and only comparison with a copy known to be perfect will reveal the defects.

Chaucer had many imitators but no real successor, and by the 16th century the influence of the Renaissance was clearly apparent in English literature. The fashion for the sonnet, an Italian verse form, was introduced by Sir Thomas

Wyatt (1503–42) and the Earl of Surrey, Henry Howard (1517?–47). Both featured largely in *Tottell's Miscellany,* the earliest edition of which, dated 1557, is known by a copy in the Bodleian Library, Oxford. At least eight new editions appeared in the following 30 years. *The Vision of Pierce Plowman,* by William Langland (1330?–1400?) or rather attributed to him under this title, was printed in 1550, a second edition appearing the same year. Meanwhile poetical miscellanies were flourishing under a variety of eye-catching titles. *A Mirror for Magistrates,* forming a link between medieval and modern literature, appeared in 1559, edited by William Baldwin. *The Paradyse of Daynty Devises,* 1576, *A Gorgeous Gallery of Gallant Inventions,* 1578, and *A Handful of Pleasant Delites,* 1584, and many others that were to follow in their wake are now of a rarity that precludes them forming part of a private collection. Meanwhile Edmund Spenser (*c.* 1552–99) reflected the passing of the age of chivalry with his unfinished allegorical epic *The Faerie Queene,* 1590, the second part, containing the fourth, fifth, and sixth books, appearing in 1596. I have had to be content with his first collected works, published in 1611; Mathew Lownes, the publisher, made use of the separate folio editions of the different titles of Spenser's works that he had in stock, binding them up with a specially printed and engraved title-page. *The Shepheards Calender,* with its delightful woodcut illustrations, *Prosopopoia; or Mother Hubberds Tale,* and *Colin Clouts Come Home Againe,* as well as minor pieces, are all contained in this folio, making it a most desirable addition to any library.

The first collected edition of Shakespeare's *Poems,* 1640, has as the portrait-frontispiece a reversed copy, by Marshall, of the Droeshout portrait found in the folios. At least 50 copies of this edition are known, no less than ten being in the Folger Shakespeare Library, Washington, D.C.

The Countesse of Pembrokes Arcadia, 1590, by Sir Philip Sidney (1554–86), and so called because it was written for, and revised by, his sister Mary Herbert, Countess of Pembroke, was not published until four years after the poet's death. His collected works appeared in 1598, and with these we arrive at the start of the age of Milton, although his greatest work did not appear until 1660 and the end of the Commonwealth. Early 17th-century lyric poetry is really a continuation of the Elizabethan, with the Cavalier poets, such as Thomas Carew (1598–1638), Sir John Suckling (1609–42), and Richard Lovelace (1618–58), contributing elegant and amorous lyrics that were an echo of a previous age. Suckling's *Ballad: Upon a Wedding,* found in his *Fragmenta Aurea,* 1646, is particularly memorable.

Much of the poetry of the period is strongly religious; Dr. Johnson called it 'metaphysical'. John Donne (1573–1631), Dean of St Paul's, was its chief exponent, breaking the Petrarchan tradition with powerful stanzas burning with an intense and fiery spirit of passionate argument. *Poems by J. D.* appeared in 1633, while his *Poems on Several Occasions,* was not published until 1719. Donne's prose works and sermons are avidly sought in first edition form by many collectors and have risen tremendously in price since 1960. John Milton (1608–74) wrote the greatest religious poem in the English language, *Paradise Lost,* first published in 1667. The earliest issue of the title-page has Milton's name printed in large capitals, although this point of issue is disputed by some bibliographers. There are at least six recorded variants of the first edition title-page. *Paradise Regain'd,* 1671, has a misprint 'loah', on page 67, line 2, which if uncorrected denotes the copy to be of earliest issue.

Students of early American verse discover their first established poet in Mistress Anne Bradstreet (1612–72), whose *Tenth Muse Lately Sprung Up,* 1650, was first published in London. She and her husband came to Massachusetts Bay in 1630 with Winthrop's party, later settling in North Andover, Mass. Her volume of verse was the first book of poems by an Englishwoman in America. The first native poet to address himself successfully to an audience of his countrymen was Michael Wigglesworth (1631–1705), a Congregational clergyman who came to America as a boy before graduating from Harvard in 1651. He was the author, among other works, of *The Day of Doom,* 1662, a long Calvinistic poem full of threats of hell-fire and the wrath to come. Nevertheless, the work became the first American literary best-seller. His diary has been published under the sub-title of *The Diary of a Seventeenth-Century Puritan.* Anne Bradstreet's *Works* were reprinted at Harvard in 1967, and she is the subject of *Homage to Mistress Bradstreet* by the modern

OVID's
EPISTLES,
TRANSLATED
BY
SEVERAL HANDS.

Vel tibi composita cantetur Epistola voce :
Ignotum hoc aliis ille novavit opus. Ovid.

LONDON,

Printed for *Jacob Tonson* at the Sign of the
Judges Head in *Chancery Lane*, near
Fleet-Street. 1680.

American poet John Berryman. But the colonial poets of America are now mostly read in extracts in anthologies. In the 17th and early 18th centuries they show the influence of Milton and other contemporary English poets rather than any distinctive New England style of their own.

My next English first edition is represented by a copy of *Poems,* 1656, by Abraham Cowley (1618–67). This contains his *Miscellanies, The Mistress, or Love Verses,* his *Pindarique Odes,* and *Davideis, or, A Sacred Poem of the Troubles of David.* This folio, collated in fours, represents the first collected edition of his works. Copies exist on large-paper, and in its time the work was so highly thought of that eight folio editions appeared in the space of a single generation. A copy might still be purchased for as little as £40 ($96).

John Dryden (1631–1700) can claim to be the first officially appointed Poet Laureate, although Ben Jonson could be considered to have held the honour in the modern sense of the term. After Dryden the list, in chronological order, reads as follows: Shadwell, Tate, Rowe, Eusden, Cibber, Whitehead, T. Warton, Pye, Southey, Wordsworth, A. Tennyson, A. Austin, Bridges, Masefield, C. Day Lewis. Dryden's term of office extended from 1670–88, and, by adopting the heroic couplet, he set a fashion that was to last for well over a century. His fame rests not only on his brilliant satires such as *Absolom and Achitophel,* 1681, but on plays such as his *All for Love.* He was one of the greatest literary all-rounders. His *Essay on Dramatic Poesie,* 1668, reveals an incisive and critical mind; it confirms him as the leader of almost every literary movement in the 40 years between the Restoration and the start of the 18th century. *Mac Flecknoe,* 1682, and *The Hind and the Panther,* 1687, I have searched for but never found at a price I could afford.

I have space to name only a few of the most important names before 1700. Robert Wild (1609–79) produced *Iter Boreale,* 1660, the edition of 1661 adding

A rare poetical miscellany, with contributions by Dryden, Nahum Tate, Thomas Flatman, Thomas Otway, Mrs Aphra Behn, etc.

Size of title-page:
18.7cm × 11.5cm.

20 new poems. The first collected edition of his poems did not appear until 1870. Nahum Tate (1652–1715), *Poems,* 1677: Andrew Marvell (1621–78), *Miscellaneous Poems,* 1681: Charles Cotton (1630–87), *Poems on Several Occassions,* 1689, of which I have a fine copy in contemporary calf: and John Pomfret (1667–1702), *The Choice,* 1700, bring us in time to William Wycherley whose works I will discuss in the chapter on drama (see p. 61).

Mathew Prior's *Poems on Several Occasions* first appeared in 1707 in a pirated and unauthorised edition put out by the notorious Edmund Curll. I have the massive 1718 edition, one of the tallest poetical folios ever produced, but a handsome volume finely printed and with a pictorial frontispiece and chapter headings. His *Miscellaneous Works* appeared in two volumes in 1740. John Gay (1685–1732) published *Wine: A Poem,* in 1708, and it contains the first specimen of printed music from type produced at Oxford. I often re-read his *Trivia: Or, the Art of Walking the Streets of London* (1716), a poem giving us an intimate glimpse of the London of his day. The title means what it says, the poem starting with advice on how:

> Through winter streets to steer your course aright,
> How to walk clean by Day, and safe by Night,
> How jostling Crouds, with Prudence to decline,
> When to assert the Wall, and when resign.

The title-page is undated, and large-paper copies contain a variant vignette at the head of the first page of text. John Phillips (1676–1709) is represented in the collection by *Cyder: A Poem,* 1708.

Alexander Pope (1688–1744) followed Dryden in his use of the heroic couplet. His mock-heroic poem *The Rape of the Lock,* 1712 (in two-canto form), first appeared in Lintot's *Miscellaneous Poems and Translations,* of that date, and again under a Dublin imprint the following year. As a separate publication, this time in five cantos, it was issued in 1714; three editions, plus another Dublin imprint, appeared that year. *An Essay on Man* (1733), generally held to be Pope's masterpiece, was issued in three separate parts. I have the first collected edition of his *Works,* 1717, with the large folding frontispiece intended to fit the few large-paper copies that were issued.

The title-page of *Poems on Several Occasions,* 1722, by Dr Thomas Parnell (1679–1718) is printed in red and black. It was edited by Alexander Pope and he supplied a four-page dedication in verse. Parnell was a member of the Scriblerus Club and a close friend of Pope, Swift and Gay. My copy is in a binding of contemporary gilt-panelled red morocco, with the marbled

An uncut copy of the first edition of *Cyder,* 1708, by John Phillips. The inscription to his memory in Westminster Abbey is ornamented with an apple-tree to commemorate this poem. Size from top to bottom of title-page: 20.5cm.

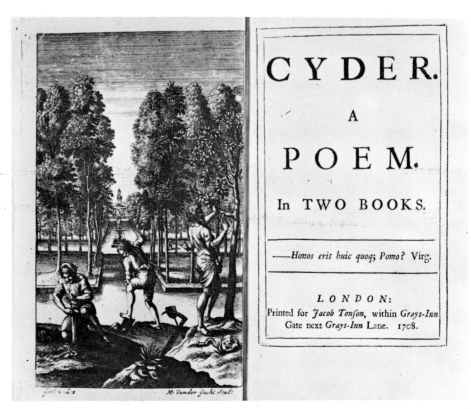

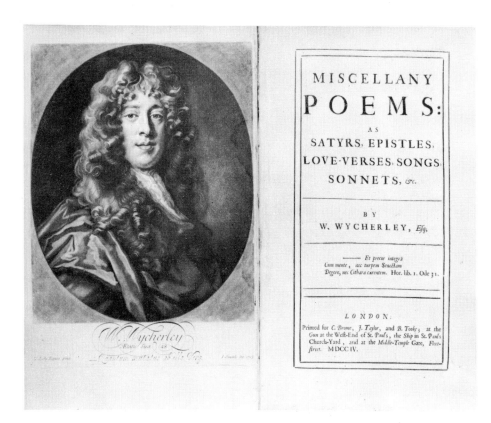

MISCELLANY
POEMS:
AS
SATYRS, EPISTLES,
LOVE-VERSES, SONGS,
SONNETS, &c.

BY
W. WYCHERLEY, Esq;

———— Et precor integrâ
Cum mente , nec turpem Senectam
Degere, nec Cithara carentem. Hor. lib. 1. Ode 31.

LONDON.
Printed for C. Brome, J. Taylor, and B. Tooke; at the
Gun at the West-End of St. Paul's, the Ship in St. Paul's
Church-Yard , and at the Middle-Temple Gate, Fleet-
street. MDCCIV.

Despite the sensuality displayed in the frontispiece, William Wycherley is regarded as a confirmed misanthrope, with the knack of making any sort of immorality appear more than a little ridiculous. His play *The Country Wife*, 1675, is a masterpiece of English comedy.

Size of title-page:
32cm × 20.5cm.

end-papers that were so fashionable at that time. A limited edition of 200 copies was issued by the Cuala Press, Dublin, in 1927. When we turn to James Thomson (1700–48) we think immediately of *The Seasons,* although his *Castle of Indolence,* 1748, written in imitation of Spenser, is almost as well known. The first collected edition of Thomson's *Seasons* actually appears in his *Works,* a two-volume quarto set published 1730–6. But to find each part of the set of four seasons as they first appeared is an extremely difficult and expensive task. *Winter: A Poem* was the first to be published, and was issued in wrappers, in 1726. This part of the quartette is rendered even scarcer by the fact that, like the first part of Young's *Night-Thoughts,* it was issued in a larger format than the instalments that followed after, and therefore could not be bound up with them. In 1727 the next part, *Summer,* was published, as an octavo-sized pamphlet, and the following year saw the appearance of *Spring.* The final part, *Autumn,* was not printed until the publication of the first collected edition of *The Seasons* in 1730. Of this edition there were two issues, one in quarto for subscribers, and the other in octavo size. Thomson kept adding to what he had written and the definitive and complete edition of *The Seasons* did not appear until 1746. My copy of the four parts is bound up in octavo size, together with a leaf marked 'Proposals for Printing by Subscription the Four Seasons'. The completed quarto, printed on 'superfine Royal Paper, and adorned with Copper-Plates', was to cost subscribers one guinea. It became an 18th-century best-seller.

I have copies of *The Chace,* 1735, by William Somerville (1675–1742); and of the much rarer *The Spleen,* 1737, by Matthew Green (1696–1737). The genuine first edition has the words 'Price One Shilling' at the foot of the title-page, and has 46 pages of text as against 24 in a piracy that appeared the same year. The price does not appear on the spurious edition's title-page, which otherwise reads exactly the same. *Poems Upon Various Occasions,* 1737, by William Shenstone (1714–63) is a rare find for any collector, for he took 'uncommon pains to suppress it, by collecting and destroying copies wherever he met with them'. I have a fine copy, in the original boards with uncut edges, of *Letters Written by the late . . . Lady Luxborough to William Shenstone, Esq.,* published by Dodsley in 1775, a most readable collection that tells us much about the poet's life and aspirations. *The Poetical Works of Samuel Johnson,* 1785, were published and edited by G. Kearsley, and I hunted for several years before being lucky enough to find a copy in a contemporary binding. It appeared as a small octavo of some 196 pages, and gives the text of *London: A Poem,* first published in 1738, and of *The Vanity of Human Wishes,* 1749, both of which are

The first edition of Thomas Percy's *Reliques of Ancient English Poetry*, 3 vols. 1765, now affectionately known as Percy's *Reliques*, did more to revive interest in our older poetry than any work of its age. The dedication, although signed by Percy, is entirely from Johnson's pen.

Size of title-page:
17.4cm × 11cm.

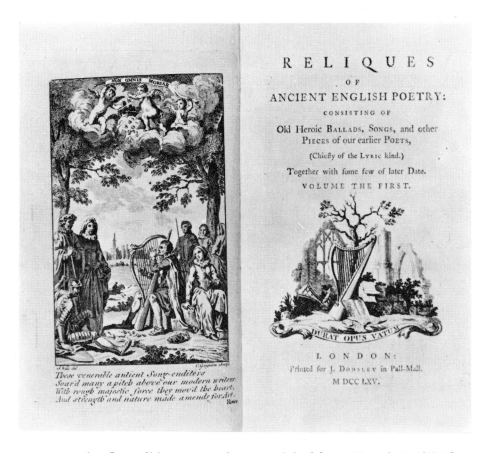

very expensive first editions to purchase in original form. Kearsley's 1785 first collected edition is now seldom priced at less than £100 ($240) in the catalogues of antiquarian booksellers. There is an issue point which states that the reading 'their' in the third line of leaf A2 was later altered to 'its'. A weightier work, which a deputation of London booksellers persuaded Johnson to undertake at the age of sixty-seven, was *The Lives of the Poets,* in many ways his masterpiece, being perhaps the greatest distillation of critical opinion yet written in the English language. The first edition appeared in Dublin in three volumes in 1779; but the first London edition, a four-volume work of 1781, with the famous copperplate portrait of Johnson after the painting by Sir Joshua Reynolds, is the set I prefer to have in my library. The rest of my Johnson collection comprises his *Political Tracts,* 1776, which contains *The False Alarm, Falkland's Islands, The Patriot,* and *Taxation No Tyranny,* all of which had been previously issued separately, his *Debates in Parliament,* 2 vols. 1787, his *Letters,* 2 vols. 1788, *A Journey to the Western Islands of Scotland,* 1775, and his *Prayers and Meditations,* 1785.

To try and give details of the many first editions in my collection of 18th-century poetry is an impossible task in a work of this scope, but the dates of important works will be useful to the collector who perhaps lacks the specialised bibliographies needed for a detailed assessment of the points to look for in these once plentiful quartos. Many appeared as folios or octavos, but one associates poetry of the 18th century with the calf-bound quartos once crowding the shelves of every antiquarian bookseller. Those days are gone forever, and happy is the man who took advantage of the years of plenty. I managed to rescue quite a few, but was a decade or so too late to avoid the scramble that has since developed. Now I concentrate on the lesser poets, and I have moved up a century to the Victorian age where there is still an opportunity of finding the original verse in the original cloth.

An Elegy Wrote in a Country Church-Yard by Thomas Gray (1716–71) is a 'first' I am never likely to possess. Apart from a Latin poem in honour of the Prince of Wales's marriage, this represents the first appearance of Gray in print. It is by far the scarcest of the original editions of his works, and less than a dozen copies are known to have survived. Issued in wrappers, it would now fetch over £1,000 ($2,400) at auction. I am content with the poem's third appearance in *Designs by Mr. R. Bentley, for Six Poems by Mr. T. Gray,* 1753, a large folio issued by R. Dodsley. An issue point is contained in the half-title, the first issue of this edition having the word 'Drawings, &c.' later changed to 'Designs, &c.' Some of

Gray's poems appear for the first time in this publication. *Odes, by Mr. Gray,* 1757, was printed at Horace Walpole's famous Strawberry-Hill, being the first book printed there.

The Fleece, 1757, by John Dyer (1700–58), *The Shrubs of Parnassus,* 1760, by William Woty (1731?–91), and *Poems Chiefly Pastoral,* 1766, by John Cunningham, are all books that I have managed to find since 1960. The frontispiece to Cunningham's *Poems* is one of the most delightful pastoral scenes to appear in any 18th-century volume, matching the mood of his verse:

> Swiftly from the mountain's brow,
>   Shadows, nurs'd by night, retire:
> And the peeping sun-beam, now
>   Paints with gold the village spire.

An uncut copy in the original boards of *Poems, Supposed to have been Written at Bristol, by Thomas Rowley,* 1777, in reality by Thomas Chatterton (1752–70), is all I have of the original work of this remarkable young genius, whose first collection of poems appeared when he was still only 12 years of age. At the age of 17, reduced to despair by poverty, he poisoned himself with arsenic. His collected works appeared in three volumes in 1803. The first collected works of William Blake (1757–1827) were published in a slim little cloth bound volume by William Pickering in 1839, under the title of *Songs of Innocence and of Experience.* My copy is of the first issue, containing on the recto of F4 the poem *The Little Vagabond.* This starts:

> Dear mother! dear mother! the church is cold,
> But the ale-house is healthy, and pleasant, and warm;
> Besides I can tell when I am used well;
> Such usage in heaven will never do well.

and gave such offence to the Establishment of the time that Pickering was forced to cancel the offending leaf. In the second issue it is blank.

George Crabbe (1754–1832), Erasmus Darwin (1731–1802), Thomas Campbell (1777–1844), and Robert Bloomfield (1766–1823) are still not difficult to find in first edition form. *An Evening Walk,* 1793, by William Wordsworth (1770–1850) was the poet's first publication and is extremely rare. The first issue of the first edition of *Lyrical Ballads,* with the Bristol imprint, a collection of poems by Wordsworth and S. T. Coleridge (1772–1834) published in 1798 is also rare. It contains the first printing of *The Rime of the Ancyent Marinere.* The second issue of the first edition was published in

Right
A rare item of Churchilliana, published in paperback in Hodder & Stoughton's *Sixpenny Novels, c.* 1910. This rather tattered copy is one of the few to have survived.

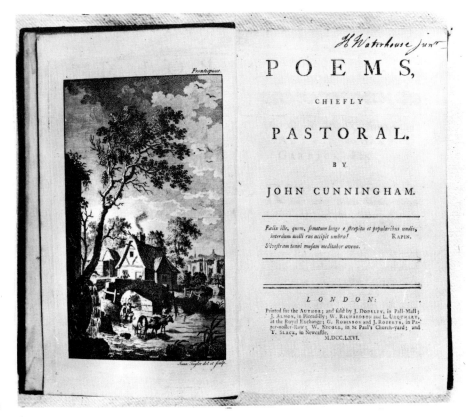

The first edition of Cunningham's *Poems,* 1766. A handsome piece of book production, notable for its intelligent use of type-ornament, and containing Isaac Taylor's charming pastoral frontispiece.

Size of title-page:
20cm × 12cm.

MY AFRICAN JOURNEY

BY THE RIGHT HON.
WINSTON S. CHURCHILL, M.P.

A PRESENT FROM THE CRYSTAL PALACE

Designed by
Sir Jos. Paxton, M.P.
Opened by the Queen
May 10th 1854.

LENGTH OF PALACE 1392 FT.
BREADTH 384 FT.
HEIGHT OF ROOF 200 FT.
AREA OF PARK 192 ACRES.
LENGTH OF HOT WATER PIPES-
18 MILES.
HEIGHT OF WATER TOWER 284 FT.
WATER IN TOWER TANKS 2500 TONS.

MARRIED AT
St GEORGE'S CHAPEL
WINDSOR
MARCH 10 1863

THEIR ROYAL HIGHNESSES
ALBERT EDWARD
AND
ALEXANDRA
PRINCE AND PRINCESS
OF WALES

THE LATE
EARL OF
BEACONSFIELD

RICHMOND 1865
Vicksburg
Fort Donelson

GENERAL U.S. GRANT
"I WILL FIGHT IT OUT
ON THIS LINE."

THE BLESSING

The LORD bless
thee, and keep thee:
The LORD make
his face shine upon
thee, and be gra-
-cious unto thee:
The LORD lift up
his countenance
upon thee, and give
thee peace.

TO MY DARLING

MARY HAD A LITTLE LAMB,
ITS FLEECE WAS WHITE AS SNOW,
AND EVERYWHERE
THAT MARY WENT,
THE LAMB WAS SURE TO GO.
HE FOLLOWED HER TO
SCHOOL ONE DAY,-
THAT WAS AGAINST THE RULE;
IT MADE THE CHILDREN
LAUGH AND PLAY
TO SEE A LAMB AT SCHOOL.

"WHAT MAKES THE LAMB
LOVE MARY SO?"
THE EAGER CHILDREN CRY;
"OH, MARY LOVES THE LAMB,
YOU KNOW,"
THE TEACHER DID REPLY.
AND YOU, EACH GENTLE ANIMAL
IN CONFIDENCE MAY BIND,
AND MAKE THEM FOLLOW
AT YOUR CALL,
IF YOU ARE
ALWAYS
KIND.

HANDEL
FESTIVAL

SACRED HARMONIC SOCIETY

CRYSTAL
PALACE
JUNE
1862

We praise
Thee
O God

The first issue of the collected poems of William Blake, *Songs of Innocence and of Experience,* 1839, published in a slim octavo by William Pickering, London, contains the poem 'The Little Vagabond'. In later issues of the first edition this leaf was cancelled and left blank.

Size of right-hand page: 19cm × 10.5 cm.

70   SONGS OF EXPERIENCE.

THE SICK ROSE.
—
O ROSE! thou art sick!
The invisible worm,
That flies in the night,
In the howling storm,

Has found out thy bed,
Of crimson joy,
And his dark secret love,
Does thy life destroy.

SONGS OF EXPERIENCE.   71

THE LITTLE VAGABOND.

DEAR mother! dear mother! the church is cold,
But the ale-house is healthy, and pleasant, and warm;
Besides I can tell when I am used well;
Such usage in heaven will never do well.

But if at the church they would give us some ale,
And a pleasant fire our souls to regale,
We'd sing and we'd pray all the live-long day,
Nor ever once wish from the church to stray.

Then the parson might preach, and drink, and sing,
And we'd be as happy as birds in the spring,
And modest dame Lurch, who is always at church,
Would not have bandy children, nor fasting, nor birch.

And God, like a father, rejoicing to see
His children as pleasant and happy as He,
Would have no more quarrel with the devil or the barrel,
But kiss him and give him both drink and apparel.

THE END OF THE SONGS OF EXPERIENCE.

The engraved title-page for *The Grave, A Poem,* 1808, by Robert Blair, designed by the poet William Blake.

Size of engraving: 34.5cm × 27cm.

Left
One of the periphery benefits of book-collecting. Some of the woven silk bookmarks the author has discovered while collating his books. Most were made by Thomas Stevens (d. 1888), of Coventry, now justly famous for his silk pictures.

Size of bookmark on extreme left, down to bottom point, but not including yellow tassel: 25cm × 5.3cm.

London in the same year, but Wordworth's famous 'Preface' was not added until the second edition of 1800, published in two volumes. I have a matching pair: Volume 1 is the third edition of 1802, and Volume 2 the first edition of 1800. All the early editions are difficult to find, and the latest cataloguing of the second issue of Volume 1 (with the London imprint) 1798, and the first edition of Volume 2, 1800, is priced by a London bookseller at £350 ($840). *Poems* by William Wordsworth appeared in two volumes in 1807. On Volume 1 of my copy is the presentation inscription 'Francis Wrangham, 1807. From the author'. This was Wordsworth's second major collection of poems, containing many of his most famous lyrics, including 'Sonnet Composed upon Westminster Bridge', and 'I Wandered lonely as a cloud'.

Samuel Rogers (1765–1855) is a special favourite of mine, not because of the quality of his verse, for the high position he attained among men of letters was at a period when the standard of poetry was generally at a low ebb. He was the first author whose works I set out to collect in first edition form, purchasing many of them for a few shillings, and the rest usually for only a pound or two. From the date of my discovering his first quarto pamphlet, *An Ode to Superstition,* 1786, which I still consider contains the best work he ever wrote, dates also my acknowledgement of joining the ranks of bibliophiles. Now I have Rogers all but complete.

His books are here in my study, some of them presentation copies: *The Pleasures of Memory,* 1792, which went through four editions in a few months, his *Poems,* 1812, *Italy, A Poem,* 1822 (Part the Second 1828), both these latter works later being illustrated in a series of steel-engravings by J. M. W. Turner and T. Stothard 'at an enormous expense'; *Human Life,* 1819, the first edition issued in quarto size, with a second edition, in octavo, dated the same year, and the very readable *Recollections of the Table-talk of Samuel Rogers,* 1856, edited by A. Dyce.

Percy Bysshe Shelley (1792–1822), Leigh Hunt (1784–1859), John Keats (1795–1821) and John Clare (1793–1864) are all represented by first editions or early texts. Clare I have all but complete, and mostly in the original bindings of paper-covered boards with uncut edges.

I have never discovered a copy of *Poems on Various Occasions,* 1807, by Lord Byron (1788–1824). It was privately printed and preceded only by his *Fugitive Pieces* (Newark, 1806), of which only a handful of copies have survived. But I do have a copy of the poet's third work, in fact his first published work, *Hours of Idleness,* 1807, also published at Newark. Only 100 copies were printed. *Poems Original and Translated,* 1808, is designated on the title-page as 'second

First editions, in the original paper-covered boards, of Tennyson's *Poems,* 1842, and John Clare's *The Village Minstrel,* 1821, the binding styles being similar although over 20 years separate the issues.

Size of 1 volume of
Tennyson's *Poems:*
17.5cm × 2cm.

An uncut copy, in the original boards, of the first edition of John Clare's *The Village Minstrel,* 1821, published in two volumes.

Size of title-page:
18cm × 10.5cm.

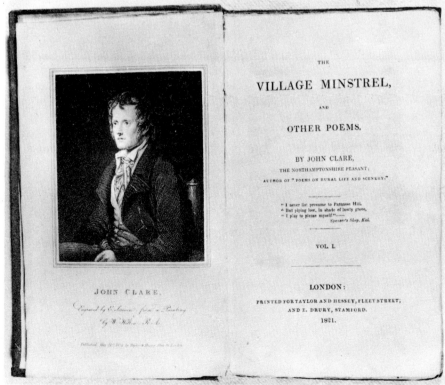

THE PRINCE'S PROGRESS
AND OTHER POEMS
BY CHRISTINA ROSSETTI

The long hours go and come and go

MACMILLAN & CO. 1866

W.J. LINTON SC.

You should have wept her yesterday

D. G. Rossetti's designs for the frontispiece and title-page of the first edition of Christina Rossetti's *The Prince's Progress*, 1866.
Size of title-page:
17cm × 10.5cm.

edition', although at least five of the poems appear here for the first time. *English Bards and Scotch Reviewers,* a biting satire, was published undated but appeared in 1809. At least three counterfeit editions appeared the same year. Space forbids mention of the rest of his poetical works, except perhaps that notorious rarity *Waltz: an apostrophic hymn,* by Horace Hornem esq., 1813. *Childe Harold's Pilgrimage, The Giaour,* and *Don Juan,* will present little difficulty after you have tracked down the elusive *Waltz,* but the search will be long.

Thomas Hood's *The Plea of the Midsummer Fairies,* 1827, stands next on my shelf to John Keble's *The Christian Year,* two vols. 1827, the first volumes of verse to be published in a full-cloth binding, with paper-labelled spines. My copy is the only one I know to have survived in the original state. It contains the first printing of some well-loved hymns, including *New Every Morning is the Love.* Amongst hymnologists I have *Remains of the Late Rev. Lyte,* 1850, containing the first printing of *Abide with Me,* a small cloth-bound octavo that seems to have been ignored by bibliographers.

Elizabeth Barrett Browning (1806–61) and her husband Robert Browning (1812–89) have both been favourites with poetry collectors since the late 19th century. Many of their works in first edition form can be found easily enough, but, as with every other author whose output extends over many years, there are always difficult (or impossible) titles. Elizabeth's first book, *The Battle of Marathon: a Poem,* 1820, is almost unknown, and her *Essay on Mind,* 1826, is also rare. I have had to be content with *Poems,* 1844, in the original green cloth, a two-volume work that now fetches over £100 ($240) if complete with the eight pages of inserted advertisements. *Aurora Leigh,* 1857, *The Seraphim,* 1838, and her later works should present little difficulty if you are prepared to wait and watch. Robert Browning has so far eluded me with his *Bells and Pomegranates*, issued in eight parts under differing titles, the first being *Pippa Passes*, 1841. Nearly everything else he published is in my collection, including *Dramatis Personae*, 1864, *Men and Women*, two vols. 1855, and *The Ring and the Book*, 4 vols. 1868-9. *Pauline*, 1833, and *Paracelsus*, 1835, have never yet come within stalking distance.

To find a fine copy in the original cloth of *Lays of Ancient Rome*, 1842, by Lord Macaulay (1800-59) took many years, as did *The Prince's Progress and Other Poems*, 1866, by Christina Rossetti (1830-94), but *London Lyrics*, 1857, by Frederick Locker (later, Frederick Locker-Lampson, 1821-95) is a most difficult 'first'. It forms the basis of all the various editions of that title that followed, the author constantly adding and changing to the end of his writing career. *The Defence of Guenevere*, 1858, by William Morris (1834-96) I consider a very under-priced book, only about 250 copies being sold when it was first published. Despite this one can still purchase a good copy in the original cloth for as little as £10 ($24). Yet the edition of the same work dated 1892 published by the Kelmscott Press, founded by Morris in 1890, commands as much as £60 ($144). *Atalanta in Calydon*, by Algernon Charles Swinburne, was first published in a limited edition of 100 copies in 1865. Issued in a binding of cream buckram over bevelled boards, it is a difficult 'first' to find in clean and acceptable state, and now fetches in the region of £50 ($120). His *Poems and Ballads*, 1866, must have the imprint of Edward Moxon & Co., to qualify as a first edition (of which there are two separate issues). Hotten, the publisher to whom Moxon transferred the book after the outcry of public protest, re-issued it with a fresh setting of type, but without any indication that this was in fact a second edition. So a collector must be on his guard.

It grieves me to have to run my eye along so many shelves of poetry, both major and minor, of which I can make no mention. *Verses on Various Occasions*, 1868, by Cardinal Newman (1801-90) asks to be brought to your attention to make clear the facts regarding the two distinct editions that both appeared the same year, with no indication on the title-page of the second edition that the book had already appeared. The first edition has 340 pages, the second 368. Newman's name is not mentioned on the title-page. Alfred, Lord Tennyson, has a shelf to himself. I lack a 'first' of *Poems, by Two Brothers*, 1827 (the second edition did not appear until Macmillan & Co., issued a limited edition of 300 copies in 1893). *Timbuctoo*, the poet's first separately published work, and always referred to by its sub-title, appeared in 1829. Most of the rest of his large output I have been able to find fairly easily, with his two-volume *Poems*, 1842, in the original boards, and *In Memoriam*, 1850, taking pride of place.

In America William Cullen Bryant (1794-1878) was for 50 years editor of the *New York Evening Post*; but he began to make a name for himself as a poet as early as 1817 with the publication of *Thanatopsis*, still his best known poem. It owes much to the influence of William Wordsworth, as does nearly all of his poetical work. He confirmed his reputation as the leading American poet of the day with his *Poems*, 1821. The first edition of *A Forest Hymn* appeared in quarto form in New York (1860); his *Hymns* in the same city (1864); as did *Thirty Poems*, 1864. One of the best known abroad of America's poets is Henry Wadsworth Longfellow (1807-82), whose rare command of metre allowed him to contrive metrical effects that jingle the memory years after his poems are first read. In many cases his first editions appeared under a London imprint before their issue in America. *The Song of Hiawatha*, 1855, was first published by David Bogue, London, a few days before Ticknor, Reed & Fields, Boston, issued the American sheets. *Voices of the Night*, 1839, and *Evangeline*, 1847, are titles that command high figures at auction. *The Golden Legend*, 1851, *The Courtship of Miles Standish*, 1858, and *Tales of a Wayside Inn*, 1863, can all be purchased for moderate sums, but the latest auction price for the true first edition of *Hiawatha* is close to £150 ($360). Especially desirable is a copy of the magnificently produced first collected edition of his poems, published by Carey & Hart, Philadelphia, 1845, a limited number of copies being issued in a publisher's binding of full-morocco, heavily gilt.

John Greenleaf Whittier (1807-92), born in the same year as Longfellow, was a Quaker poet. His early work includes *Lays of My Home*, 1843, *Songs of Labour*, 1850, and *Panorama*, 1856. *Snow-Bound*, first issued in Boston in 1866,

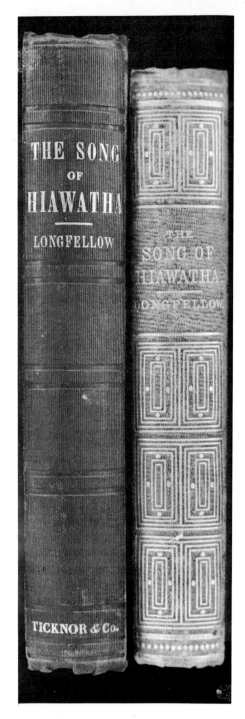

The first edition of Longfellow's *The Song of Hiawatha*, 1855, is the English edition (on the right); the American edition, published by Ticknor, Reed & Fields, Boston, being issued 10 days later (on 10 November 1855). The first (English) edition is much the more difficult of the two issues to find, but either will now cost a collector about £30 ($72).

Size of left-hand spine: 18.5cm × 3cm.

with its vivid descriptions and felicity of phrase, is undoubtedly his masterpiece, with its conjured projection of an old Puritan Colonial interior taking the reader back in time to the early settlers in Massachusetts. Copies of the first edition can not now be obtained in original condition (or thereabouts) for much less than £150 ($360).

Mosada, 1886, by William Butler Yeats (1865–1939) is in fact a privately printed offprint of the poet's first published work, which had appeared in the June 1886 issue of the *Dublin University Review.* Only about 100 copies are believed to have been printed and very few of these appear to have withstood the test of time. This six-leaf pamphlet now fetches anything up to £1,000 ($2,400) at auction, and all Yeats' first editions have rocketed in price during the last decade. Robert Louis Stevenson's *A Child's Garden of Verses,* 1885, is a well-loved little book, difficult to find in first edition form, as is *A Shropshire Lad,* 1896, by A. E. Housman (1859–1936). The binding is rather fragile, and I keep my copy in a specially made folding box to preserve the paper label and the paper-covered boards. My copy of *Verses and Sonnets,* 1896, by Hilaire Belloc (1870–1953), the poet's first book, contains a tipped-in letter from the author to a Mr Charles Wilson, dated 2 December 1930, which reads:

My first published book was a badly printed very small book of verse which contained more than one piece which I thought below the sufficient standard,

53

so that I have long withdrawn it from publication and had the copies destroyed . . .

My copy, in mint condition and still in its original plain-paper dust-wrapper, must have escaped, as have several others I know of. The paper used is most unusual, being almost a stiff board in feel and appearance. Despite the imprint of Ward & Downey, London, I strongly suspect that Belloc paid F. N. Evans & Co., Crystal Palace, London, to print the work for him and that the book was published at his own expense.

Thomas Hardy (1840–1928) is represented by his *Wessex Poems,* 1898, and his *Satires of Circumstance,* 1914; while Oscar Wilde (1856–1900) I have all but complete. *The Ballad of Reading Gaol,* 1898, by C.3.3., was published by Leonard Smithers, in an edition of 800 copies on handmade paper, and 30 copies on Japanese vellum. Several piracies appeared almost identical in appearance with the genuine first edition. 'C.3.3.' was Wilde's number in Reading Gaol, indicating that he occupied Cell 3 on the third landing of Gallery C.

A. E. Housman's influence on the poetry of the Georgian period can be seen in the work of many who followed him. George Orwell wrote that Housman stood for 'a kind of bitter, defiant paganism, a conviction that life is short and the gods are against you . . .' John Masefield (1878–1967), who succeeded Robert Bridges as Poet Laureate in 1930, and many of the poets of the First World War, reflect in some degree the sentiments expressed in *The Shropshire Lad,* a preoccupation with unhappy love, murder, sudden death, and the futility of life.

These poets of the early part of the 20th century make an interesting school to collect, although in almost every case their first published works are difficult and expensive books to find in first edition form. I have *The Listeners,* 1912, by Walter de la Mare, but have never been able to afford a copy of *Songs of Childhood,* 1902, published under his pseudonym of 'Walter Ramal'. *1914 and Other Poems,* 1915, by Rupert Brooke (1887–1915) is not easy to find in a first impression, but re-prints in exactly the same format are legion. John Masefield's *Salt-Water Ballads,* 1902, has always been difficult to find in fine condition as the spine of blue cloth is very subject to fading. His *Ballads and Poems,* 1910, and *Reynard the Fox* (1919), contain much of his finest poetry, although the first named work reprints pieces from *Salt-Water Ballads,* including his famous *Sea-Fever.* James Elroy Flecker (1884–1915) is best remembered for his *The Golden Journey to Samarkand,* 1913, not a difficult 'first' to find, although the limited issue with a vellum spine was restricted to only 50 copies. Despite the fact that D. H. Lawrence (1885–1930) lived in Zennor, Cornwall, within a mile from my home (his stone cottage is in almost the identical condition to when he left it in 1917), I have not yet acquired a copy of his *Love Poems and Others,* 1913, his first book of poems, or, for that matter, his novel *Women in Love,* 1920, most of which he wrote here in Cornwall.

A now elderly collector of poetry whom I know well, purchased *The Mother and Other Poems,* 1915, by Edith Sitwell (1887–1964), as a new little book at the published price of sixpence (6 cents). The only copy I have seen offered for sale in recent years was priced at £50 ($120). I suppose much the same could have occurred with the perceptive purchaser of T. S. Eliot's *Prufrock and Other Observations,* 1917, issued in paper wrappers at one shilling a copy and now fetching anything up to £100 ($240). His *The Waste Land,* 1922, was first published in New York. It has the misprint 'mount in' for 'mountain' on page 41, in the earliest issues. The first English edition, hand-printed at the Hogarth Press, Richmond, Surrey, was not published until September 1923. *Over the Brazier,* 1916, by Robert Graves, is a most elusive first edition. It was published by Harold Munro at his Poetry Bookshop, and, a fragile production, originally issued at eightpence (8 cents), it now fetches anything up to £180 ($432). My copy is considerably less than fine, and is only holding the fort until I discover another in the original printed wrappers. *Ardours and Endurances,* 1917, by Robert Nichols (1893–1944), the poet's second book, is common and inexpensive; but I have only seen one copy of *Invocation,* 1915, which preceded it.

The *Poems* of Gerard Manley Hopkins (1844–89) were not published until long after his death. The date, 1918, appears on the half-title, and the work was

18
POEMS

DYLAN THOMAS

Published by
THE SUNDAY REFEREE and
THE PARTON BOOKSHOP
PARTON STREET, LONDON. W.C.I

The poet's first book, published in 1934. Copies of the first issue, shown here, can now be valued at about £100 ($240), and continue to rise steeply in price with each passing year.

Size of title-page:
21.5cm × 14cm.

Frontispiece of *Readings in Poetry*, the first English poetical miscellany to contain the work of American poets, including James G. Whittier, William Bryant, N. P. Willis, R. H. Dana, W. H. Longfellow, James G. Percival, and many others, few, if any, of whose works had appeared in England before this date. *Readings in Poetry*, 1833, was possibly edited by William Cooke Taylor (1800–49.)

Size of title-page:
17cm × 10.7cm.

edited by Robert Bridges. In several respects Hopkins was one of the greatest of the poets of the Victorian age, *The Windhover* and *The Wreck of the Deutschland* showing him at his most powerful; but Bridges, his literary executor, retained the manuscripts for nearly 30 years before allowing them to be printed.

Running my eyes down my shelves of modern poetry I finish by mentioning *Poems*, 1930, by W. H. Auden; *Poems*, 1920, by Wilfred Owen (1893–1918); and then to a man I have complete in his major work, Dylan Thomas (1914–53). The first issue of the first edition of his *18 Poems*, 1934, issued at 3/6d (42 cents), is still in its dust-wrapper, as are all his other 'firsts'. Any modern work dating from the last 40 years or so should be looked for in its original dust-jacket, and copies without this protection should be replaced when the opportunity affords. Although not part of the book, these eye-catching selling aids do lend emphasis to the age in which the volume first appeared, and to the feel of the era in which the author wrote. They change in colour and design as quickly as do the fashions in women's clothes and now employ the talents of the most creative of artists and designers. Most of Thomas's other works range beside my copy of his *18 Poems*; the most difficult to acquire have been *Conversation about Christmas*, 1954, an inconsiderable little eight-page pamphlet issued for the friends of J. Laughlin and *New Directions*; and *Deaths and Entrances*, 1946, a demy 16mo, bound in bright orange cloth. *Under Milk Wood*, 1954, should not prove difficult to acquire, but is rising in price with each and every catalogue.

David Gascoyne (b. 1916), the first English poet to be deeply influenced by the surrealism of the 1930s, produced his *Short Survey of Surrealism*, in 1935; a work that was preceded only by Georges Hugnet's *Petite Anthologie du Surrealisme*, 1934. 'The disastrous decade. Infiltration of literature by destructive influences of Surrealism', Cyril Connolly called the 1930s in his book *The Modern Movement*, 1965. 'Nevertheless a good period to be young in.' Gascoyne was 14 years of age in 1930, yet published his first book of poetry, *Roman Balcony and Other Poems*, in 1932, a remarkable achievement for one so young. *Man's Life is this Meat*, 1936, was followed by *Poems: 1937–1942*, 1943, illustrated in characteristic style by Graham Sutherland. *Hölderlin's Madness*, 1938, *A Vagrant and Other Poems*, 1951, and *Night Thoughts*, 1956, are other of Gascoyne's poetical works I have in my collection. His autobiographical *Opening Day*, 1933, is his first prose work.

Like most collectors of modern first editions, I keep my eye on the literary reviews as a guide when adding new books to my shelves. John Berryman, Allen Ginsberg, Philip Larkin, R. S. Thomas, Ted Hughes, John Updike, and other contemporary poets are bought new, read, and slipped into their steadily filling rows.

There are many specialist bibliographies that the collector of poetry can consult, each dealing with the works of a single poet, or of a period or group. *Seven XVIIIth Century Bibliographies*, 1924, by Iola A. Williams, is one such; but an all-embracing work covering the entire field can be found in *English Poetry*, 1950, by John Hayward, of which the illustrated edition was limited to 550 copies.

POETS' CORNER, WESTMINSTER ABBEY.

Drama

Although my collection of first and early editions of verse, some 2,000 volumes, is superior, both in numbers and in quality, to my books on the theatre and drama, I have managed to amass a shelf of plays and theatrical works to which I am still adding. I need hardly say that amongst the works of the greatest poets and playwrights, William Shakespeare (1564–1616) takes pride of place.

We are indebted to a paragraph by Francis Meres (1565–1647), a Cambridge divine and schoolmaster, written in his *Palladis Tamia: Wits Treasury,* published in 1598, for our ability to date with certainty, as being early or late in the Shakespeare canon, a number of the plays he wrote. As the relevant passage allows me a chance to illustrate the factual evidence by means of which bibliographers are able to make dogmatic assertions I will quote it in full. It must be remembered that Meres' book appeared during Shakespeare's lifetime and that the greatest of his works remained as yet unwritten. It enables us to recognise that he was acknowledged by his contemporaries as the author of plays which Baconians once tried to assign elsewhere.

As *Plautus* and *Seneca* are accounted the best for Comedy and Tragedy among the Latines: so *Shakespeare* among ye English is the most excellent in both kinds for the stage; for Comedy, witnes his *Gentlemen of Verona,* his *Errors,* his *Love Labors lost,* his *Love Labours wonne,* his *Midsummers Night Dreame,* & his *Merchant of Venice:* for Tragedy his *Richard the 2. Richard the 3. Henry the 4. King John, Titus Andronicus* and his *Romeo and Juliet.*

No play by the name of *Love Labours wonne* has ever been discovered; but the other eleven plays in Meres' list are, of course, well known. This perceptive Cambridge schoolmaster had no hesitation in placing Shakespeare (with his best work still to be written) at the head of the 80 or so other English writers he cites. For a contemporary critic to do this shows that Shakespeare was already recognised as the genius we now know him to have been, and that his own day and age were already applauding in decisive fashion the work of the actor from Stratford-upon-Avon.

By the 16th century play-going had become an accepted part of town and country life in England, whenever amateur players or companies of professional actors visited the district. The halls of large country houses served the amateur players, while the galleried yards of inns proved ideal for the strolling players who made their living by the stage. The first London playhouse was erected in 1576. It was called simply The Theatre, and was built in Shoreditch, just outside the Bishopsgate entrance to the City. Before long The Curtain, London's second theatre, was built alongside to cope with the ever-growing crowds who packed every performance. Others soon appeared, including The Newington Theatre; The Rose, belonging to Philip Henslowe, where the famous Edward Alleyn used to appear; The Swan; and the most renowned of all Elizabethan play-houses, The Globe, in Bankside, Southwark. Here it was that the Lord Chamberlain's men played to audiences that came from far and wide, with Will Shakespeare as one of the cast. First opened in 1599, it soon established a reputation that made it the most famous theatre in the country. It was burnt down in 1613, but was re-built and remained in use until 1642. Like most of the other major theatres of the time, The Globe was a great deal larger than most of us today would imagine and audiences of up to 3,000 people were said to have attended the most popular plays.

The title-page of the first octavo, and first illustrated, Shakespeare, edited by Nicholas Rowe, published in 1709 in six volumes, a seventh volume, unauthorised, appearing 1710.

Size of printed title-page: 19.5cm × 12cm.

THE
WORKS
OF
Mr. *William Shakefpear*;
IN
SIX VOLUMES.

ADORN'D with CUTS.

Revis'd and Corrected, with an Account of
the Life and Writings of the Author.

By *N. ROWE*, Efq;

LONDON:

Printed for *Jacob Tonfon*, within *Grays-Inn*
Gate, next *Grays-Inn* Lane. MDCCIX.

Mr P. Gucht Sculp.

Of Shakespeare's contemporaries, Christopher Marlowe (1564–93) wrote
Tamburlaine the Great, printed anonymously in 1590, but acted two or three
years earlier. *The Troublesome reigne of Edward the second*, 1594, *The Tragicall
History of D. Faustus*, 1604, and *The Famous History of the Rich Jew of Malta*,
1633, were three others of his plays that are occasionally revived today; but they
are unlikely to concern the collector of plays in first edition form as their
extreme rarity makes them almost unknown in the auction room. One can be
content with the first appearance of his collected works, published in three

Copperplate engraved frontispiece to *Hamlet* in the first illustrated Shakespeare, edited by Nicholas Rowe.

volumes in 1826, and obtainable for £40 to £50 ($96 to $120). Marlowe's contemporary, Thomas Kyd (1558–94) is remembered for his *Cornelia*, 1594 (re-issued as *Pompey the Great* in 1595), and for *The Spanish Tragedie* (1594?). His collected works did not appear in print until 1901.

The Comedy of Errors (*c.* 1592) and *Titus Andronicus* (*c.* 1593) are two of Shakespeare's earliest plays, with *Cymbeline, The Winter's Tale,* and *The Tempest,* coming at the end of his writing career. The dramatic companies that performed his plays and those of other playwrights developed from the entertainers who once formed an integral part of royal and aristocratic households. The two most important companies in Elizabeth's day were 'the Admiral's men' and 'the Chamberlain's men'. Alleyn was considered the most talented actor amongst the Admiral's men, and Richard Burbage the greatest of the Chamberlain's company. Plays were usually bought outright by the company from the author, and the original manuscripts formed part of the troupe's stock-in-trade. The author seldom had the chance to print his play for the world to read: to do so would allow other companies to act it, thus destroying the sole performing rights vested in the actors who had bought it from him. It is not surprising therefore, that 16th- and early 17th-century plays rarely appeared in print until several years after they had first been written and acted, and then, more often than not, in pirated and garbled form.

The plays of William Shakespeare were first printed in quarto, the last to appear being *Othello,* 1622, issued after his death. But many did not appear in print until the publication of the noble volume of his collected works, the great First Folio, issued in 1623. This book, one of the glories of English literature, was compiled by Shakespeare's old friends and fellow actors John Heming and Henry Condell. One must remember that these two men were actors and not writers, and the collection of the text and the laborious task of preparing the manuscript for the press must have been a tedious and exacting discipline extending over many months. Without their hard work as many as 20 now world-famous plays might well have been lost to us forever, for not one of them had ever appeared in print before. In 1619, W. Jaggard and T. Pavier had attempted to make a quick financial killing by binding up real and spurious plays in an unauthorised collection of Shakespeare's works. Many were issued with false dates. It was the appearance of this 'false folio' as it has come to be known that spurred Heming and Condell into action. The result was the First Folio of 1623, with its prefatory remarks castigating Jaggard and his partner, although not by name, as being responsible for 'stolne and surreptitious copies, maimed and deformed by the frauds and stealthes of injurious impostors that expos'd them.'

For a collector to aspire to add to his library an original first printing of a play by Shakespeare in quarto form, issued before the appearance of the First Folio, is a dream that will never be realised, silver spoon, oil-wells, diamond mines, or what you will. He will almost certainly have to be content with a set of the four folio editions, issued in 1623, 1632, 1664, and 1685, with the proviso that he has the equivalent of £50,000 ($120,000) to pay for his purchase. Even then he may have to accept a leaf or two in facsimile, for a set of the four folios, all in complete and unsophisticated condition, is an event in the auction rooms that sets the world's press voicing the news across a front page column. As one would expect, the First Folio is the volume that commands the greatest price, a complete copy easily making a five-figure sum. When I state that, a year or two ago, a leading London dealer paid £3,000 ($7,200) under the hammer for a copy with nine of the preliminary leaves and the last five leaves in facsimile, 47 other leaves added to make up the text (these taken from the second and third Folio Editions) and the volume sold with other faults, you will realise that the bottom of the barrel is being scraped for any morsel that the past has left for us. Before World War II such a copy would have not made £50 ($120).

One will have to consult the specialist bibliographies to discover all the points to look for in the varying states of issue of the four folios. Each has as a frontispiece a copperplate portrait of Shakespeare by Droeshout, believed to be a likeness approved by those who had actually been friends and acquaintances of the author, although it is unlikely that the artist ever met him. This portrait, and the leaf of verses by Ben Jonson, are the two leaves most often missing, although all the preliminary leaves, and those at the end of the text, often have to be supplied in facsimile. The Third Folio of 1664 has the reputation of being as rare as the First, as many copies perished in the Great Fire of London in 1666.

After the four folios came the edition of which I have managed to acquire two sets, although I do not normally make a practice of keeping two identical editions of the same work on my shelves. However, the seven-volume 1709 edition of Shakespeare's works is of such importance, and is becoming so rare, that I have made an exception with a set of volumes that seem of prime interest to visiting book-collectors and friends. They delight in examining the work, and I make sure they handle my second-best copy in the manner that Jean Grolier stipulated in gentle fashion in the mid-16th century. He was a generous-hearted man and instructed his binder to add the words *Io Grolierii et*

Amicorum (of Jean Grolier and his friends) after his *ex libris* mark of ownership. Nicholas Rowe's 1709 edition was a pioneering work that displays considerable scholarship, and is an amazing achievement by a man who laid no claim to be an academic or even a literary critic. He was first and foremost a poet and dramatist, and received the laureateship in 1715. Rowe (1674–1718), had intended the collection to be a six-volume edition, but in 1710 a seventh volume appeared under the imprint of Edmund Curll, carefully designed to range with Rowe's set of volumes. 'Volume the Seventh' contained *Venus and Adonis*; *Tarquin and Lucrece*; and the *Sonnets* and *Miscellany Poems*. It is much the rarest of the numbered volumes in the set, and, if offered alone, as it sometimes is, it commands prices as high as £50 ($120). But to return to Rowe's pioneer work: it recorded an almost embarrassing succession of first printings, in the sense that the following innovations first appeared in this edition. It was the:

first illustrated edition

first octavo edition

first edition to contain a Life of Shakespeare

first edited edition

first edition to list the dramatis personae

first edition to attempt the division and location of scenes

first edition to clearly denote entrances and exits

first edition to contain a criticism of the works of Shakespeare

first edition to give details of the actors' costumes

first edition to tell the story of Lucy and the deer stealing

For the first time it made intelligible to readers and actors of a later age an abstruse and difficult mass of Elizabethan literature. His contemporaries accorded him little praise, although most of his emendations and clarifications were later appropriated by those who came after him. Curll's seventh volume of 1710 was printed without Rowe's authority. It was, however, incorporated in the third issue of Rowe's second edition which appeared in nine volumes in 1714. It is an interesting point that Rowe chose to illustrate his editions with full-page copperplate engravings showing the actors in contemporary dress (of the period of Queen Anne), rather than in the period in which the plays were originally written.

Shakespeare's next editor, Alexander Pope (1688–1744), produced a version in six volumes dated 1723–5. It said little new and textually is unimportant; although he did add several omitted passages from the quartos and identified lines printed as prose that the author had written as verse. A set of Pope's edition now fetches in the region of £20 ($48). But the first really important critic and reviser of the original printed texts was Lewis Theobald (1688–1744), poet, translator, and dramatist, who published in 1726 his *Shakespeare Restored; or, A Specimen of the many Errors as well Committed as unamended by Mr Pope*. He followed this in 1733 with his seven-volume *Works of Shakespeare* (re-issued under a Dublin imprint in 1739). We owe to Theobald many valuable restorations in the text, and many of his conjectural emendations have been applauded by the eminent literary historians and critics who followed where he had shown the way. Alexander Pope was furious at being deflated as a literary critic by a fellow poet and dramatist, and he made Theobald the hero of his satirical poem directed against dullness and indolence entitled *The Dunciad*, of which three books were published anonymously in 1728. *The Dunciad, Variorum*, the first collected edition of the three books, was published in 1729, and he followed this with *The New Dunciad*, 1742, the fourth book in the series, but with the playwright and poet laureate Colley Cibber (1671–1757) enthroned as hero in Theobald's stead. A set of the first edition of Theobald's *Shakespeare* now fetches about £80 ($192).

He was followed by Sir Thomas Hanmer (1677–1746), whose *Works of Shakespeare*, issued in six volumes at Oxford, 1743–4, were described as being 'carefully revised and corrected'. In fact he had nothing new to say. William Warburton (1698–1779), was the next to try his hand. He was Bishop of Gloucester, and a literary bully who tried to conceal his lack of scholarship under a smoke-screen of fist-shaking at the ignoramuses who, he told his readers, had handled the Shakespearean texts before he himself took up the pen. He entitled his eight-volume work, which appeared in 1747, and was followed almost immediately by a Dublin imprint of the same year, *The Works of Shakespeare. The Genuine Text, collated with all the former editions and then corrected and emended, is here settled; being restored from the Blunders of the First Editors.* As a text the edition is of little value, but it drew from Thomas Edwards the following year an ironical rejoinder in the form of a supplement. Re-issued as *The Canons of Criticism* it brilliantly exposed Warburton's grotesque absurdities and revealed the way he had tortured the text to bend it to his own arguments. Yet Dr Johnson, a friend of Warburton, while admitting that Edwards had scored points, compared him to a mere fly stinging 'a stately horse'.

Samuel Johnson's eight-volume edition of the *Plays of William Shakespeare*, published in 1765 (10 vols. Dublin, 1766), is remarkable for its great preface, now accorded the laurels as being one of the major landmarks in literary criticism. A set in a contemporary binding would now cost about £120 ($288). It has a portrait frontispiece in Volume 1, as do almost all sets of collected works, no matter who the author may be. Lowndes *Bibliographer's Manual of English Literature,* can be consulted regarding frontispieces and other plates required in major works that have appeared at auction before the 1850s, but for more intimate details the collector will have to refer to specialist bibliographies.

Shakespeare is so well loved, and finds a place in nearly every home where a shelf or two of books await their readers, that I have dealt with his collected works at length. A list of the other important editions reads as follows:

Edward Capell (1713–81)	10 vols.	1767–8
George Steevens (1736–1800)	10 vols.	1778
Edmund Malone (1741–1812)	10 vols.	1790
Alexander Dyce (1798–1869)	6 vols.	1857

From this time onwards editions multiplied to an extent that makes further entries impossible. *The Cambridge Shakespeare,* edited by W. G. Clark and J. Glover, was for long a standard text, superseded by *The New Cambridge Shakespeare* (1921–66), edited by Sir Arthur Quiller-Couch, John Dover Wilson, and others. A fine set for the collector is the Nonesuch Press edition, 1929–33, bound in niger morocco and published in seven volumes. The editor was Herbert Farjeon. Such a set in fine condition will now cost in the region of £200 ($480). But the four-volume Nonesuch Press edition, published in 1953 in a binding of marbled boards with cloth spines, is an excellent buy at £20 ($48).

The most noteworthy friend of Shakespeare's of whom we have knowledge was Ben Jonson (1572–1637) who wrote intricate plots around characters displaying what he termed 'comedy of humours'. His *Workes* appeared as a first collected edition in 1616; a good copy in contemporary calf binding fetching anything up to £400 ($960). Several of his individual plays, originally issued in quarto form, were reprinted by private presses. *A Croppe of Kisses* appeared as a limited edition by the Golden Cockerel Press in 1937, and is sought after by collectors. So is his *Volpone: or the Foxe,* with a frontispiece and other illustrations by Aubrey Beardsley, issued as a quarto in 1898.

Francis Beaumont (1584–1616), and John Fletcher (1579–1625), wrote in such close collaboration that modern scholarship has still not decided exactly who wrote which of the plays. The first collected edition of their *Workes* was issued as a folio in 1647, with the second edition following in 1679. Philip Massinger (1583–1640), is remembered for his comedy *A New Way to Pay Old Debts,* 1633; but the collected edition of his *Dramatic Works,* in four volumes; did not appear until 1759. With James Shirley (c. 1596–1666) an era came to an end as far as drama was concerned, all the theatres being closed by order of the Puritan parliament in 1642.

Among the dramatists whose works were performed after the Restoration of 1666, I have a fine copy of *The Works of the Ingenious Mr. William Wycherley,* 1713. This contains *The Plain-Dealer, The Country Wife, The Gentleman Dancing-master,* and *Love in a Wood.* To match this I have his *Miscellany Poems,* 1704, a fine folio in contemporary blind-stamped sprinkled-calf, with the magnificent portrait frontispiece after Sir Peter Lely. This very lively collection of poems by one of the wittiest of the Restoration dramatists contains much of Wycherley's best work. Others who contributed their quota of bawdy plays that

15, VICARAGE GARDENS,
KENSINGTON,
LONDON, W.

re OSCAR WILDE deceased

Dear Sir,

As the Administrator of the estate and effects of the late Mr. Oscar Wilde, my attention has been called to the very large number of unauthorised prints of the Author's Works being offered for sale in various parts of London _____ country at the present time.

I am well aware that for _____ late Mr. Wilde's death in 1900, and pr_____ trator of his estate in 1906, _____ authorities to put a stop to _____ authorised prints; and I ha_____ in question have been offere_____ various members of the bo_____ the belief that they were _____

The sale of these _____ affects prejudicially the _____ interests of Messrs. Me_____ the authorised editions _____ take the necessary _____ unauthorised prints. _____

I am therefo_____ of the book trade, _____ faith in the mat_____ of their being f_____ otherwise deali_____ Works, legal _____ doing so.

Herewith you_____ of the authorised editions whic_____ _____om.

I remain,

Your obedient ser_____

ROBERT ROSS.

July, 1908.

[P.T.O.

OSCAR WILDE.

ALFRED ELLIS & WALERY

51 BAKER STREET LONDON W

delighted the audiences of an age intent on forgetting Cromwell and his Puritans were William Congreve (1670–1730), whose first collected works were issued in three volumes in 1710; Sir John Vanbrugh (1664–1726); and George Farquhar (1678–1707). I am well content with my Baskerville edition of Congreve's works, 3 vols. 1761, a beautifully printed text with frontispieces to each of the several plays. Jeremy Collier condemned the indecency of the age in his *Short View of the Immorality and Profaneness of the English Stage*, 1698, but a fashion had been set that the public was not to see abandoned lightly.

An Apology for the Life of Mr. Colley Cibber, Comedian, 1740, which was written by Cibber (1671–1757) himself, is one of the shrewdest and most kindly records of the contemporary stage that has come down to us. It is a book that can be read today with as much pleasure as when it first appeared. This wide-margined quarto, complete with its copperplate frontispiece of the author, is now commanding well over £100 ($240). Jonathan Swift is said to have sat up all night to read the book through, and even Samuel Johnson gave it grudging praise. Oliver Goldsmith (1730–74) although well represented in my collection by his prose works, is not shown by his successful play *She Stoops to Conquer,* 1773; or by his *The Good Natur'd Man,* 1768. R. B. Sheridan (1751–1816) is a difficult author to collect in first edition form, but I have managed to acquire a copy of the first printing of his collected works, a 12mo complete with portrait frontispiece, printed in Dublin in 1792.

Ballad opera, as exemplified by John Gay (1685–1732), with his extremely successful *Beggar's Opera,* 1728, foreshadowed the comic operas of Gilbert and Sullivan. David Garrick (1717–79), the greatest actor the century produced, also wrote 20 or more plays, as well as a large number of adaptions from the great playwrights who had gone before. The first collected edition of his dramatic works appeared in three volumes, 1768.

Dickens' *Nicholas Nickleby* affords us an intimate glimpse of the theatre in the early part of the 19th century, but I have little of the period in my library until the appearance of Irving, Wyndham and the Bancrofts. Arthur Wing Pinero (1859–1934), despite churning out a host of minor drama, is not now collected to any great extent; but the works of Oscar Wilde (1854–1900) fetch high prices whenever they appear for sale. *The Importance of Being Earnest,* 1895, produced the year he was arrested, is often revived and has stood the test of time as a comedy of the most enduring humour.

The shelf containing my collections of the writings of George Bernard Shaw (1856–1950), whose works can still be obtained for quite small sums, has also those of his fellow-Irishman J. M. Synge (1871–1909). John Galsworthy (1867–1933), and T. S. Eliot (1888–1965), bring me as near to the moderns as I have yet ventured. Except, that is, for *Look Back in Anger,* 1957, by John Osborne.

Science & Medicine

'The Art itself is Nature'
Shakespeare

Detail from the title page of *A Sketch of the Origin and Progress of Steam Navigation* by Bennet Woodcroft. This work appeared in 1848, and contains full-page illustrations of the author's then recently invented variable pitch screw-propeller, as well as a remarkable series of lithographic plates of steamships of the past.

The invention of printing from movable metal type marks a great advance in the development of Western civilisation. The use man makes of newly discovered technical devices, fresh knowledge in the field of physics, biology, medicine, geology, or the finding of an easier way of accomplishing tasks essential for his survival, is increased and added to when the know-how is imparted to the rest of experimenting humanity. The invention by Gutenberg of an efficient printing press, supported by rapid improvements in paper-making, stimulated an insistent demand for books that imparted scientific knowledge handed down not only by the ancients, but by modern scholarship and contemporary researchers. Early scientific and medical books have in recent years appreciated in value more rapidly than any other field of collected books. These works had set out to make the sum of knowledge available to the enquiring minds of the rest of intelligent mankind. The cultivated layman and the student of science benefited in equal degree, and they, in their turn, added pages to the encyclopedia of human progress. The tardy realisation of the important part the printed word played in the distribution of scientific and medical knowledge has caused an upsurge of interest in the 'first' books on every aspect of human endeavour, each and every publication giving details of a new discovery in any one of a dozen scientific, mathematical, medical, or mechanical spheres, seeming to at least double in price every few years. This is a reflection of the previous disregard by scholars and collectors for a class of books that probably made the greatest impact on the mind of man, shaping his reasoning and moulding the philosophies by which he steadies his way forward. I shall name some of the most important works, and give details of those I have been able to add to my own collection.

The first book printed with illustrations of a technical and scientific nature was *De re Militari*, 1472, by Robertus Valturius. It is also the first book containing woodcuts made by a contemporary Italian artist. One could best describe it as being a handbook of engines-of-war, a manual for the military engineer, with pictures of battering-rams, catapults, 15th-century portable bridges, gun turrets, and a diver's suit. The second edition appeared in 1483, and even this fetches well over £1,000 ($2,400) at auction. The first edition to be printed in Italian, *Del Arte Militare*, appeared later in the same year.

Modern surgery can be said to have started with Guy de Chauliac (1300–68) whose *Chirurgia*, 1478, was printed at Lyons. The author wrote the work in Latin in or about 1363, but the Latin text was not printed until 1498 at Venice. The first edition of 1478, printed in French, is so rare that very few of the largest national institutions possess a copy, and I know of no copy in private hands.

The first complete Latin edition of *Opera*, by Hippocrates (460?–337? B.C.), appeared in Rome in 1525. Aldus published an edition in Greek the following year. Hippocrates, a native of the island of Cos, is known as the 'Father of Medicine'. To him is ascribed the authorship of the Hippocratic Oath, the earliest statement on medical ethics. Nicholas Copernicus (1473–1543), founder of modern astronomy, was the first to propound the theory of the planetary orbits. *De Revolutionibus Orbium Coelestium*, 1543, published in Nuremberg by Johannes Petreius, revealed one of the greatest advances in human thought. Its English title is *On the Revolution of the Celestial Spheres*. His proof that the Earth was not after all the central point around which the entire Universe revolved helped to reorient the whole outlook of enquiring mankind,

Right
'The Collier', one of the 41 full-page hand-coloured plates from *The Costume of Yorkshire*, 1814, by George Walker and R. & D. Havell. This illustration shows the first printed view of a steam-engine on rails, that of John Blenkinsop's locomotive of 1812. Originally issued in 10 paper-wrappered monthly parts; the book now fetches in excess of £200 ($480) at auction.

Size of coloured surface: 30cm broad × 20cm high.

Taking in Water at Parkside.
(The Station where Mr Huskisson fell.)

London, Pub.d by R. ACKERMANN, 96 Strand 1831.

and knocked a prop from beneath certain religious superstitions. Geortius Agricola (1494–1555), wrote one of the earliest technological treatises of modern times. His *De re Metallica,* 1556, published in Basel, defines mining and metallurgy in scientific terms, with a host of chemical processes explained for the first time. The book contains nearly 300 woodcuts, many depicting early mechanical devices of the most absorbing interest. A first edition, complete and in a contemporary or early binding, would fetch well over £500 ($1,200).

Decimal fractions received their first systematic treatment in a 36-page pamphlet *De Thiende,* 1585, by Simon Stevin (1548–1620), published at Leiden. The modern atlas was born with the appearance of *Atlas sive Cosmographicae Meditationes de Fabrica Mundi,* 3 vols. *c.* 1585–95, by Gerardus Mercator (1512–94). Using what has come to be known as 'Mercator's Projection', the schoolboy, the sailor, or the armchair traveller, can plot a course by pencilling a straight line with a ruler, and, as developed by Edward Wright, the system has been used for all nautical charts until the most recent times.

Some years ago, I hesitated a day too long when offered for the sum of £100 ($240) an excellent copy of *De Magnete,* 1600, by William Gilbert (1544–1603). I have made a point, throughout my career as a book-collector, to acquire as many first statements in book form on as many important subjects as my shelves could hold and my pocket could afford. I knew that Gilbert's book, 'On the Magnet', was the first major English scientific treatise printed (based on experiments he had made), and that he had coined the name 'electricity' to describe the mysterious force occurring in certain phenomena which he described. In fact it was with Gilbert, who was physician to Queen Elizabeth I, that the study of magnetism and electricity started. The memory of the woodcuts and the folding diagram in the small folio volume the bookseller had opened before me sent me back to the shop next day, armed with my cheque book and three or four valuable duplicates which I hoped to sell and so mitigate the asking price. But the precious volume was no longer in the glass-fronted case. It had gone on approval to a university library, and it never came back. There is now a gap on my shelves that I shall never be able to fill, for the latest auction cataloguing of the first edition of *De Magnete* is just under £2,000 ($4,800). The next complete and perfect copy will make at least half as much again. So I shall have to be content with a facsimile reproduction.

Galileo Galilei (1564–1642) published his *Sidereus Nuncius* in Venice in 1610, a pamphlet of only 24 pages, yet containing many important astronomical discoveries. He was the first to use the telescope for scientific purposes (although he did not himself invent the instrument). All his first and early editions are eagerly sought and highly priced, and his 'Mathematical Discourses', published in Leiden by the Elzivir Press in 1638, as *Discorsi e Dimostrazioni Matematiche Inforno,* has made £1,000 ($2,400) at auction. Another mathematical discourse, unique in the history of science in that it was the result of unaided original deduction, was 'Description of the Wonderful Table of Logarithms'. First published in Edinburgh under its Latin title of *Mirifici Logarithmorum Canonis Descriptio,* 1614, it was the brain-child of a brilliant Scottish mathematician, John Napier (1550–1617), and, as later modified, gave us the first tables of decimal logarithms.

The discovery of the circulation of the blood was made by William Harvey (1578–1657) a successful physician and surgeon at St Bartholomew's Hospital, London. *Exercitatio Anatomica de Motu Cordis et Sanguinis in Animalibus,* 1628, was first published in Frankfurt, Germany, and is now so highly priced that the best a private collector can hope for would be either the facsimile reprint of 1894, or perhaps the finely printed Nonesuch Press edition, 1928. The first English edition of his *Anatomical Exercitations,* 1653, has been catalogued at over £500 ($1,200), reflecting the continuing rise in the price of important books in the field of science and medicine. Perhaps this fact is illustrated to even sharper effect when we turn to the works of Robert Boyle (1627–91) easily the best-known scientific experimenter of his day. A founder-member of the Royal Society, he always described himself as a chemist, although much of his most important work took place in the field of what we would today term experimental physics. *The Sceptical Chymist,* was published in London in 1661. It was his *magnum opus,* by means of which he overthrew the Aristotelian conception of the four elements and in its place substituted the modern ideas that form the foundations of chemistry as we know it today. His collected works were published in five volumes in 1744, now being catalogued at about £150 ($360). *The Sceptical Chymist*, 1661, is a £5,000 ($12,000) book.

Micrographia, London, 1665, is the most famous of the works of Robert Hooke (1635–1703), of which there are two separate issues of the first edition. Of the 38 plates, 36 are folding, containing magnificent illustrations, by the author and others, of plant cells and other minute structures as seen through the microscope. A horologist as well as a physicist, he helped to perfect the balance-spring in a manner that enabled Thomas Tompion (1638–1713) and other eminent makers to apply the principle to clocks and watches. But the pendulum clock was the invention of Christian Huygens (1629–95) who described its workings in his *Horologium Oscillatorium*, Paris, 1673, a copy of which the author presented to Sir Isaac Newton (1642–1727), in 1673. It was not until 1687 that Newton established the principle of universal gravitation by the publication of his monumental work *Philosophiae Naturalis Principia Mathematica*, although few could grasp the implications of his reasoning at the time.

The first edition in English of *Principia Mathematica* appeared in 1729 under the title of *The Mathematical Principles of Natural Philosophy*, the translation having been made by Andrew Motte. This two-volume work has now advanced in price to about £300, and a complete copy contains two engraved frontispieces, 47 folding plates of diagrams, and two folding tables. The second edition to appear in English was published in three volumes in 1803. The true first edition of 1687 seldom appears for sale and fetches well over £1,000 ($2,400). Newton's *Opticks*, 1704, in which, for the first time, he analysed the nature of white light as being a compound of many pure elementary colours, together with his experimental proof that rays of differing colours are refracted by a prism to different extents, was published in English in London, and contained 19 folding engraved plates. The second edition was dated 1719 and the third 1721. All the early editions of Newton's scientific books fetch high prices and are likely to continue to appreciate in value.

One of the earliest and most observant experimenters with the microscope, Anthony van Leeuwenhoek (1632–1723), painstakingly ground his own lenses for his collection of over 200 instruments. By their use he discovered bacteria and made important discoveries in the anatomy of man and animals. *Arcana Naturae Detecta*, 1695–7, was published in Delft, and later under its English title of *Secrets of Nature Discovered*. Two collections of his works, one in Dutch and one in Latin, appeared during his lifetime. His 'little animals' as he called microbes, did not cause the sensation amongst the reading public of the dying years of the 17th century as did the description of the 'little men' given by Edward Tyson (1650–1708). His book *Orang-Outang; or the Anatomy of a Pygmie compared with that of a Monkey, an Ape, and a Man*, published in London in 1699, stirred the imagination of the general public as well as students of comparative morphology. Tyson's 'typical pygmy' was, in fact, an African chimpanzee but he was the first to recognise that man was closely affiliated with certain lower animals. A few years later Edmund Halley (1656–1742) was publishing his *A Synopsis of the Astronomy of Comets*, 1705, and his correct prediction of the reappearance of 'Halley's Comet' to light the sky 16 years after his own death brought astonished crowds into the streets to witness the spectacle he had promised them. The *Catalogus Stellarum Australium*, 1679, was his principal astronomical work.

The first book on modern dentistry was *Le Chirurgien Dentiste*, 2 vols. Paris, 1728, by Pierre Fauchard (1678–1761). It was more than 40 years before John Hunter (1728–93) one of the greatest surgeons of all time, published his *A Treatise on the Natural History of the Human Teeth*, 1771. Complete with its 16 plates, and with its half-title, a good copy now fetches about £120 ($288). Hunter's *A Treatise on the Venereal Disease*, appeared in 1786, complete with seven plates, and the monumental work of his elder brother William Hunter (1718–83), *Anatomy of the Human Gravid Uterus*, 1774, containing 34 life-size hand-coloured copperplate illustrations, was first published by Baskerville under its Latin title *Anatomia Uteri Humani Gravidi*. Since 1960 I have watched this book rise in price from £25 ($60) to £300 ($720). It was reprinted in 1851.

Benjamin Franklin (1706–90) was the first American scientist to achieve an international reputation. By means of his now famous demonstration with a boy's kite, he established the identity of lightning with electricity, also suggesting the use of lightning conductors on high buildings, etc. His *Experiments and Observations on Electricity* first appeared in 1751 under a London imprint. I have a particularly fine copy of his first collected works, published in three volumes by Longmans, London, in 1806, although selections had appeared previously. A glance at the index makes one realise how wide-ranging were Franklin's activities in the world of science, and what an action-filled existence was spanned by his 84 years. He used the pseudonym 'Richard Saunders' on the title-pages of some of his works, the titles of which were extremely diverse. *Observations on the Causes of Smoky Chimneys*, 1787, is now a £75 ($180) book. This work appeared only a year after the first appearance of the final volume of Joseph Priestley's *Experiments and Observations on Different Kinds of Air*, 6 vols. 1774–86, a series contributing a most important advance in our knowledge of gases. Priestley (1733–1804) discovered oxygen, although it was Lavoisier who gave the gas its modern name.

Although I have never been lucky enough to acquire a copy of the two-volume work describing the first ascent in a balloon by the Montgolfier brothers, published in Paris 1783–4, I do have *An Account of the First Aërial Voyage in England*, 1784, by Vincent Lunardi, and signed by him on the half-title (as I suspect most copies of the first edition were). It is a most interesting work, with two folding copperplate engravings showing the balloon in flight and the means by which the hydrogen gas was made. This historic flight took place on the afternoon of Wednesday 15 September 1784, the Neapolitan balloonist landing near Ware, Hertfordshire. The volume contains a fine portrait-frontispiece by Bartolozzi after Richard Cosway, depicting the first aviator ever to rise from

The first aviator ever to rise from British soil was a Neapolitan who masked his real identity behind the pseudonym 'Vincent Lunardi'. Nevertheless, he was a brave man who risked his life in a contraption of oiled-silk filled with home-made hydrogen gas. His balloon ascent and flight of several miles was made on 15 September 1784.

Size of title-page:
20.3cm × 12.2cm.

Protinus æthereà tollit inastra viâ. ... et se

VINCENT LUNARDI ESQ.
Secretary to the Neapolitan Ambassador;
and the first aërial Traveller in the
English Atmosphere
Sept. 15. 1784.

AN

ACCOUNT

OF THE

First Aërial Voyage in *England*,

In a SERIES of LETTERS
to his GUARDIAN,

Chevalier Gherardo Compagni,

Written under the Impreſſions of the various Events
that affected the Undertaking,

By VINCENT LUNARDI, Eſq.
Secretary to the Neapolitan Ambaſſador.

A non eſſe, nec fuiſſe, non datur argumentum ad non poſſe.

LONDON:

Printed for the AUTHOR: and ſold at the PANTHEON; alſo
by the Publiſher, J. BELL, at the BRITISH LIBRARY, Strand;
and at Mr. MOLINI'S, Woodſtock-Street.

M,DCC,LXXXIV.

Entered at Stationers Hall.

British soil. Both the first and second editions (issued the same year) were originally published in marbled paper-wrappers, the leaf edges being left uncut. There was a gap of 86 years before the appearance of what may almost be termed the definitive work on the subject. *Travels in the Air*, 1871, edited by James Glaisher, F.R.S. (1809–1903) had first appeared in Paris in 1870 as *Voyages Aériens*, in the preparation of which Glaisher had been assisted by Camille Flammarion, W. de Fonvielle, and Gaston Tissandier. The tall and heavy octavo format in which the first English edition appeared makes it an impressive looking volume, the pictorial cloth-covers, bound over bevelled-boards, depicting a dramatic last-minute escape from death in the basket of a rapidly climbing balloon in which the author all but lost his life. The Aeronautical Society was founded in 1866 with Glaisher as its first treasurer. A second and revised English edition of *Travels in the Air* appeared later in 1871, this time with six chromo-lithographs added to the other illustrations. Copies of either of these editions are now priced at about £30 ($72). While on the subject of aviation I can mention that I was lucky enough to acquire a bound-up run of *The Aeronautical Journal*, from the commencement in January 1897 (it was published quarterly), until October 1902. It was the first publication dealing with heavier-than-air machines, its rival in this field, *Flight*, not appearing until January 1909.

An Inquiry into the Causes and Effects of the Variolae Vaccinae, 1798, by Edward Jenner (1749–1823) a work which helped to form the basis of the modern science of immunology and gave us the word 'vaccination', has now been catalogued at over £1,000 ($2,400). There are four hand-coloured copperplate engravings, the first issue of plate 2 being watermarked '1794', and there should be a half-title and errata leaf. His *Further Observations on Variolae Vaccinae or Cow Pox* was published in 1799. Jenner was primarily responsible for the eventual defeat of smallpox, a disease that had disfigured and ravaged the face of humanity from time immemorial. The advance of medical science had already been witnessed by the publication in 1785 of *An Account of the Foxglove and Some of Its Medical Uses*, by the wealthy Birmingham physician William Withering (1741–1799), describing the use of the drug digitalis extracted from that plant. From that date onwards, digitalis has been a specific and widely used heart stimulant in cases of cardiac failure. A folding coloured plate precedes the title, and a half-title and explanation leaf is also called for in a complete copy. His *Account of the Scarlet Fever* appeared in 1779, and his important botanical work, *A Botanical Arrangement of all the Vegetables Naturally Growing in Great Britain*, was first published in two volumes in 1776, but was later revised and enlarged.

The name of Robert Brown (1773–1858), is commemorated in his discovery of what came to be known as the 'Brownian movement', revealing that gases and liquids consist of molecules in rapid motion. His privately published *A Brief Account of Microscopical Observations on the Particles contained in the Pollen of Plants* appeared in 1828, some 11 years before the first volume of *Experimental Researches in Electricity*, 3 vols. 1839, 1844, 1855, by Michael Faraday (1791–1867). Faraday's experiments advanced our knowledge of the nature and immense potential of electricity, not only through his discovery of the electric motor and the dynamo, but by the unexplored fields he opened up that finally led others to the discovery of the electron theory of matter. A title that has taken the fancy of collectors, and thus helped to elevate the price, is his *A Course of Six Lectures on the Chemical History of the Candle*, 1861, currently being catalogued at over £40 ($96).

The strongest of sunlight was needed for J. N. Niépce (1765–1833) to take the first photograph in 1826, although his feat was not made public until as late as 1841. Three separate and distinct methods of photography were in operation by 1844, and these were first described in *The Art of Engraving with the Various Modes of Operation*, 1844, by T. H. Fielding (1781–1851), the first book to have a chapter solely devoted to all aspects of photography. My copy of this tall slim octavo is still in its original red-cloth binding, complete with the ten full-page tipped-in plates. It seems to have escaped the notice of the specialist bibliographers on the subject. *The Pencil of Nature* appeared in book-form in 1846 (although dated on the title-page '1844', being the date of the first of the part-issues of the work). In it, William Henry Fox Talbot (1800–71) gives a full account of his photographic process, as well as showing 24 photographs taken by means of it. L. J. M. Daguerre (1787–1851) had preceded this by the publication of his *Historique et Description des Procédés du Daguérreotype et du Diorama,* a monograph which appeared in 1839. Nevertheless, it was Fox Talbot who unquestionably invented the negative/positive process which completely superseded Daguerre's iodised silvered-plate process. Talbot's other book on the subject, *Sun Pictures in Scotland,* a quarto containing 23 original photographs and published in 1845, is fetching anything up to £300 ($720) at auction.

The coloured illustration of my copy of the first edition of *On the Origin of Species by Means of Natural Selection,* 1859, by Charles Darwin (1809–82) will reveal to the initiated that a copy as fine as this must have spent a considerable proportion of its life protected inside a specially-made box. This is a book notoriously difficult to find in anything approaching fine condition in the original cloth. It was a work that immediately caused an international furore, refuting as it did the traditional belief, buttressed by religious superstition, in the immutability of species. *On the Origin of Species* is now recognised as one of the most important, if not *the* most important, books ever written. Darwin wrote a total of 16 full-length books, plus several pamphlets. He continued revising and altering his *magnum opus* until the definitive text appeared in the 1876 issue of the sixth edition, so all editions until that date are of importance to the collector. His *Descent of Man,* 2 vols. 1871, is really an application of the principles expounded in *The Origin of Species* to humanity itself. But T. H. Huxley had already taken the plunge eight years before this by the publication of his *Evidence as to Man's Place in Nature,* 1865, with its striking frontispiece showing skeletons of four man-like apes compared with that of man himself. *Evolution, Old and New,* 1879, by Samuel Butler, was one of the many attacks made on Darwin for daring to dispense with the hand of a purposeful God; attacks that continued with unabated fury until well into the first half of the 20th century. Today there can be no doubt of the universal acceptance of Darwinism even in the most bigoted of quarters.

Another book for which I searched for many years was the first book on the telephone, my copy being the only one known to have survived in the original pictorial wrappers. *The History of Bell's Telephone,* 1878, edited by Kate Field, was a 72-page booklet, commissioned by the Electric Telephone Company, Cannon Street, London, and published by Bradbury, Agnew & Company in April of that year. At the back of the book is printed the world's first telephone directory, containing a total of 48 subscribers in London and the provinces. On 23 January 1878, the London *Daily News* reported that 'communication was

Left
The title-page of the first edition of one of the most important books ever written. Fine copies are now catalogued at well over £500 ($1,200).
Size of title-page:
20cm × 12cm.

Right
The first book on the telephone; written by Kate Field, who was an intimate of Anthony Trollope. Issued in pictorial wrappers, printed in red and black, the title-page is dated 1878. The work contains the first telephone directory for the British Isles, with the names of 19 London subscribers, and a further 29 in the provinces.
Size of cover: 18cm
× 12cm.

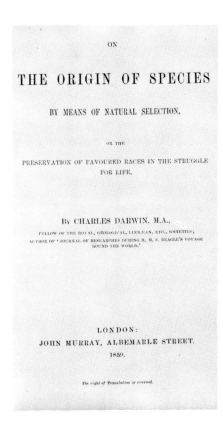

established between the House of Commons and the office of the *Daily News*, by means of the telephone, and that conversation was distinctly audible.' But it was 1907 before the General Post Office began to take over the service as a public institution.

The science of criminology is represented in the collection by the first edition of *Finger Prints*, 1892, by Francis Galton, F.R.S., the first book on the subject; although there is an interesting use of this means of identification in the thumb-print of Thomas Bewick, the engraver, as a receipt for payment of the first edition of his *The Fables of Aesop and Others*, 1818. On the periphery of this field I have copies of the first edition of *The State of the Prisons in England and Wales*, 1777, by John Howard (1726–90), the great penal-law reformer, and *Juvenile Delinquents*, 1853, by Mary Carpenter, together with a small shelf of kindred works.

FINGER PRINTS

From the title-page of *Finger Prints* by Sir Francis Galton. This work heralded the dawn of a new era in crime detection. Sir Francis Galton (1822–1911), a cousin of Charles Darwin, was one of the first men to realise that our finger-prints remain constant from childhood to death. But it was 1901 before a Finger-print Bureau was established by Scotland Yard.

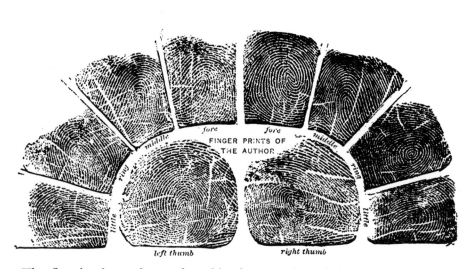

The first book on the modern bicycle was *The Velocipede*, 1869, by J.F.B. (Joseph Firth Bottomley). Blocked on the front of its blue cloth-covers are the words: 'How to Ride a Velocipede, Straddle a Saddle, then Paddle & Skedaddle'. The first book on the motor-car to appear in English I believe to be *Concise History of English Carriages*, 1896, by George Smith, published at Tunbridge Wells, a town where the first motor show ever to be held in England took place in the local Agricultural Grounds on 15 October 1895. Apparently the magazine *Cycling* had just held a ballot amongst its readers to determine the name most suitable for the new mechanically propelled vehicles and 'motor-car' came out the winner. I also have a copy of *Auto-Cars*, 1896, by D. Farman, published the same year. Within a few more years books on the subject of horseless-carriages were appearing by the dozen, but anything dated before 1930 is worth looking for.

I have never been able to track down or identify the first book to be published on the subject of wireless-telegraphy, although it is known that Guglielmo Marconi (1874–1937), applied for his provisional patent for 'improvements in transmitting electrical impulses and signals' on 2 June 1896. The first book on television was published in 1926, *Television*, by Alfred Dinsdale, with a portrait-frontispiece of its inventor, John L. Baird (1888–1946), who made little out of his electro-mechanical discovery (eventually superseded by the present high-definition system first used by the British Broadcasting Corporation in November 1936). *Radio-Activity*, by Ernest Rutherford, later Lord Rutherford (1871–1937), was published by the Cambridge University Press in 1904; the word was coined by Henri Becquerel (1852–1908) who had published works on the subject in Paris the year before. It was he who suggested to the Curies the importance of investigations into the residue of pitch-blende, a natural uranium oxide, with the result that they discovered radium. During World War I Albert Einstein (1879–1955) published details of his theory of relativity which has completely transformed the whole scientific outlook of mankind. *Die*

Grundlage der allgemeinen Relativitätstheorie, first appeared in print in *Annalen der Physik,* published in Leipzig, 1916, an off-print of which appeared the same year. A book called *The Principle of Relativity,* by E. Cunningham, was published at Cambridge in 1914; the author completely failing to grasp the implications of what he called in his preface 'the highly speculative attempt of Einstein at a generalisation of the principle in connection with the physical theory of gravitation'. *Relativity,* the first English translation of Einstein's theory, by R. W. Lawson, was published in 1920.

Penicillin – Its Practical Application, 1946, by Sir Alexander Fleming, is a surprisingly underpriced book that can still be picked up for less than £5 ($12). His paper on the subject had first appeared in 1929, but it was not until E. B. Chain and H. W. Florey, who in 1945 shared with Fleming the Nobel prize for Medicine, realised the implications of his neglected discovery of the antibacterial action of cultures of penicillium mould, that its active principle was isolated and put to startlingly dramatic curative uses. This first book on the subject was published by Butterworth & Co., London. *Miracle Drug,* 1946, by David Masters, appeared the same year, and describes in layman's language, with the help of illustrations, the inner history of penicillin. A reprint of Fleming's original paper of 1929 was made for his wife in 1940.

PENICILLIN

ITS PRACTICAL APPLICATION

Under the General Editorship of

PROFESSOR SIR ALEXANDER FLEMING
M.B., B.S., F.R.C.P., F.R.C.S., F.R.S.

PROFESSOR OF BACTERIOLOGY IN THE UNIVERSITY OF LONDON,
ST. MARY'S HOSPITAL, LONDON

LONDON
BUTTERWORTH & CO. (Publishers), LTD.
BELL YARD, TEMPLE BAR

AFRICA: BUTTERWORTH & Co. (AFRICA) LTD.
DURBAN: 1 LINCOLN'S COURT, MASONIC GROVE
AUSTRALIA: BUTTERWORTH & Co. (AUSTRALIA) LTD.
SYDNEY: 8 O'CONNELL STREET
MELBOURNE: 430 BOURKE STREET
CANADA: BUTTERWORTH & Co. (CANADA) LTD.
TORONTO: 1367 DANFORTH AVENUE
INDIA: BUTTERWORTH & Co. (INDIA) LTD.
BOMBAY: JEHANGIR BUILDING, ESPLANADE ROAD, FORT
NEW ZEALAND: BUTTERWORTH & Co. (AUSTRALIA) LTD.
WELLINGTON: 49/51 BALLANCE STREET
AUCKLAND: 35 HIGH STREET

1946

The first book on penicillin, good copies of which can still be purchased for less than £5 ($12).

Size of title-page:
21.7cm × 13.5cm.

Right
The first book on television. Published in 1926, and edited by Alfred Dinsdale, the text and illustrations give a history and progress-report of John Logie Baird's new-fangled invention.

Size of the dust-wrapper: 18.5cm × 13cm.

Travel & Topography

Early books on travel to far-distant and often unexplored lands have always exerted a fascination for the collector who likes to dream the hours away, safely ensconced in a favourite arm-chair, tracing the footsteps of long-dead trail-breakers and the discoverers of unknown continents. This class of literature is one of the most exciting types of non-fiction. The earliest circumnavigators had no charts to guide them, could calculate the latitude only by the sun, and the longitude not at all. Despite what now seem like insurmountable obstacles, they often succeeded, bringing back the first maps of unknown territories, and the first descriptions of strange races of men and even stranger species of animals. Many, like Magellan and Cook, died on the way. Some changed the face of the earth and the way of life of generations cramped in a Europe that could find no use for their talents and skills. Today's explorers are encased in the most expensive hardware this earth has ever known; but this earth is only the stepping-off place to territories man will one day read about in books that will themselves become collector's pieces.

Collecting the earliest books describing one's own village, town, or county (and someone, at sometime or other, seems to have written something about even the most obscure and inaccessible of hamlets), can be as difficult, though never as expensive, as acquiring the first works giving details of lands half the size of Europe. The reason lies in the number of copies privately printed at the expense of the local vicar, who had spent years in painstaking research before committing to print the *Parochial History of Saint Neots in Cornwall,* 1833; or *Saint Just in Penwith,* 1842, 'by the Rev. John Buller, printed at the expense of the author', three-quarters of the hopefully printed issue finishing in the trunk-maker's hands. Local histories of this description have only a limited appeal, but I know of few book-collectors who have not at least a handful of early works dealing with their own home town, usually backed up by a county history or two. It is fascinating to know what a place looked like in the days of the steam-trams, or before they removed the cobble-stones in the High Street.

The first printed guide-book developed out of the list of places to visit in Rome, compiled for the benefit of pilgrims to that city, by Benedict, Canon of St Peter's, about A.D. 1145. *Mirabilia Romae* was first printed in about 1473, the first edition to bear a date being that of 1475. 'The Wonders of Rome', to give the work its English title, gives us a valuable insight into the historic treasures that remained in medieval Rome, and of the measures already in hand to preserve for posterity, and for the attraction of tourists, as many as possible of the statues and ancient monuments there. 16th- and 17th-century editions of the work are not uncommon.

Every schoolboy knows by heart the jingle which enables him to remember that Christopher Columbus (1451–1506) discovered (or re-discovered) America in 1492. Unlike the explorers in the centuries that followed, he made little effort to rush into print, or to give the world a volume of autobiographical memoirs of his sensational discoveries in the west. All he left us was a four-page report, giving details of his 'newly discovered islands', a pamphlet first printed

GULIELMI
Ætatis. 5

The greatest of the county histories, the title-page being printed in red and black, and dated 1656. It was the result of 20 years' indefatigable research by Dugdale, in which he visited every town, village and hamlet in the county on horseback.

Size of printed title-page: 34cm × 22cm.

72

DUGDALE
Æ MDCLVI

dulcedine cunctos
non finit esse sui

THE
ANTIQUITIES
OF *Ducie*
WARWICKSHIRE
ILLUSTRATED;

From Records, Leiger-Books, Ma-
nuſcripts, Charters, Evidences,
Tombes, and Armes:

BEAUTIFIED

With Maps, Proſpects and Portraictures

By *WILLIAM DVGDALE.*

MANTUAN,

Cuncta aperit ſecreta dies, ex tempore verum
Naſcitur, & veniens ætas abſcondita pandit.

LONDON,
Printed by *Thomas VVarren*, in the year of our Lord
God, M. DC. LVI.

at Barcelona, 1493, and known as 'The Columbus Letter'. To the end of his life Columbus believed that he had discovered merely the outlying islands of the Indies, and not a new continent. *Epistola de Insulis nuper inventis* is known by only a single copy of the first edition (discovered in Spain in 1889, and now in the New York Public Library), although a total of nine separate editions appeared before the turn of the century. The equally famous Marco Polo (1254?–1324) also wrote no account of his travels; but in 1298–9, while a prisoner-of-war, he narrated his story to a writer from Pisa, and the text was soon circulating in manuscript. *Buch des edlen Ritters und Landfahrers Marco Polo,* was first printed in Nuremberg, as early as 1477. It was not long before the story of the adventures of one of the greatest travellers of all time was translated into every European language. 'The Wonders of the World', by Marco Polo, is still in print today, the standard translation, *The Book of Ser Marco Polo*, 2 vols., London 1903, edited by Sir H. Yule, being followed by a supplement by H. Cordier, 1920.

The first printed collection of voyages and travels, *Paesi Novamente Retrovati*, 1507, by Fracan da Montalboddo, appeared in English as 'The New Found Lands'. The work was one of the most important of the Renaissance travel books, giving to the traders and merchants of Europe their first news of the wealth and natural resources of the newly discovered lands in the east and west. Voyages of Alvise Cadamos, the first navigator to make astral calculations using the Southern Cross; Pedro Cabral, who first discovered Brazil; Vincente Yanez Pinzon, who, in 1500, discovered the Amazon delta; Columbus (three voyages); Amerigo Vespucci, after whom America is probably named; and Vasco da Gama, the earliest printed account of his travels, are all narrated in this collection. Complete copies of the first edition now fetch in the region of £3,000 ($7,200). *Isolario*, by Bartolommeo Dalli Sonetti, printed in Venice *c.* 1485, is the first book to contain printed nautical charts. There are 49 woodcut maps of varying accuracy, the price of a first edition being as much as £4,000 ($9,600). But of both of these works there are later editions that the collector of means can acquire for very much less than these sums, and both pale into financial insignificance when compared with the prices paid for the account of the first voyage around the world. *Le Voyage et Navigation faict par les Espaignolz es Isles de Mollucques*, published in Paris in about 1525, was compiled by Francesco Antonio Pigafetta (1491?–1534?). It gives us much the best and most detailed account of the voyages and adventures of perhaps the greatest seaman the world has ever known, the intrepid Fernando Magellan (1480–1521). 'The Voyage and Navigation of the Spaniards to the Molucca Islands' is an authoritative account of the first circumnavigation of the earth, written by Pigafetta, who had himself accompanied Magellan on the voyage. Magellan had set out on 10 August 1519 with five ships, had eventually discovered the eastern end of the strait that now bears his name, and had entered the Pacific Ocean and reached the Philippines. There he was killed by natives in April 1521, and, out of his entire flotilla only one ship and 18 men reached home. But he had linked east Asia with Europe, and had proved the linear circumference of the earth, as well as the length of a degree of latitude. Although a first edition will cost the collector of travel books about £25,000 ($60,000), he can always turn to the definitive English text in J. A. Robertson's three-volume edition, published in Cleveland, U.S.A. 1906. Entitled *Magellan's Voyage around the World*, with the text in English and Italian, it contains facsimile plates and maps, and may be purchased for £25 ($60).

Atlases and maps can be mentioned only briefly in a work of this length, for although they form part of the library of many collectors, they are not books in the accepted sense. An atlas was published in Bologna, Italy, as early as 1477, containing 27 maps by Claudius Ptolemy. These are the earliest printed maps. The discovery of the art of map-printing by means of wood-blocks, or by copperplate engraving, caused a boom in production and in demand. Time could be spent in ensuring the accuracy of the original plate, and then each print would be identical in outline with those that had been printed before, and was not subject to the variations and modifications caused by hand-copying one manuscript plan from another. At first the Italians held almost a monopoly in map production, but it was to Holland and the Low Countries that travellers and seamen later turned for their charts. Due to the development of new techniques, and the continual improvement in the accuracy of the maps they printed, the Flemish and the Dutch map-makers came to be acknowledged as the best in the world. In 1570 Abraham Ortelius printed the first edition of his *Theatrum Orbis Terrarum*, which in less than 45 years passed through almost as many editions. It was the first collection of maps issued in uniformly sized volume form, and covered all parts of the known world. It contained 70 maps, increasing to nearly 170 as succeeding editions appeared. The issue with the text in English did not appear until 1606.

Gerard Mercator's famous atlas appeared in 1585, a second part being published in 1590, and the final portion in 1595, a year after his death. He is known to every schoolboy by reason of 'Mercator's Projection', the system he devised of projecting a map with lines of latitude and longitude set at right-angles. In the 17th century appeared one of the great monuments of map production, the atlas of Johannes and Guilelmus Blaeu, *Le Theatre du Monde ou Nouvel Atlas,* 1646-7. It contained a total of 328 double-page and four single-page maps, the accuracy and beauty of which for centuries remained unsurpassed in the history of cartography. The series of atlases gradually expanded to fill 11 large folio volumes, most of the issue being hand-coloured. They contained fine cartouches showing the people of the countries they depicted, their trades, coats-of-arms, and plans and views of towns. The first complete edition of 1662, in 11 volumes, now fetches about £7,000 ($16,800).

By this time the English had started their own map production, and Christopher Saxton (1540?-1608?), the father of English map-making, had already begun his surveying by 1573. His first maps were issued as separate sheets, bearing dates from 1574-9, in which latter year his *Atlas of England and Wales,* containing a general map and 34 double-page maps of counties, first made its appearance. Its price at auction is now about £3,000 ($7,200). The atlas was re-issued by William Webb in 1645, with the arms of Queen Elizabeth I changed to those of Charles I. John Norden, a contemporary of Saxton's, issued county maps showing, for the first time, the main roads of Britain, and also triangular distance-tables which gave the miles between given places. John Speed (1552-1629) was fortunate in having the wealthy Sir Fulke Greville as his patron, whose financial allowance left him free to write a history of Great Britain, published in 1611. Accompanying it was his renowned *The Theatre of the Empire of Great Britain,* which contained the maps with which his name is associated. It had 67 double-page maps, some of which had appeared as single sheets from 1603 onwards. Copies are found coloured and heightened in effect by the use of gold. A clean and complete set will now cost about £2,500 ($6,000). Further editions appeared in 1614, 1616 (text in Latin), 1627, 1646, 1662, 1676 (possibly the most common edition), 1713, and 1770. John Ogilby was granted the title of King's Cosmographer and Geographic Printer soon after the Great Fire of London, but it was not until 1675 that his *Britannia* was issued. Here, for the first time, the network of main roads was accurately marked, with the distances between towns incorporated in the legend. Many of his signs and symbols are still in use today by the Ordnance Survey. Two further editions appeared the same year, and the fourth in 1698. The one-volume first edition is now priced at about £800 ($1,920). It contains 100 double-page maps.

The maps and atlases produced in the 18th and 19th centuries can be purchased much more cheaply; those of Herman Moll appearing soon after the turn of the 18th century. His *The World Described; or a New and Complete Atlas,* contains a series of 27 large folding maps. The single sheet *New Map of North America,* 1715, in which he still shows California as an island, now fetches around £300 ($720). His rival in trade, John Senex, published his *New General Atlas,* 1721, a folio edition of 34 double-page maps, plus three engraved plans, the maps coloured in outline, which has now risen to £450 ($1,080) for a complete copy. His *Actual Survey of all the Principal Roads of England,* 2 vols. 1719, is an octavo reduction of Ogilby's road maps, and can be bought for about £60 ($144). Probably the finest county maps to appear in the 18th century were contained in the *Large English Atlas,* 1755, produced by Emanuel Bowen, Thomas Kitchin, and R. W. Seale. Kitchin is remembered for his general atlas of 1768, with its four magnificent sheet-maps of the continents, finely detailed and carefully engraved, and decorated with large cartouches picturing the way of life of the inhabitants of the countries shown. The brothers Christopher and John Greenwood carried out a fresh survey before engraving and printing their fine series of county maps, issued in 1834. The volume contains 47 county maps, and sells for about £200 ($480). Finally, I must mention Thomas Moule, whose series of decorative county maps of England appeared in 1836. In later editions, up to 1852, railways are shown, but the earlier editions, usually coloured, are sought by collectors and can still be purchased for less than £10 ($24) per single map.

The best of the county histories is undoubtedly *The Antiquities of Warwickshire,* 1656, by William Dugdale, a folio of some 840 pages, and containing numerous engravings of views and monumental effigies, plans of towns, and finely-engraved historical scenes of past events. Dugdale (1605-86), was Garter King-at-Arms; he also published *The History of St Paul's Cathedral,* 1658, and many other works. The second edition of his *Warwickshire* appeared in two volumes in 1730, was enlarged by the addition of a magnificent series of double-page views, and, at about £150 ($360) a copy, fetches more than the first edition. Robert Plot's *Natural History of Oxford-Shire,* 1677, and *Natural History of Stafford-Shire,* 1686, William Borlase's *Antiquities of Cornwall,* 1754, and *Natural History of Cornwall,* 1758, are representative of the many works of this type that appeared during the 17th and 18th centuries. Most contain maps, and engraved views, and too often fall into the hands of the breakers of books, a class of trader who frames anything saleable and discards the rest. Thomas Pennant's *Of London,* 1790, is happily found extra-illustrated in so many cases that it must have been a favourite subject for Grangerisation, and in such condition is more often preserved than broken.

My copy of *The History of the Worthies of England,* 1662, by Thomas Fuller, has the inscription 'J. Langham ex dono Authoris' at the head of the title-page; but as the author was dead before the massive folio volume appeared, it is difficult to understand how he could have presented a copy to the mysterious Mr Langham. This work, the first attempt at a national biography, surveys the natural resources, manufactures, and geography of each county in England and Wales, and is important also for containing the first biography of William Shakespeare. An index was compiled in the 18th century and is sometimes found bound at the end of the volume. A copy in a contemporary full-leather binding would now be priced at about £100 ($240) in the catalogues of antiquarian booksellers. One of the finest series of copperplate engraved views of towns and cities is contained in *Antiquities in England and Wales,* 3 vols. 1774, by Samuel and Nathaniel Buck, in which there are a total of 511 plates, 83 of

The first attempt at a national biography, and the first to contain a biography of Shakespeare. The work surveys the natural resources, manufactures, and geography, of each of the English and Welsh counties.

Size of title-page:
33cm × 22cm.

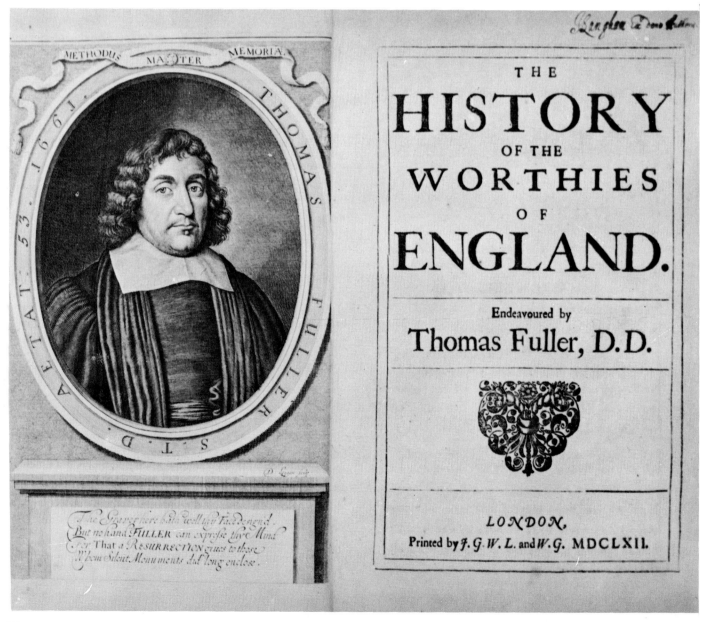

Many of the annuals that appeared during the first half of the 19th century could be classed as travel books, and the quality of their engraved illustrations was usually of a high order. *The American in Paris* was the title of *Heath's Picturesque Annual for 1844*, with 18 plates, one of which, 'The Family Concert', is shown.

Size of engraved surface: 16.5cm × 11cm.

which are double-paged. These oblong folios, in a contemporary morocco binding, are usually priced at well over £1,000 ($2,400). Their *Panoramic View of London*, 1749, issued on five sheets, cannot now be purchased for less than £120 ($288) on the open market.

I have space only to enumerate a cross-section of books in my collection that come under this chapter heading. *Purchas his Pilgrimage*, 1613, by Samuel Purchas (1575–1626), is the sort of book that can be dipped into anywhere and at any time, with the certainty that one is sure to alight on a passage of absorbing interest. Here are set forth narratives of voyages to India, China, Japan, Africa, the Mediterranean, and (most interesting of all) 'of New France, Virginia, Florida, New Spaine, with other Regions of America, and Mexicana'. The first edition of John Leland's *Itinerary*, 1710, was limited to only 120 copies, and is now all but unobtainable. The second edition of 1744 (Volume 1 is dated '1745') is also a most difficult set of nine volumes to obtain, as this edition, too, was limited – to 350 copies. He was the earliest of modern English antiquaries, and his extensive tour through England between 1534 and 1543, resulted in a mass of undigested notes that his subsequent insanity in 1550 left unresolved. But his tour makes fascinating reading, and such towns as Birmingham are here described in print for the first time in any detail.

I was lucky enough to obtain R. M. Ballantyne's copy of *Voyages from Montreal . . . through the Continent of North America*, 1801, by Alexander Mackenzie, which he used for checking data when writing his many boys' adventure stories set in Canada and Rupert's Land. This quarto is now a comparatively rare book as is the later *Narrative of the Surveying Voyages of H.M. ships Adventure and Beagle*, 1839–40, which appeared in three volumes plus an appendix, containing nine folding charts and maps. A difficult set to obtain in the original dark-blue cloth; as is *The Zoology of Voyage of H.M.S. Beagle*, in five parts (usually in three volumes, with 166 plates, 82 of which are coloured) 1840–3, also by Captain Robert Fitzroy. Much of the interest of these sets lies in the fact that Charles Darwin was an active member of the scientific complement of the surveying ships, and obtained the facts and information that led him to write his *On the Origin of Species*, 1859, (see p. 69), as well as a number of other important works. *Authentic Narrative of a Voyage from the Cape of Good Hope to Brasil*, 1808, by Thomas Lindley, is a random selection from a shelf of similar 19th-century works that, until a few years ago, could be picked up by the handful for quite small amounts. Today, any original work dealing with travel and exploration, especially in North or South

America, commands sums that make one think twice before despatching an order. Nevertheless, I have still been able to obtain a number of worthwhile books, all in the original cloth, that can be picked from the shelf and read with a deal of pleasure and enjoyment. *Missionary Travels and Researches in South Africa,* 1857, by David Livingstone, must have the folding frontispiece coloured to be a first issue. *How I found Livingstone,* 1872, by H. M. Stanley, embellished with the latest refinement in book illustration – a photographic pasted-in frontispiece-portrait of the author, is also difficult to find in anything approaching original condition in the pictorial cloth binding in which it first appeared. Next to these two volumes, and out of chronological order, stand Sir Walter Scott's copy of *Paris during July, 1815,* 1815, by W. D. Fellowes, which the Wizard of the North doubtless used during his stay there that year, and *Journal of a Tour in Asia Minor,* 1824, by W. M. Leake, with the large folding map of the territory which is so often missing. The end of the shelf is occupied by the first English edition of *The Perillous and most Unhappy Voyages of John Struys,* 1683, translated by John Morrison, of which once again and with good reason, plates are often lacking, usually the horrific one entitled 'A Woman flayed alive'.

Works which I hope one day to add to my collection include *A Generall Historie of Virginia,* 1624, by John Smith, an adventurer who accompanied the colonists on their voyage to America in 1607. In 1616 he published *A Description of New England,* with a map of surprising accuracy. Neither of these rare works will I ever be able to afford as first editions: the former now makes about £7,500 ($18,000) at auction (if complete with its four maps), and the latter about £2,500 ($6,000). Captain James Cook (1728–79), one of the greatest of explorers, laid the foundations of British Australia and opened up the Pacific Ocean to western civilisation. *A Voyage towards the South Pole, and*

Three works difficult to find in good condition in the original cloth bindings: Livingstone's *Missionary Travels,* 1857 (which must have two folding maps, and folding frontispiece), Stanley's *How I Found Livingstone,* 1872 (five maps), and Paul du Chaillu's *Equatorial Africa,* 1861 (one map). The folding or full-page maps must be present in a complete copy, but are sometimes missing.

Height of right-hand book: 23cm.

round the World, 2 vols. 1777, contains 64 plates. It was followed by *A Voyage to the Pacific Ocean,* 3 vols. plus a folio volume of plates, 1784. A complete set of Cook's *Voyages* totals nine volumes (including the atlas), dated variously between 1773 and 1784, and is now priced at £350 ($840) or more. Another 'first' that has so far eluded me is *Travels in the Interior Districts of Africa,* 1799, by Mungo Park (1771–1806). Before the publication of Park's book, little, if anything, was known about the heart of the Dark Continent. In 1805 he set out on another exploration, this time of the Niger, but he and his companions were killed by natives after their canoe had been crushed in rapids. More fortunate was Samuel White Baker (1821–93), whose work *The Albert N'yanza, Great Basin of the Nile,* 2 vols. 1866, first gave news of Lake Albert and the Nile Basin. He survived to be made Governor-General of the region; but his book can still be purchased for very little, and is grossly underpriced for such an important work of travel and exploration.

The shelves in my library on which the books of travel and topography stand contain a haphazard mixture of voyages, travellers' guides, county histories, and the memoirs of those sons and daughters of the landed gentry who had undertaken the Grand Tour. I still view with affection R. M. Ballantyne's first literary effort, an autobiographical account of his experiences in Rupert's Land, and the first travel book I acquired. *Hudson's Bay; or Every-Day Life in the Wilds of North America,* 1848, led me on a collecting path that did not finish until I had written its author's biography. On the shelf directly below it stands *The Moon,* by James Nasmyth, published in 1874. How this work strayed amongst the travel books is a mystery. But I have decided, for the future, to leave it there.

'Opium Smoking' – one of the full-page illustrations by Gustave Doré for *London: A Pilgrimage,* 1872, the text being by Blanchard Jerrold. This large folio volume contains some of Doré's finest work.

Size of engraved surface: 23.5cm × 19cm.

Natural History

I must set at the head of this chapter the only work of natural history ever to achieve the distinction of being acknowledged as a classic in the field of English literature. I refer, of course, to *The Natural History and Antiquities of Selborne*, 1789, by Gilbert White (1720–93). He spent most of his life as curate of Selborne in Hampshire, refusing more lucrative livings in order to remain in his beloved birthplace. He began in 1751 to keep a 'Garden Kalendar', and then a 'Naturalist's Journal'; later forming a friendship with two distinguished naturalists, Thomas Pennant and the Hon. Daines Barrington. It was with these two men that he carried on a correspondence which formed the basis of his world-famous work, making him the writer of an English classic without the slightest intention or desire on his part that this event should occur. The long series of letters he wrote, extending over 20 years (1767–87), contained his observations on natural phenomena and the habits of animals and birds. Although Barrington suggested publication as early as 1770, White remained indifferent, and it was not until 1789 that the quarto finally appeared, complete

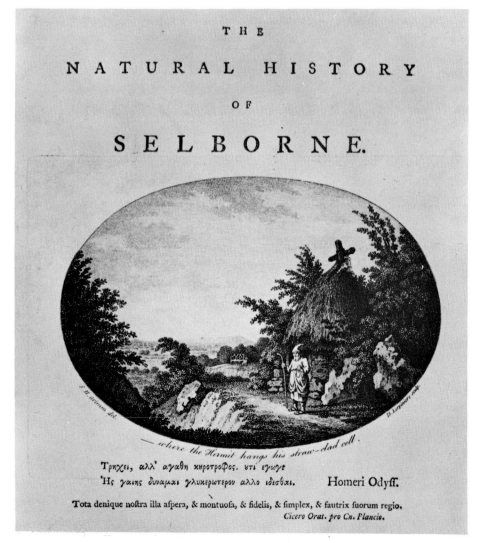

From the engraved title-page of Gilbert White's *The Natural History of Selborne,* 1789, the first work on natural history accepted as a classic of English literature.

Right, above
Fore-edge paintings remain concealed beneath the gilt on the fore-edges of the leaves of the book. When the leaves are splayed open the picture comes into view.

Right, below
One of the magnificent series of 80 full-page hand-coloured lithographs contained in *The Seat of the War in the East,* 1855, by William Simpson. This massive folio was issued in two volumes by Colnaghi & Co. Here Florence Nightingale is seen entering one of the wards of the military hospital at Scutari during the Crimean War.

Size of original coloured surface: 43.5 cm broad × 28cm high.

THE LIBRARY.

2   PLATE IV.

3

4

1

1.   TEALIA CRASSICORNIS   4.   B. BALLII
2.3   BUNODES GEMMACEA   5.6   B. THALLIA

6   IN COLOURS BY W. DICKES

with a large folding-frontispiece that is sometimes missing. The charm of this endearing work is unfading, and it is a book that one can read time and again with as much pleasure as at first acquaintance. The Selborne Society, for the preservation of wild life such as birds and plants, was founded in his memory in 1885. Happily, the village of Selborne stands today as unspoilt as when White himself lived there: the famous yew tree still towers over the plestor, the church has been saved from modernising fingers, and White's house is much as he left it. *A Naturalist's Calendar*, 1795, followed soon after his death, and must contain the strange-coloured copperplate-engraving of 'A Hybrid Bird' to be complete. His *Selborne* went through so many editions that an entire bibliography was devoted to the work (published by the Roxburghe Press, 1897). The edition of 1875, edited by Frank Buckland, and with illustrations by P. H. Delamotte, was issued in 'Sixties' book style, the heavily gilt pictorial covers being bound over bevelled-boards, and is much the most desirable of the many reprints.

To begin at the beginning we must go back to the middle of the 16th century, and to one of the most celebrated and beautiful herbals ever printed. 'Commentaries on the Histories of Plants' by Leonhard Fuchs (1501–66) was first published under its Latin title *De Historia Stirpium Commentarii*, 1542. This monumental work contains a total of 512 superb woodcut illustrations. The fuchsia was named after the author. All the drawings were based on actual observation of living plants, and the freshness and clarity of the illustrations ensured an immediate and lasting success for the work. But there was a need for a more scientific classification of plants, instead of just listing them in alphabetical order as Fuchs had done. With the publication of *De Plantis*, 1583, by Andreas Caesalpinus (1519–1603), came the first attempt to classify his botanical specimens in a systematic and logical manner, and 'On Plants', to give the work its English name, was the forerunner of the scientific botanical works that followed after. The next important advance came 40 years later, with the publication of 'The World of Botany Illustrated', which appeared under a Basle imprint as *Pinax Theatri Botanici*, 1623, by Caspar Bauhinus. Six thousand different species of plants were described, and the book could be nominated as the first attempt at a 'natural' classification founded on general morphology, a system of nomenclature that later formed the structure of Carl Linnaeus' method. It was this latter botanist whose *Systema Naturae*, 1735, set the seal on the modern system of botanical and zoological classification. 'The System of Nature' was issued as a slim folio of only seven leaves, and of these fourteen pages two are blank; yet its present-day value is well over £5,000 ($12,000), a sum reflecting the importance in which the work is held. The first English edition of his collected works appeared under a Lichfield imprint, dated 1782, 1783, and 1787, being the *System of Vegetables*, 2 vols. 11 plates, and *Families of Plants*, 2 vols.; a set of the four volumes is now priced at about £150 ($360). His *Hortus Cliffortianus*, 1737, a folio with 36 full-page plates of plants and flowers, now fetches £600 ($1,440).

All these early botanical books had only a limited appeal, having been produced primarily for the specialist with scientific knowledge. The first work of any importance to be published with the avowed intention of popularising natural history was *Histoire Naturelle*, by Comte de Buffon (1707–88), which appeared in a long run of 44 volumes during the period 1749–1804. Buffon's 'Natural History' made an instant appeal and continued in print in various editions well into the 19th century. Most were embellished with hand-coloured plates, and are therefore sought by book-breakers, the illustrations being removed and framed before being offered for sale. A complete run of the first edition seldom fetches less than £2,000 ($4,800) by auction, especially if bound in contemporary French morocco, as is often the case. His *Histoire Naturelle des Oiseaux*, 10 vols. 1770–86, containing 973 hand-coloured plates of birds (a further 35 non-ornithological plates are found in some copies), is also catalogued at anything up to £2,000 ($4,800). In the book-trade, birds are best sellers, with humming-birds way out in front. Flowers come next, with the animal kingdom making a bad third. Why this should be so perhaps a psychologist could explain. Buffon's works, in a condensed and modified form, were popular with children, the editions with uncoloured pictures of birds and animals exciting the younger members of the family with the prospect of applying their own colour-schemes to the copperplate engravings. 'Some of the plates coloured by a contemporary hand', as the booksellers apologetically inform their clients – but the results never compare with the professional shop-coloured issues. The desire to brighten nature with vivid greens and skies of electric blue, to say nothing of sparrows like robin-redbreasts, jars the pastel-shaded minds of bibliophiles brought up on a more conservative diet of muted tints and pale-washed backgrounds. I do not know which of the mid-19th-century publishers first conceived the idea of producing pictures in outline for children to colour with paints and crayons, but all the earliest books of this type are of birds, animals, and flowers. The same rule applies today, but the juvenile editions of Buffon's 'Natural History' published in the early 1800s seem to have started the fashion.

Undoubtedly the most highly prized and most highly priced set of bird books is the magnificent four-volume set of *The Birds of America*, 1827–38, by John James Laforest Audubon. It was published by the author in the massive double elephant-folio size (about 960 mm × 640 mm) in order that all the birds could be depicted life-size. Plate 1, of the wild turkey, must have presented problems to the engraver, and to the book-binder, for the tail-feathers of this very large bird extend to the edge of the plate, with the result that almost all copies have the plate-number and the extreme tips of the feathers shaved slightly with some loss of printed surface. The four volumes contain a total of 435 plates engraved in aquatint and coloured by hand. On the rare occasions when a complete set in fine condition appears in the auction rooms the book-trade holds its breath. £100,000 ($240,000) would not be a surprising figure for this greatest of all illustrated works of ornithology, thus valuing the individual plates at about £250 ($600) each. For works of art of this quality this may be judged as moderate compared with the prices ruling elsewhere in the same field. A smaller version of this work is the first octavo edition, published in seven volumes, 1840–4. This contains 500 coloured plates and is now catalogued at about £2,000 ($4,800).

The most important illustrated work on indigenous birds to appear in England was *Birds of Great Britain*, 1862–73, by John Gould (1804–81). A one-time gardener at Windsor Castle, and then an amateur taxidermist before gaining a post in this capacity at the newly formed Zoological Society of London, Gould started supplying sketches of birds for his wife to transfer to lithographic stones for printing and hand-colouring. The quality of the works they produced made Gould's bird books famous, and their compiler earned a fortune. Before he died he had published over 40 folio volumes, containing over 3,000 plates. *Birds of Great Britain* was originally issued in 25 separate parts, bound in printed boards, but is usually met with in a five-volume set that is now catalogued at anything up to £2,500 ($6,500). The complete work contains 367 hand-coloured lithographic plates, the birds being shown life-size. Some of Gould's other works make a great deal more than this: *Birds of Asia*, 1850–3, a seven-volume set with 530 coloured plates, about £8,000 ($19,200); *Birds of Australia*, 8 vols. (including the supplement), 1840–69, 681 coloured plates, £7,000 ($16,800); and other selective titles devoted to families and species such as the humming-birds fetching anything up to the figures just given. This puts them beyond the reach of the average collector of fine bird books, but he may be well content to possess a copy of the less expensive works that are, nevertheless, most desirable acquisitions to any library of books of natural history.

Foremost amongst these are the works of Thomas Bewick (1753–1828), the 'Burns of painting', as Ruskin called him. The old and neglected art of wood-engraving was revived by Bewick, whose genius totally transformed the craft in a manner that makes any book illustrated by him a collector's piece in its own right. He was apprenticed to Ralph Beilby, a Newcastle engraver, with whom he later entered into partnership; but he first established his reputation with his *A General History of Quadrupeds*, 1790 (the most difficult of his major works to find in first edition form), the vignettes and tail-pieces of which display to the full his unequalled powers of observation of the dramas and comedies of everyday life in rural England. His technical mastery of a difficult art, and the virile humour that is seldom absent in his illustrations are most conspicuous in his *History of British Birds*, 2 vols. 1797–1804, the quality of the wood-engraving never having been equalled before or since.

The first issue of Volume 1 contains an engraving that was considered vulgar, and on which an extra, discreetly placed, bar was drawn in later issues.

The receipt signed by Thomas Bewick, and impressed with a facsimile of his thumb-mark, which appears at the front of his *Fables of Aesop*, 1818.

Size of page: 22.7cm × 13.5cm.

The two-volume work, if found in the original boards with uncut leaf-edges, would be a bargain at anything less than £100 ($240). A two-part supplement was published in 1821. *Figures of British Land Birds,* Vol. 1, 1800, was, in fact, the only volume published under this title. I also have a fine copy of his *The Fables of Aesop and Others,* 1818, the early editions of which are signed by Bewick, as well as having a facsimile of his thumb-print. This work is now catalogued at about £60 ($144). It is the impulse that wood-engraving received from the individual genius of Bewick that led to the widespread use of the medium for book-illustration. Any of the early editions of his works are well worth acquiring. Following in the same tradition is a work that is still in print, *British Birds in their Haunts,* 1862, by Rev. C. A. Johns, copies of which, in the original pictorial cloth binding, can be found for as little as £8 ($19.2). The author produced many popular scientific and educational books, none of which cost more than that. Standing next to them on my shelves is *The Rural Life of England,* 2 vols. 1838, by William Howitt, a delightful work to read, written by the husband of the famous Mary Howitt, who was one of the first to translate Hans Andersen's tales into English. William's *Book of the Seasons, or Calendar of*

Nature, 1831, was a best-seller for many years. So was *The Recreations of Christopher North,* 3 vols. 1842, by John Wilson, full of fascinating tales about birds and animals in the countryside he loved so well. *Rural Sketches,* 1839, by Thomas Miller, who also wrote *A Day in the Woods,* 1836, and a number of botanical guides, is another of the inexpensive countryside books, all of which have expressive and finely executed woodcut illustrations, and which can be purchased for only a pound or two. Those with hand-coloured plates always fetch a great deal more proportionately than those with black-and-white illustrations, but even some of these titles can be acquired for modest sums. I have an affection for Sir William Jardine's *Naturalist's Library,* issued in 40 volumes, 1833–43, a full set of which now sells at about £150 ($360). There were three publisher's bindings, priced when new according to the finished style. The cloth binding was the cheapest, but the buyer could also choose between half-morocco, or full-morocco. The two volumes devoted to humming-birds, when sold separately, make as much as any six other titles in the series. My own full-morocco set took several years to complete.

The nearest I shall ever approach to owning the splendidly illustrated flower and botanical books that were once a part of every gentleman's library, is perhaps the acquiring of a single plate, or one of the lavishly produced facsimiles that can sometimes cost more than the original work once did. Mention flower books to a collector, and sooner or later the conversation will turn to the magnificent works produced by P. J. Redouté, whose *Les Liliacêes,* 8 vols. 1802–16 and *Les Roses,* 3 vols. 1817–24, make anything up to £10,000 ($24,000) a set. The first contains 487 plates, and the second 169. The stipple-engravings, printed in the most delicate of colourings that exactly suit their subjects, were finished by hand.

The first octavo edition of *Les Roses,* that at one time was just within stretching distance, is now well past the £1,000 ($2,400) mark. It has 160 coloured plates, and was published in three volumes, 1824–6. In contrast, *The Temple of Flora,* three separate parts (often bound in only one or two volumes), 1799–1807, by Robert John Thornton (1768?–1837), containing a total of 31 coloured plates, seems to have been printed and engraved by so many different processes that it is difficult to find two copies alike. Aquatint, mezzotint, stipple- and line-engraving, all methods were used, and the impressions taken from them were printed in colour before being finished by hand. Some of the plates have as many as four different 'states'. Copies of this folio edition are now priced at around £3,000 ($7,200), while the much inferior reprint of 1812, called the Lottery Edition, is now offered at about £300 ($720).

A small shelf of books on gardening has a miscellany of works that have attracted me, either by their texts or the quality and interest of their illustrations. *The Gardener's Pocket-Calendar,* 1776, by Thomas Ellis, is one of a host of such works that appeared in various forms during the 18th and 19th centuries. Most can still be bought for very little and I gave only £1.25 for *The New and Improved Practical Gardener,* 1848, by Charles M'Intosh, its text of nearly 1,000 pages concealing the fact that there were 10 full-page hand-coloured plates of flowers tipped in at the extreme end. One accepts such strokes of luck without comment. My interest in publisher's binding styles led me to purchase *Familiar Wild Flowers,* 5 vols., by F. E. Hulme, *c.* 1877, originally issued in parts, each of which contains a chromo-lithograph. The volume issue, on each front cover, has a hand-painted picture of a flowering plant, and this is one of the few works of the period issued by the publishers embellished in this fashion. *Familiar Garden Flowers,* 5 vols., by the same author, appeared the following year, the complete series of ten volumes fetching about £10 ($24). Another fine example of a cloth binding of the same period is to be found on the two-volume folio *British Fresh-Water Fishes,* 1879, by Rev. W. Houghton, although the value of this particular work lies in the extremely fine series of hand-finished colour-printed full-page plates of fishes by A. F. Lydon. It is a difficult work to find in good condition in the original cloth, such copies now being priced at about £50 ($120): Houghton also wrote *Country Walks of a Naturalist with his Children,* 1869, and *Sea-Side Walks of a Naturalist with his Children,* 1870, as well as several other works aimed at popularising natural history among the young. The coloured plates in the two above-mentioned titles are among the best that Benjamin Fawcett ever produced, rivalling Baxter in the quality of the colour-printing.

The standard household text on the subject of this chapter, during the latter end of the 19th century and the beginning of the 20th, was *The Royal Natural History,* 6 vols. 1893–96, edited by Richard Lydekker. The 72 full-page coloured plates, plus the 1,600 black-and-white engravings, made it a work that could be dipped into at any time by those interested in birds, animals and plants, without having to wade through technical prose and difficult scientific descriptions. It was, in fact, a popular household encyclopedia of natural history, but has now become an interesting set to acquire for a library devoted to the subject, fine copies being priced at about £20 ($48). It is a work that I consider underpriced, and one that will shortly be changing hands at several times that sum. Lydekker's *Animal Portraiture,* 1912, is a book that fetches only a tenth of his *Deer of All Lands,* 1898; although *Great and Small Game of Europe,* 1901; and *Great and Small Game of India,* 1900, are both now £70 ($168) books. *Wild Oxen,* 1898, appeared in a limited signed edition, and copies in the original cloth now fetch at least £100 ($240).

I have space only to mention one other author whose works are still available at prices that today are considered moderate. Mrs Jane Loudon devoted her life to the flower garden, and to writing books about her favourite subject. *British Wild Flowers,* 1846, appeared in an edition with 60 hand-coloured lithographs, and can still be purchased for less than £40 ($96). *The Ladies' Flower Garden of Ornamental Annuals,* with 48 coloured plates, is now a sought-after book that regularly fetches £80 ($192) or more. The first edition appeared in 1840, but later editions command much the same price. *Ornamental Bulbous Plants,* 1841, with 58 coloured plates, is priced at about £100 ($240); her *Ornamental Greenhouse Plants,* 1848, is a good buy at half as much again. *Ornamental Perennials,* 2 vols. 1844, has made as much as £150 ($360).

I have a representative collection of many of the works mentioned above; but I most enjoy acquiring the books produced for children and young people in the field of natural history. All the best of the early ones have hand-coloured plates, and, provided you do not venture earlier than the beginning of the 19th century, most of them can be bought for below £10 ($24); many for as little as £1.5. Some of the ones in my own collection I have mentioned in the chapter on early children's books; but any bibliophile who keeps his eye on the catalogues of antiquarian booksellers who specialise in this field will not have to wait too long before being offered items in the period 1830 to 1860. The best appeared in quarto size, the plates being remarkably true-to-life considering that many of the artists employed could not have seen a great number of the animals and birds they depicted so vividly. Two of my favourites retain their place by being amongst the first books on natural history that I bought, in the late 1940s: *The Tower Menagerie,* 1829, first published in roan-backed boards; and *The Gardens and Menagerie,* 2 vols. 1831, which is now a rare work in the original glazed-cloth with paper labelled spines. Both were illustrated in black-and-white by that master of animal portraiture, William Harvey, whose woodcuts rival those of Bewick in accurate detail and technical excellence. These two works, and another favourite, *The Trees of Great Britain and Ireland,* 8 vols. (including index), by H. J. & H. A. Elwes, a work that first appeared in a series of 15 parts in printed wrappers, 1906–13, and is now valued at about £300 ($720), I hope never to have to part with.

'And the pig got up and slowly walked away!' One of the intimate tailpieces used by Thomas Bewick in his *History of British Birds,* 1797. Condemned as vulgar, later issues of the same edition had the offending posterior discreetly masked by a bar.

Size of the original small woodcut: 7cm broad × 4cm high.

Early Children's Books

'Once upon a time . . .' Memories of the lost delights of childhood are conjured back from a past that is now all too far away as soon as we hear those four magical words. The stories and tales we read and heard as children made an impression on our memories that is indelible. We still remember the plots and dramatic incidents, often blood-curdling, from the fairy-stories and folk-tales in the first books we were allowed to handle, long after the novels and romances we read in adult life have faded and been forgotten.

Perhaps that is one of the reasons why the volumes in which our great-great-great-grandparents first spelled out the story of *Cinderella*, or *The Butterfly's Ball*, or of the tales of 'Peter Parley', or of the brothers Grimm, have exerted such a strong fascination over me. In fact, these ephemeral and often elusive little books, with their hand-coloured frontispieces, and woodcut and copperplate engravings, have brought me more pleasure than most of the massive folios and important-looking quartos that line the bottom shelves of my study walls.

One of the full-page woodcut illustrations from the earliest printed picture book for children. *Kunst und Lehrbüchlein*, 1580, by Jost Amman ('Book of Art and Instruction for Young People'), contains amongst its 93 full-page plates this picture of a little girl holding a doll, believed to be the first printed picture of a child with a doll, and, *Right:* the first printed picture of a child using a horn-book.

Size of page: 16.5cm × 13cm.

86

Many of the books described and illustrated in this chapter have been bought for almost nothing, although some of the rarer and better known first editions will be expensive for the present-day collector to acquire. The earlier you go back in time the higher the cost will mount; but if you know what to look for and where to look at least part of the battle is won. Early children's books can still be discovered, often in the most unpromising places, although the condition of those whose popularity had led them to pass through the loving fingers of several generations of youthful hands often leaves much to be desired. Those of the Victorian and Edwardian eras must be found complete and unsullied and in their original bindings; but the further back you step in time the less likely are you to find fine copies of stories and picture-books that have once been cherished by juvenile owners. This observation applies, of course, to all classes of literature – the older the book the less likely is it to have survived intact – but with children's books, especially well-loved titles, it refers with special force. It is surprising how many have, in fact, withstood the ravages of time and have survived to stand in serrated rows of talls and shorts, stouts and thins, emblazoned and plain, on the shelves of the collectors of 'juveniles', as the antiquarian-booksellers head this section of their catalogues.

The earliest book in my collection that was specially compiled and published for the benefit of children and young people is nearly 400 years old. It is the first picture-book ever produced for children, and was published in Germany in 1580. *Kunst und Lehrbüchlein* displayed the world in pictures before the eyes of young people three-quarters of a century before its nearest rival attempted to do the same. The finely-executed full-page woodcuts, of which I illustrate two examples, were the work of Jost Amman (1539–91) who spent the early part of his life in Zurich, Switzerland. The publisher was Sigmund Feyerabend (1528–90), who is today acknowledged as one of the greatest and most enterprising publishers that 16th-century Europe produced. *Kunst und Lehrbüchlein,* the first part of its full-page title can be translated as 'Book of Art and Instruction for Young People', is also the first book known to have a printed picture of a child holding a doll, and of a young scholar using a horn-book. This consisted of a piece of paper or parchment let into a recess in a tablet of

leather or wood, or, in rare cases, of metal or bone. A slice of thin transparent horn covered the paper, thus protecting it from the grubby fingers of the young reader. On the sheet of paper there was either printed or written the Lord's Prayer, the alphabet, and perhaps a set of Roman numerals. These were then studied in the manner in which the boy in Amman's picture is applying himself. Authentic examples of horn-books are rarely met with today, and those that do come on the market are eagerly sought by collectors of juveniles. *Kunst und Lehrbüchlein* first appeared in 1578, but was then composed of a hotch-potch of illustrations culled from books which Feyerabend had issued under a variety of titles during the course of the previous decade. The 1580 edition was specially prepared for young people, Jost Amman drawing a fresh set of illustrations on the wood-blocks for the woodcutter to carve. A limited edition in collotype-facsimile of this first picture-book for children has recently been issued by the Eugrammia Press, London.

Very few books for the amusement of children came into existence before the middle of the 18th century. Juvenile literature consisted of devotional manuals, courtesy-books and books used in the classroom. Even Amman's delightfully illustrated book, quoted above, was meant to be didactic and instructional in its primary intent, as was the next children's book, the *Orbis Sensualium Pictus,* compiled by Johannes Amos Comenius (1592–1671), a philosopher and educationalist, who expressed the hope that his little book might 'entice knowledgeable children . . . to read more easily than hitherto'. The work first appeared in Nuremburg, Germany, in 1657, written in Latin and High Dutch. It proved so popular that an English translation, by Charles Hoole, was published over a London imprint in 1658: *Visible World; or, A nomenclature, and pictures, of all the chief things that are in the world, and of men's employments therein; in above 150 cuts . . .* as the translator entitled it, and new editions continued to be called for until well after the end of the 18th century. Comenius (more correctly Komensky) was at one time Bishop of Leszno, Poland, and a leading member of the Moravian Brethren. The crudely executed woodcut illustrations in his book show many points of similarity in the scenes they depict with those of Amman's far earlier work. But the artistic ability and technical merit fluently displayed in Jost Amman's woodcuts is so immeasurably superior to anything we can find in *Orbis Sensualium Pictus* that no valid comparison is possible.

In the early days children read for pleasure what they considered the more interesting of their instructional and school-books, the intelligent amongst them dipping into any adult work they could find. John Bunyan's *Pilgrim's Progress,* 1679, *Robinson Crusoe* by Alexander Defoe, 1719, and Dean Swift's *Gulliver's Travels,* 1726, were soon claimed as their own by the young, especially when abridged versions, luridly illustrated, appeared in the bookshops. Debased chap-book versions of traditional folk-tales, romances, travel books, bestiaries, and stories like *Gesta Romanorum,* together with compendiums produced for the literate cottager rather than for children, were devoured by the young who had little else to satisfy their craving for something to read. Many of them knew the entire series of *Aesop's Fables* by heart. In his *Boke of Nurture* (c. 1545) Hugh Rodes thundered that, at all costs, parents must keep children 'from reading feigned fables, vain fantasies, and wanton stories, and songs of love, which bring much mischief to youth'. Poor youth! Black-browed divines, sheltering under such genial pseudonyms as 'Mr. Lovechild', sent fire and brimstone through the nursery and condemned to eternal damnation all who so much as thought of fleshly sins. James Janaway's *Token for Children* (1671) gave what he described as 'an exact account of the conversion, holy and exemplary lives, and joyful deaths of several young children . . .' Religious fanatics such as Janaway mentally tortured the more pious of their juvenile believers with prophesies of an early death to be followed by inescapable hell-fire for transgressions in thought, word, or deed.

It was little wonder that children turned from the crackling agonies confronting them in macabre detail in the folio copperplate engravings of Foxe's *Book of Martyrs,* a constantly recommended volume for the repentant young. They were forced to look to the chapmen and pedlars to supply reading matter in which self-righteous piety took a less prominent place and the good became heroes by strength of arm rather than by strength of belief. It was in these little pamphlets, usually no more than 16 pages in length, that they read of the Arthurian legends, and of the princesses and the dragons of the Middle

In the William Morris tradition, the frontispiece and title-page of *A Book of Nursery Songs and Rhymes,* 1895, were ornamented with woodcut borders and illustrations by members of the Birmingham Art School, who established an international reputation for the quality of their book production.

Size of right-hand title-page: 20cm × 12.2cm.

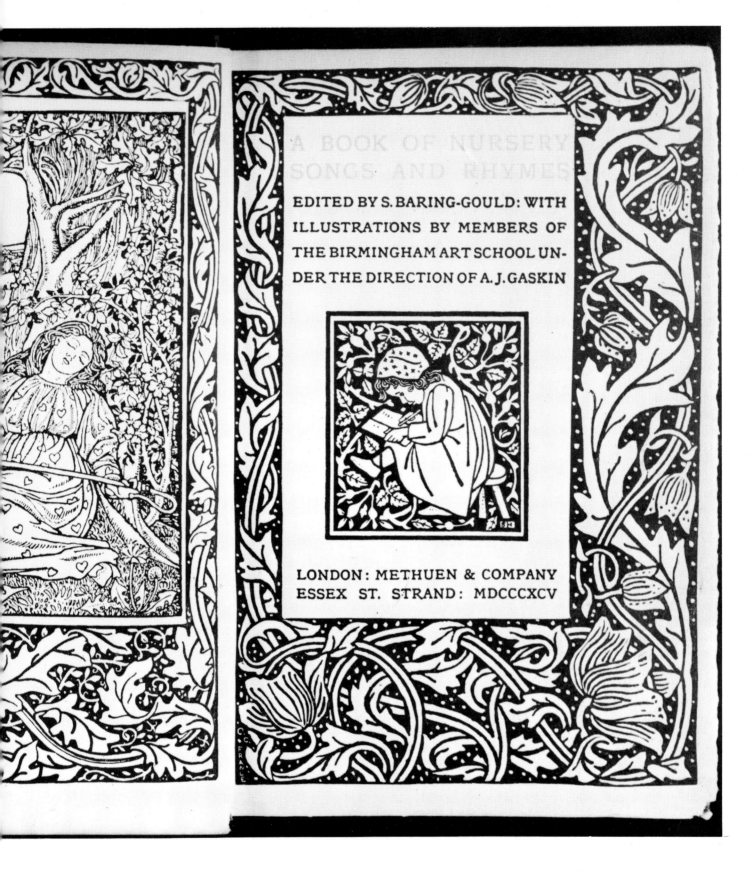

Ages. The tales they read were often coarsely told, clanking with armour and the groans of the fallen, and loud with oaths as earthy as the hawkers who sold them. But the children loved them, devouring the stories like a modern child his comic. In these penny-plain, twopenny-coloured booklets, beneath the dignity of regular booksellers to handle, children could live out their dreams. *The History of Guy of Warwick, Tom Thumb, Springheel Jack, Tom Hickathrift, Robin Hood, Friar Bacon,* and a hundred others; these were the titles the pedlars kept in string-tied bundles in their crowded packs. Romances printed on a single folio sheet could be purchased for a halfpenny. Printed on the coarsest and cheapest rough-edged paper, with a crudely executed woodcut illustration to top the tale, these were almost identical in appearance with the ballad-sheets printed by S. Hazard for the Cheap Repository, or by the famous James Catnach of Seven Dials.

France contributed much to the development of children's books. Some of the traditional folk-tales told by the countryfolk, and the delightful *contes* of Charles Perrault (1628–1703), were first translated into English by Robert Samber in about 1730. Perrault was a member of the French Academy, and is supposed to have first been introduced to the stories by his own little son – who may well have heard them from the lips of his nurse. *Histoires ou Contes du Temps Passé* he called them, and they were first published in Paris in 1697, the frontispiece having the legend *Contes de ma Mère l'Oye,* although who the original Mother Goose may have been we shall never know. From the 1730s onwards, children took to their hearts the stories of Red Riding Hood, Cinderella, Blue-beard, the Sleeping Beauty, Puss-in-Boots, and the rest of the tales told by Mother Goose, and they have kept them there ever since. Fairy-tales were also translated into English from the works of Mme d'Aulony (1650?–1705), Mme Leprince de Beaumont (1711–80), and a few others.

Before the middle of the 18th century collections of nursery rhymes had appeared in print. *Tommy Thumb's Pretty Song Book* had been published in two miniature volumes about 1744. The date is conjectural, and so for that matter is the existence of a copy of Volume I, for only part of the work is known to have survived. This is in the British Museum, but comprises Volume II only, and we are lucky to have even this small fragment. Small it certainly is, measuring only 3in. × 1¾in., a crudely printed relic of an age from which little in the way of original children's books has escaped the destructive fingers of time and youthful owners. It probably cost the original purchaser about 4d (4 cents), but what remains is today worth several times its weight in solid gold. There, for the first time in print, we read of 'Bah, Bah, a black sheep'; 'There was a little Man, And he had a little Gun'; 'Who did kill Cock Robin?'; and over 30 other songs, most of them illustrated with woodcuts the Georgian artist thought appropriate to the rhyme.

The earliest songs for children contained in my own collection is *Little Master's Miscellany,* 1750, published in Birmingham, one of the first (if not the earliest) poetical and prose miscellanies produced specially for the young. The copy is of the third edition, the first having appeared in 1743. Although complete with all its copperplate engravings it lacks the final leaf of text. But no collector would disdain a children's book dating from the reign of George II in slightly incomplete state. Any fragment of this period is worth keeping, for in many cases titles have totally disappeared. Until recently no copy of the first edition of *Goody Two-Shoes,* 1765, had ever been discovered, but happily the British Museum now possesses the only known copy. The famous nursery tale is said to have been written by Oliver Goldsmith, and was one of the publications of the enterprising and far-seeing John Newbery (1713–67), a publisher and bookseller, who established himself in 1744 in St Paul's Churchyard, London. He originated the specialist publication of children's books, appreciating before his rivals the vast market awaiting the house that was first to produce books intended for the entertainment of youth, rather than the instructional and didactic tracts that had been published in the past. Probably the first to appear in this field under his imprint was *A Little Pretty Pocket Book,* 1744. He started the *Lilliputian Magazine,* published in parts at a few pence an issue, as early as 1751. *Mother Goose's Tales* appeared in about 1765. Thomas Carnan (d. 1788), the stepson of John Newbery, succeeded to the business in partnership with his half-brother. He, too, was an innovator, altering the format in which many of his little books were sold, and advising his young clients that, for an extra penny a copy, they could have real vellum spines (always stained green) that would out-wear the old Dutch-paper bindings by many years. In 1801 this famous publishing house passed to John Harris (1756–1846), who maintained the Newbery tradition by continuing to specialise in publishing children's books.

One of the most famous letter writers of his age, Philip Stanhope, fourth Earl of Chesterfield (1694–1773), compiled a voluminous correspondence to his son and his godson. These were private letters, instructional in character, warning the two young men of the perils they might well encounter in the world. They make fascinating reading, and when published in two massive quarto volumes in 1774 comprised a work that young people could read, learn, and also enjoy. As such Chesterfield's *Letters to his Son,* 1774, published by

Eugenia Stanhope from the originals, deserves a place in this chapter, although his strictures of book-collecting in Volume I, page 567, directly conflict with most of what I have so far written.

'When you return here', he writes to his son, 'I am apt to think that you will find something better to do, than to run to Mr. Osborne's at Gray's Inn, to pick up scarce books. Buy good books, and read them; the best books are the commonest, and the last editions are always the best . . . But take care not to understand editions and title-pages too well. It always smells of pedantry, and not always of learning. Beware of the *Bibliomanie.*'

His *Miscellaneous Works* appeared in two volumes in 1777, with 'Volume the Third' (really a separate, and much rarer, work) being published in 1778.

In May 1802 appeared the first monthly-issue of *The Guardian of Education*, the first publication of any kind to review books published for children and young people. It was edited by the formidable Mrs Sarah Trimmer (1741–1810), although her name did not appear on the title-page until issue No. 9 in January 1803. Her object was 'so to criticize and examine educational and children's books that only good ones might spread abroad'. A total of 28 numbers of the magazine appeared, the last being published in September 1806. I have a complete set of this ephemeral publication, and find it invaluable as a guide to juvenile books in that early period in their history, giving as it does not only details of their contents, but much bibliographical information as to bindings, published price, and general format. Many of the works described have not survived and are known only through the lists she gives. Mrs Trimmer, herself the mother of 12 children, wrote at least one notable book for juveniles, her famous *Fabulous Histories; Designed for the Instruction of Children, respecting their Treatment of Animals*, 1786 (a second edition appeared the same year), the title later being changed to the more familiar *The History of the Robins*. She was a pioneer in the education of small children by the use of pictures, all her little books being crowded with full-page engravings depicting scenes from everyday life and historical times. She criticised *Cinderella* as being 'a compendium of vice', and would have nothing to do with fairy-stories in any shape or form.

The period which ended about 1830 can be described as having witnessed a battle royal between the strait-laced moral and didactic juvenile tract, and the fairy-story. Mrs M. M. Sherwood sided with Mrs Trimmer against the fairies, and her *The Fairchild Family*, published in three separate parts 1818–47, although widely read, was soon ridiculed and condemned by those with the interests of children's literature at heart. Maria Edgeworth, devoted, like her father, to the teachings of Rousseau, produced *The Parent's Assistant: or, stories for Children*, 3 vols. 1795, of which no complete copy is known to have survived. *Early Lessons*, 1801, came out in several differently titled parts, the complete work being re-issued in ten volumes in 1803. Meanwhile, another disciple of Rousseau, the unconventional Thomas Day (1748–89), had written *The History of Sandford and Merton*, 3 vols. 1783–9, a succession of episodic adventures in which the rich prig Tommy Merton is contrasted with the too-good-to-be-true Harry Sandford. Volume I is especially difficult to find in first edition form. Charles and Mary Lamb had co-operated in the writing of *Tales from Shakespeare, designed for the use of young persons*, 2 vols. 1807, although only Charles' name appears on the title-page. My copy of his *The Adventures of Ulysses*, 1808, mentions that *Tales from Shakespeare* were 'just published in eight single numbers, each number being adorned with three plates, beautifully coloured, price Sixpence. The remainder will speedily follow.' I know of no copy of this part-issue, which must, in fact, rank as the second edition. *Mrs. Leicester's School*, another famous story, appeared in 1809, only three of the ten stories being by Charles, the rest coming from the pen of his sister.

Despite the finger-wagging moralists, children demanded fairy-tales, and there were authors and publishers eager to fulfil the demand. William Roscoe's *The Butterfly's Ball and the Grasshopper's Feast* appeared in 1807, and proved immensely popular. R. M. Ballantyne rewrote the verses and re-issued the work in 1857, as he had done a year earlier with the nursery rhyme *The Three Little Kittens*, which had first appeared in *New Nursery Songs for all good Children*,

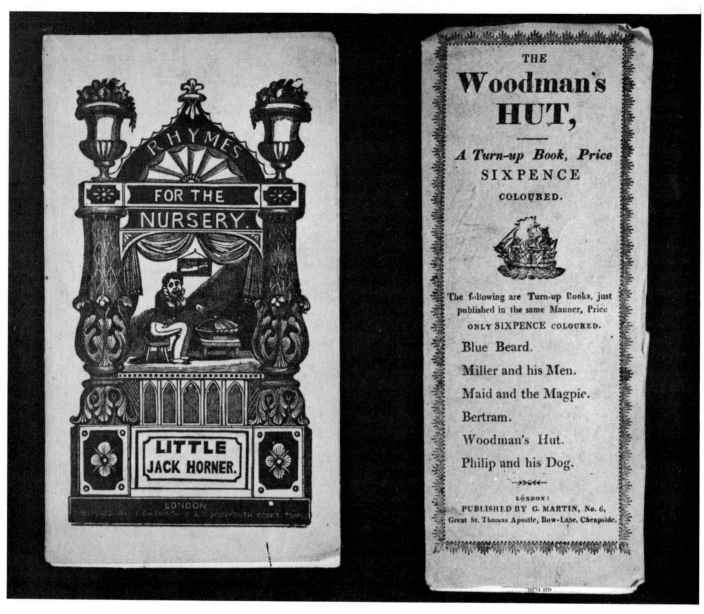

1843, by Eliza Fallen (1787–1860), printed in the United States of America. German folk-tales, collected by the brothers Grimm under the title of *Kinder- und Hausmärchen*, were first published in three volumes between 1812 and 1818. In 1819 a second edition appeared, this time specially prepared for children. The first English edition, illustrated by George Cruikshank, was published in two volumes under the title *German Popular Stories*, 1823. The first English edition of *The Pentamerone, or The Story of Stories*, 1848, was also illustrated by Cruikshank. This collection of Italian fairy-stories, translated by John Taylor, is one of the most difficult children's books of the period to find in the original cloth binding. *Wonderful Stories for Children*, 1846, is the first translation into English of the stories of Hans Christian Andersen, issued with four full-page coloured plates, the text having been translated by Mary Howitt. Two other translations appeared the same year, with the result that Mary Howitt's version did not repay the cost of printing.

· Books on natural history, specially written for children, had appeared during the last quarter of the 18th century. *The Natural History of Birds; intended for the Amusement and Instruction of Children*, 3 vols. 1791, by Samuel Galton, is delightfully illustrated with 116 full-page copperplate engravings, each coloured by hand. Galton was a member of the Lunar Society, the scientific society which met in Birmingham, and his *Natural History of Quadrupeds for the Instruction of Young Persons* followed in two volumes in 1801. *The Boy's Country-Book*, 1839, by William Howitt, is one of the most readable works of its type, and is really an autobiographical account of Howitt's early life. Travel and exploration were taken care of by William Mavor (1758–1837), in his *Historical Account of the most celebrated Voyages, Travels and Discoveries*, 1796. Originally published by E. Newbery in ten volumes it proved so successful that a further

Above and above right
Typical of the chap-books and cheaply printed children's books issued before and during the first quarter of the 19th century, are the four items shown here. *Valentine and Orson* dates from 1785; the rest are all before 1820.

Size of bottom right book 'A Present. . .': 15.5cm × 10cm.

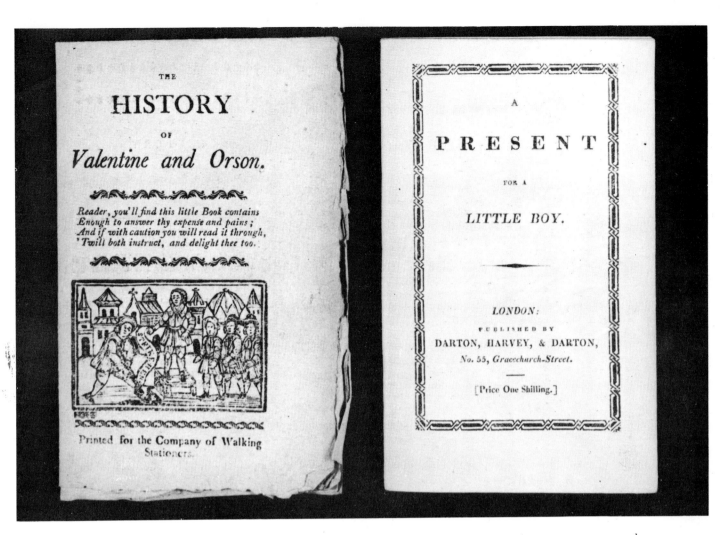

THE

HISTORY

OF

Valentine and Orson.

Reader, you'll find this little Book contains
Enough to answer thy expense and pains;
And if with caution you will read it through,
'Twill both instruct, and delight thee too.

Printed for the Company of Walking
Stationers.

A

PRESENT

FOR A

LITTLE BOY.

LONDON:
PUBLISHED BY
DARTON, HARVEY, & DARTON,
No. 55, Gracechurch-Street.

[Price One Shilling.]

ten volumes followed in 1797, again followed by a further set to make up a total of 25. Miss Priscilla Wakefield (1751–1832), did not lag far behind with her *The Juvenile Travellers,* 1801, complete with a large folding hand-coloured map of the world, and *Excursions in North America,* 1806, similarly embellished.

Original stories inspired by fairy-tales had, by the middle of the century, become far less didactic; John Ruskin's *The King of the Golden River,* 1851, published anonymously, and William Makepeace Thackeray's *The Rose and the Ring,* 1855, published under his pseudonym of 'M. A. Titmarsh', both moved away from mere teaching and instruction. *The Water Babies,* 1863, by Charles Kingsley, had a moral to preach, but with *Alice's Adventures in Wonderland,* 1865, and *Through the Looking-Glass,* 1872, by 'Lewis Carroll', we reach the culminating point of pure fantasy bounded by a dream-like logic that has proved itself beyond the reach of any writer who followed. Revd. C. L. Dodgson ('Lewis Carroll') objected to the quality of the printing of the first edition of *Alice,* 1865, and insisted that the issue be withdrawn. So did John Tenniel who had drawn the memorable illustrations, and Macmillan, the publishers, were forced to acquiesce. All the copies that could be retrieved of the 1865 edition were sent to a children's hospital, the book being re-published in 1866, an issue now referred to as the 'first published edition'. An 1865 *Alice* now fetches in excess of £1,000 ($2,400), being, for obvious reasons, extremely rare in any condition. The 1866 edition costs about £100, with the first American edition, dated also 1866, about twice that amount. This American edition is actually the second issue of the plates and text of the 1865 edition, with a new title-page giving the American imprint, the publishers having thriftily disposed of the remainder of the offending sheets far from Dodgson and Tenniel's eyes. In reverse, the first American writer of children's books to be widely read in England (and extensively pirated and copied) was Samuel Griswold Goodrich (1793–1860), who wrote under the pseudonym of 'Peter Parley'. Dozens of different stories appeared with this name on their title-pages, and a series of *Peter Parley Annuals* continued from 1840 to 1894. The first annual for children, other than a few inconsequential religious tracts, was *The Excitement,* 1830, published by Waugh & Innes, Edinburgh, in pictorial paper-covered

The pictorial cloth-cover by Henry Holiday of Lewis Carroll's *The Hunting of the Snark*, 1876. Size of cover: 18.7 × 12.5cm.

boards with a gilt morocco spine. Adam Keys was the editor, and it ran from 1830 to 1841, a quarrel between the owners resulting in a rival, *The New Excitement*, 1838, running side by side with the old title.

One of the first books to show a markedly lenient attitude towards the bubbling high spirits of the young, and plain naughtiness in children, was *Holiday House*, 1839. The authoress was a Miss Catherine Sinclair (1800–64), a lady as much as 50 years in advance of her time as a writer. She preferred her children to be like 'wild horses on the prairies, rather than like well-broken hacks on the road'. For the first time in a children's book she set misbehaviour in an amusing and totally understandable light. Other landmarks of the period were Sir Henry Cole's *The Home Treasury of Books*, which he published under the pseudonym of 'Felix Summerly'. The first of the series to appear was *Bible Events*, 1843; but after that worthy title he went on to such extravagances as *Little Red Riding Hood, Reynard the Fox,* and *Beauty and the Beast,* all thoroughly enjoyed by his young readers. Illustrated limerick verse came with the appearance of *A Book of Nonesense,* 1846, by Edward Lear.

Meanwhile, writers of ability were following the lead set by Catherine Sinclair and her true-to-life children. Charlotte Yonge (1823–1901), gave older girls *The Daisy Chain,* 2 vols. 1856, in the midst of her 150 or so novels and tales; Louisa M. Alcott (1832–88) produced *Little Women,* 1868, which must rank as one of the most popular juvenile books ever written; and Mary Louisa Molesworth (1839–1921), author of over 100 'child novels', gave children *Four Winds Farm,* 1887, *Carrots – just a Little Boy,* 1876, and *The Rectory Children,* 1889. Francis Hodgson Burnett (1849–1924), wrote her cloyingly sentimental story of *Little Lord Fauntleroy* as a serial in *St. Nicholas Magazine,* later to appear in book-form dated 1886. The story 'ran through England like a sickly fever', the model for the hero being the author's second son Vivian. It was dramatised in 1888, and a film version appeared in the late 1930s. *The Secret Garden,* 1911, shows her insight into child psychology.

The latter half of the 19th century witnessed the birth of the adventure story for boys. In this field R. M. Ballantyne (1825–94) was a pioneer, and from the 1850s onwards he opened for the sons of the rapidly expanding *literati* of middle- and working-class families, an exciting new vista of a world spiced with romance and danger which lay waiting for the young men of Britain to grow up and explore. He was one of the first to write straightforward adventure stories set in well-researched factual surroundings, the youthful heroes of his books being left to fend for themselves in the plots he created, without the curbing hands or interfering restrictions of pious uncles and moralising aunts. His first book, *Hudson's Bay,* 1848, was privately printed; but with the appearance of *Snowflakes and Sunbeams; or, The Young Fur Traders,* 1856, began a writing career devoted to boys' adventure stories that was to result in the publication of well over 100 books. He is remembered best for his *The Coral Island,* 1858, a

Frontispiece of the privately printed first edition of R. M. Ballantyne's first book, *Hudson's Bay,* a notorious rarity in the field of early children's books. Published in 1848, it is an autobiographical account of the young author's adventures in Rupert's Land, while in the service of the Hudson's Bay Company.

book which exerted a strong influence over the young Robert Louis Stevenson (1850–94), promoting his love for the islands of the South Seas that resulted in that immortal classic of romance, unmoralised and unashamed, *Treasure Island,* 1883, a book which brought him fame and fortune. Frederick Marryat, R.N. (1792–1848), who in the 20 years following 1829 had written a series of instructional adventure stories for young people, undoubtedly influenced Ballantyne's work and those who followed him. Amongst these were W. H. G. Kingston (1814–1880), remembered for *Peter the Whaler,* 1851, *Digby Heathcote,* 1860, *In the Wilds of Florida,* 1882, and at least 150 others, mostly tales of the sea. G. A. Henty (1832–1902), was a follower of Sir Walter Scott rather than Ballantyne, writing boys' adventure stories set in a factual historical background, *With Clive in India,* 1884, *Under Wellington's Command,* 1899, and *Out With Garibaldi,* 1901, being typical titles. Rider Haggard's *King Solomon's Mines,* 1885, and *Allan Quatermain,* 1887, were both favourite titles with young people, as were the science fiction books of H. G. Wells with the generation that followed.

School stories flourished during the same period. *Tom Brown's Schooldays,* 1857, by Thomas Hughes (1822–96), depicted schoolboy cruelties and firm-chinned loyalties effectively enough to influence English ideas on public schools. *Tom Brown at Oxford,* 1861, was far less successful, but both are difficult first editions to acquire in anything approaching original condition. So is a copy

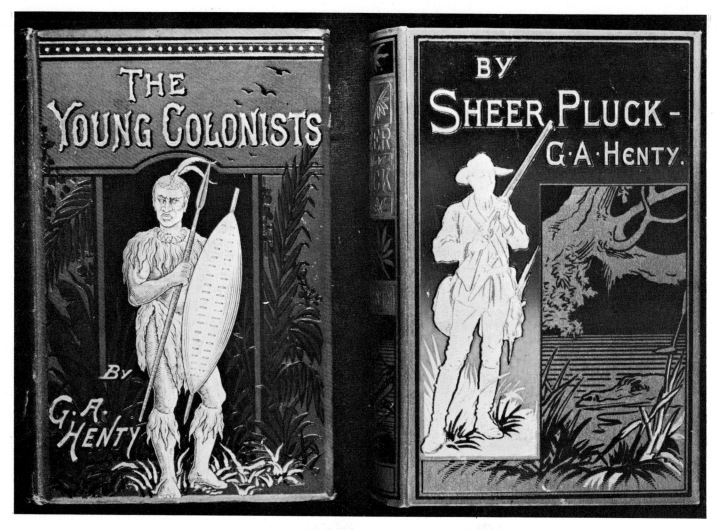

Typical of the binding styles employed for tales for young people, these two examples are pictorially blocked in gold and colours, and are both 'difficult' Henty first editions. *The Young Colonists*, 1885, published by George Routledge, is especially rare; *By Sheer Pluck* is dated 1884.

Height of book: 19cm.

of *Eric, or Little by Little,* 1858, by F. W. Farrar (1831–1903), written when the author was a master at Harrow School. Talbot Baines Reed (1852–93) reacted against both Hughes and Farrar's sentiments by producing his *The Fifth Form at St Dominics,* 1887, *The Cockhouse at Fellsgarth* (1893), and *The Master of the Shell* (1894). His *The Adventures of a Three-Guinea Watch* (1883), appeared undated under an R.T.S. imprint, as did the previous two titles. Rudyard Kipling (1865–1936), upset all the accepted traditions with his *Stalky & Co,* 1899, having previously provided constantly reprinted classics with his *The Jungle Book,* 1894, and *The Second Jungle Book,* 1895, a fine pair of which, in the original blue cloth, will cost the collector well over £60 ($144). His *Just So Stories,* 1902, a book intended for younger children, is difficult to find in clean state, the white paint of the pictorial cloth-covers soon soiling. The tradition of 'man the friend of animals' was carried on with *Tarzan of the Apes,* 1914, by Edgar Rice Burroughs, which must have the imprint of A. C. McClurg & Co., Chicago, to be a first edition. As early as 1877, Anna Sewell's autobiographical story of a horse, *Black Beauty,* was told in the equine first person singular.

Children's poetry of the same period included Christina Rossetti's *Sing-Song,* 1872, delightfully illustrated by Arthur Hughes, as was her *Speaking Likenesses,* 1874; Stevenson's *A Child's Garden of Verses,* 1885, Belloc's *A Bad Child's Book of Beasts* (1896), *More Beasts for Worse Children* (1897), and *The Moral Alphabet* (1899). The tradition has been continued through Walter de la Mare, Eleanor Farjeon and A. A. Milne, to T. S. Eliot (1888–1965), with his *Old Possum's Book of Practical Cats,* 1939.

Kate Greenaway (1846–1901), is represented in the collection by half a shelf of slim volumes in assorted sizes, starting with the first book she illustrated, *Diamonds and Toads,* 1871. It was not until *Under the Window,* 1878, made its appearance in its glazed pictorially-printed boards, engraved by the famous Edmund Evans, that her name became a household word. Despite the fact that a first edition of 20,000 copies was printed, the volume is still difficult to find in clean original condition, and now fetches anything up to £25 ($60). *A Day in a Child's Life* (1881), *Mother Goose* (1881), *Language of Flowers* (1884), and *Queen* of the Pirate Isle (1886), are all illustrated in her delightful later style, the last being described by Ruskin as 'The best thing you have ever done – it is so real and natural.'

Collections of fairy-tales continued to appear at regular intervals. Joseph Jacobs, editor of the magazine *Folk-lore,* supplied an original collection of five volumes, starting with *English Fairy Tales,* 1890. The limited edition in large-paper of this collection, printed on japon vellum, is particularly attractive. Andrew Lang's 12-volume collection of 'coloured' fairy books, the first of which (and the hardest to find) was *The Blue Fairy Book,* 1889, looks best in the brightly gilt and colourful cloth-bound issue, rather than the soberly-clad large-paper edition which appears drab and uninteresting by the side of its gaily-coloured shelf-mates. First edition dates of Lang's most eagerly sought-after collection are: *Blue,* 1889, *Red,* 1890, *Green,* 1892, *Yellow,* 1894, *Pink,* 1897, *Grey,* 1900, *Violet,* 1901, *Crimson,* 1903, *Brown,* 1904, *Orange,* 1906, *Olive,* 1907, and *Lilac,* 1910. All were reprinted many times.

Beatrix Potter (1866–1943), wrote and illustrated little books. She insisted they should remain tiny to suit the little hands into which they were meant to find their way. She lived in the Lake District, near Ambleside, Westmorland, and there, at 'Hill Top' Farm, she produced the diminutive volumes that young children the world over have loved and enjoyed ever since. *The Tale of Peter Rabbit* (1901), was the first to appear, privately-printed by Strangeways & Sons in an edition of 250 copies, to be followed by a second privately-printed edition of 200 copies in February 1902, with the text revised and corrected. It was when the first published edition of 1902 appeared, under the imprint of Frederick Warne & Co., that success was quickly apparent. In the meantime Beatrix Potter had written and privately-published *The Tailor of Gloucester,* 1902, a story she described as being her 'favourite among the little books'. It, too, was later published by Warne, dated 1903, continuing a run of her works that became famous as the 'Peter Rabbit' books. First editions carry the Warne imprint and are dated on their title-pages as well as having a copyright inscription on the verso. The first privately-printed issues fetch anything up to £100 ($240); the rest vary from £5 ($12) to £20 ($48).

A period of nearly 400 years has been lightly covered in this chapter, dating from the time when Jost Amman first cut his initials on the woodblocks that were prepared for printing *Kunst und Lehrbüchlein* in the 16th century.

To compress four centuries into a single chapter inevitably means passing over many important landmarks in the story of children's books. I have just looked again at the hundreds of volumes standing unmentioned on their shelves. They are to have their due recognition in *The Collector's Book of Children's Books,* a companion volume to this present work.

Collectors in this field can consult: *The Child and His Book,* 1891, by E. M. Field; *Pages and Pictures from Forgotten Children's Books,* 1898, by A. W. Tuer; *Les Livres de L'Enfance* (1930), 2 vols., published by Gumuchian & Co., Paris; *Children's Books in England,* 1932, by F. J. H. Darton; *English Children's Books,* 1954, by Percy Muir; and *Osborne Collection of Early Children's Books,* 1958, edited by Judith St. John, published by Toronto Public Library, Canada.

Detail from the frontispiece of G. A. Henty's first book for boys. Published in 1871, *Out on the Pampas* was the fore-runner of a long list of juvenile best-sellers.

Detective Fiction

The creator of Sherlock Holmes, taken when Dr Conan Doyle was 33 years of age. This recently discovered photograph was taken in 1893.

Opposite page:
Top left
The murderer unmasked! The frontispiece of an early work of detective fiction, with the unlikely title of *Where the Rail Runs Now: A Story of Coaching Days,* by F. Frankfort Moore, published in 1876.

Size of engraved surface: 13cm × 9.5cm.

Top right
The first English edition of one of the most successful crime and detective stories ever written. This is a fine copy of a work published in flimsy pictorially-printed paper-wrappers, few of which have survived in anything like an acceptable state. It was originally published in Melbourne, Australia, in 1886.

Size of front cover: 18.5cm × 12cm.

Bottom left
George Cruikshank's spirited engraving for the first part of *Clement Lorimer,* 1849, by Angus B. Reach, later used as the frontispiece for the cloth-bound-volume edition of the same year. This was the first full-length novel of crime, mystery and modern detection to appear in England, and was written by a newspaper reporter employed at the Central Criminal Court, London.

Size of engraved surface: 17cm × 11cm.

Bottom right
One of the 12 full-page engraved plates by George Cruikshank for *Clement Lorimer; or, The Book With the Iron Clasps,* 1849, by Angus B. Reach.

Size of engraved surface from top of circle to bottom of wording: 15cm.

Early detective fiction is now a quarry hunted with persistence by specialist book-collectors throughout Britain and the United States of America. Books that in the late 1930s could have been bought by the boxful for less than the price of a deerstalker hat now command figures that have promoted individual items to full-page rating in the catalogues of antiquarian booksellers. Yet there is still plenty of scope for the collector of only average means to fill his shelves with first editions of detective fiction. Some of the books he can discover hidden on the shelves or in the lists of the smaller and less exalted booksellers will certainly excite the admiration and perhaps the envy of later generations of collectors in the same field. One needs a flair for spotting books of mystery, crime and detection other than the high-spots that have become household names. Many of the earliest and most covetable items masquerade under titles that give no clue to the fact that their covers conceal a dark web of conspiracy, murder and inexplicable goings-on. One of my most fortunate acquisitions in this field was *Where the Rail Runs Now: A Story of Coaching Days,* by F. Frankfort Moore, 1876, which I bought as an early railroad item. When I read the story it turned out to be a first-class tale of detective fiction, complete with a heavily disguised Scotland Yard officer to carry out the final arrest. Yet it is a title that has so far escaped the notice of bibliographers.

It is difficult to define exactly what constitutes an authentic detective story, despite the fact that most collectors are eager enough, when asked, to set out their own terms of reference. Obviously the story must be largely occupied with the solution of the mystery surrounding a crime or a series of them, this task being the concern of an amateur or professional detective. In the story he may bungle the job and fail ignominiously; he may triumph and live to see his erstwhile adversary standing handcuffed in the dock; or, with honours even, he may topple over the edge of the precipitous Reichenbach Falls, locked in a death-grapple with the infamous Professor Moriarty. Win or lose, the detective, male or female – for lady detectives have been quick to assert their rights in the pages of detective fiction – must have spent a considerable portion of his or her time in the story detecting crime and/or thwarting the designs of the criminally minded. Occasionally he is himself the victim and presents the reader with the solution from the prison cell or the grave. But only very occasionally, for the detective-writer sees to it that his creation is mentally a little too quick on the draw for even a master-mind of crime.

To Edgar Allan Poe go the honours for the invention of the modern detective story. Although the scene of his *The Mystery of Marie Roget,* published as early as 1845, is set in Paris, France, in reality Poe was giving his readers a picture of the murder of the unfortunate Mary Cecilia Rogers which had recently taken place in New York. To what one imagines must have been the embarrassment of certain members of the New York City Police, the author not only gave a correct solution to the problems surrounding the crime, but by literary detective work gave clues that eventually led to the arrest of the real-life murderer.

Poe is now extremely difficult and expensive to collect in first edition form, whether one looks for his prose or poetical work. Some indication of the esteem accorded to his early works by collectors in the United States of America can be realised by the fact that $10,000 (£4,170) was paid in the autumn of 1967 for a rebound copy of *Al Aaraaf, Tamerlane, and Minor Poems,* which first appeared in 1829. *The Murders in the Rue Morgue,* 1841, and *The Gold Bug,* 1843, both works of detective fiction, the latter dealing with the solution of a cryptogram,

BROUGHT TO BAY.—P. 238.

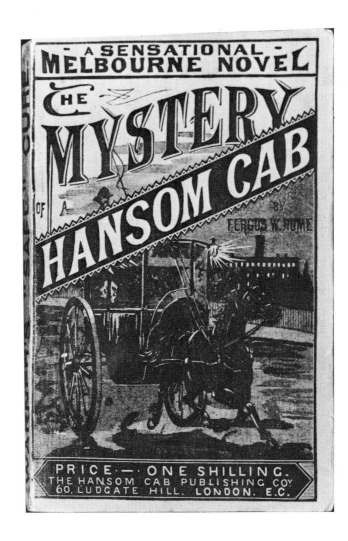

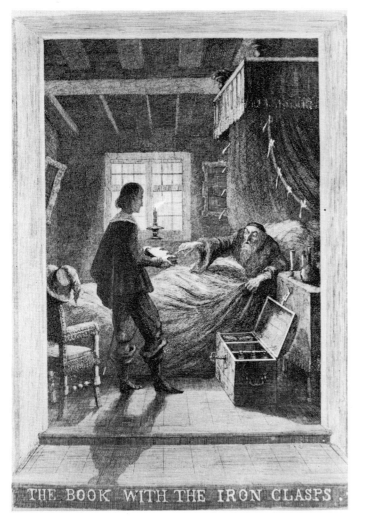

THE BOOK WITH THE IRON CLASPS.

are seldom seen in the auction room, although a copy of *Mesmerism 'in Articulo Mortis'*, 1846, in its original stitched wrappers could possibly be bought for as little as $100 (£42). *The Raven,* 1845, the first poem which brought him wide popularity, would cost the present-day collector something like six times as much if he was lucky enough to track down a copy in its original printed wrappers. His stories of mystery and detection are what interest us here: the *Purloined Letter* appeared the same year as *The Raven,* once again introducing the first fictional detective, Auguste Dupin.

The tales Poe wrote could be classed only as short stories. The distinction of having written the first full-length 'modern' crime and detection story must go to a Scotsman. Angus Bethune Reach (1821–56) was born at Inverness, Scotland, and educated at Edinburgh University, but in 1842 he and his family moved to London. There young Reach was employed as a crime reporter at the Central Criminal Court while working for the London newspaper, the *Morning Chronicle.* In 1848–9 he published in six monthly parts, a tale of vendetta, murder, racehorse doping, slow poisoning and abduction, and other dastardly deeds, under the title of *Clement Lorimer; or, The Book with the Iron Clasps.* George Cruikshank contributed 12 spirited full-page illustrations, and the publishers, David Bogue, Fleet Street, London, issued the work in book-form from the sheets of the monthly parts, in heavily gilt and blind-stamped maroon cloth. The original stab-holes used in stitching the paper covers to the part-issue can be easily seen in the inside margins. The book itself was published in the autumn of 1849, in time for the Christmas market. It was by no means Reach's first literary work, as at least six lighthearted satires on the 'bores, humbugs, tuft-hunters and toadies' of his day had appeared during the previous two or three years, most of which had originally been printed in magazines. But *Clement Lorimer* was his first and only mystery story, with the unravelling of the tangled skein of clues left only partly in the hands of the holder of the title-role. On page 130, detectives are described for the first time as 'sleuth-hounds of the law', a fact that has apparently escaped the notice of the compilers of the Oxford English Dictionary. Copies of the first edition had been hunted down by Cruikshank collectors long before collectors of books of crime and detection started their hunt. Present-day collectors may have to be content with the 1856 reprint, although the title appears to be unknown to bibliographers of detective fiction.

One of the most prized copies of detective fiction in my collection is an all but mint specimen of the first issue of the first edition of *Recollections of a Detective Police-Officer,* by 'Waters', the pseudonym of William Russell. This ephemeral little 'yellowback' is dated 1856, and is still in much the same condition as when J. & C. Brown & Company, Ave Maria Lane, London, issued it over 110 years ago. Bright and resplendent in its original pictorially-printed paper-covered boards, it has survived in this state due to being enclosed in a wrapping of brown cloth almost since the day of issue. What prompted the original mid-nineteenth century owner to cosset and care for a volume he could have replaced brand-new for a tiny sum I shall never know. A copy in this condition could fetch as much as £50 ($120) at auction, perhaps even more, for it is doubtful if another volume approaching its state of perfection now exists. 'Waters' wrote a sequel to this novel, issued under the same title in 1859, and with the words 'Second Series' on the title-page. Of this I have only a copy rebound in half-morocco, picked up at a jumble-sale.

Many other titles were published under the names of a host of American and British authors during the next decade, and in 1866 Emile Gaboriau's *L'affaire Lerouge* appeared in France. With this full-length novel and others of Gaboriau's spine-chilling stories the fictional larger-than-life detective established a place in literature that brought him an ever increasing following of enthusiastic readers. And within two years there came a milestone in the annals of detective fiction. Wilkie Collins' book, *The Moonstone,* was published in England.

To read this novel is to retain a vivid recollection of the ubiquitous Sergeant Cuff. Under-paid and under-privileged, with a passion for roses and endearing eccentricities that masked an incisive and razor-like intellect, Cuff can be considered the fore-runner and prototype of the long line of odd, whimsical, commonplace, outlandish, suave, opera-loving, tone-deaf, pipe-smoking, martini-sipping sleuth-hounds that stretch forward in time a full century to the present press-button age.

A fly from the railway drove up as I reached the lodge and out got a grizzled, elderly man, so miserably lean that he looked as if he had not got an ounce of flesh on his bones in any part of him. He was dressed all in decent black, with a white cravat round his neck. His face was as sharp as a hatchet, and the skin of it was as yellow and dry and withered as an autumn leaf. His eyes, of a steely light grey, had a very disconcerting trick, when they encountered your eyes, of looking as if they expected something more from you than you were aware of yourself. His walk was soft; his voice was melancholy; his long lanky fingers were hooked like claws. He might have been a parson, or an undertaker – or anything else you like, except what he really was.

Despite the care with which Wilkie Collins drew for his readers this spidery figure of a master detective, he nevertheless allowed Cuff to make his exit from the pages of fiction when the last chapter of *The Moonstone* drew to a close. Sergeant Cuff disappeared – never to be seen again, but there were soon others of the same profession to take his place. The three-volume novel in which he made his first and only appearance in 1868 will now cost the present-day collector up to £200 ($480). That is if he insists on acquiring a copy of the first issue of the first edition, complete with its half-titles, the misprint 'treachesrouly' on page 129 in Volume 2, and with the leaves of advertisements in Volumes 2 and 3. A good copy in the original cloth binding would not be overpriced at this figure, whereas a rebound half-calf or half-morocco specimen might well prove dear at less than a quarter of the price. But any text of the first edition is hard to come by and it is a fortunate man that has the book on his shelves.

In 1874 the first of the Pinkerton detective stories, *The Expressman and the Detective,* appeared in Chicago, U.S.A., under the imprint of Keen, Cooke & Company. The author, Allan Pinkerton, was born in Glasgow, Scotland, in 1819, and settled in Illinois, U.S.A., early in the 1840s. He seems to have had his nose to the ground from the time he stepped ashore in his adopted land for in no time at all he had unmasked a gang of counterfeiters and brought them to justice. By 1846 he had succeeded in having himself made deputy-sheriff of Kane County, Illinois, and four years later was promoted to the rank of first detective in the Chicago police force. The same year (1850) he established the world-famous private detective agency that still bears his name. But it was the mid-1870s before he began churning out story after story of the profession he knew so well, nearly always with himself as the master detective, or with a Pinkerton agent as investigator. *Claude Melnotte as a Detective,* 1875, *Criminal Reminiscences and Detective Sketches,* 1878, and *The Gypsies and the Detectives,* 1879, are some of the better-known titles in this *genre* that can still be bought. Fine copies are exceedingly scarce, but this observation applies to nearly all first editions of detective fiction of the period before the end of the first quarter of the 20th century. The better-written and more popular works were literally read to death, passing from the hands of the original purchaser to those of his family and friends in a succession of reading cycles that left the book dog-eared and dejected. Library copies suffered the same fate in about a quarter of the time.

One of the most successful crime and detective stories of all time was Fergus Hume's *The Mystery of a Hansom Cab.* Notwithstanding its phenomenal success, the unfortunate author is believed to have netted less than £150 ($360) from a work that quickly established itself as a best-seller of international proportions. Ferguson Wright Hume (1859–1932), to give the New Zealand writer his full name, was born in England but educated at Otago University in his parents' native land. By the time he was 27 he was working in Melbourne, Australia, as a barrister's clerk, and intent on completing his first novel. *The Mystery of a Hansom Cab* was accepted for publication by Kemp & Boyce, Melbourne, and the first printing of 5,000 copies was sold out within weeks of its appearance in October 1886. The price was one shilling a copy. Another three impressions (each of 10,000 copies) were called for within a few months. At this stage Hume foolishly parted with the copyright of the book to a sharp-eyed businessman called Fredrick Trischler for a paltry sum. Trischler and a small group of business associates formed the Hansom Cab Publishing Company, and in the early summer of 1887 set up their headquarters in London. In July of that year they commenced printing something of the order of 25,000 copies of the book every month, but even that amount scarcely kept pace with the public demand. Within 18 months of the original appearance of the work in Melbourne more than a quarter of a million copies had been sold, a figure that has seldom been equalled up to the present day. By the turn of the century 12 foreign translations had been made.

My own copy of *The Mystery of a Hansom Cab* is of the second (or first English) edition, with the words 'One Hundreth Thousand' at the head of the title-page. The volume can be described as being in fine state (and I do not use the term 'fine' lightly) and is in the original flimsy pictorially printed paper wrappers. It is extremely unlikely that I shall ever discover an earlier or better copy, and I place its present day value at about £60 ($144). A rebound copy would be worth only about a tenth of this amount as much of the charm and character of the book is embodied in its luridly printed covers. Of the true first issue of the first edition only two copies are known to have survived. Both are in the collection of the Mitchell Library, Sydney, Australia.

Pride of place in any self-respecting collection of first editions of detective fiction will almost certainly be accorded to the Sherlock Holmes stories. The first editions in book-form of Sir Arthur Conan Doyle's inimitable collection of short stories, telling of *The Adventures of Sherlock Holmes,* 1892, and *The Memoirs of Sherlock Holmes,* 1894, make a handsome and well-matched set. The former volume is bound in smooth light-blue cloth over bevelled boards, pictorially blocked in black and gilt, while the latter is in identical format in dark-blue cloth. Both works originally appeared in issues of the *Strand Magazine,* increasing that periodical's circulation to an extent that had impatient readers queueing outside the doors of its office waiting for the monthly issue to appear. But it was in 1887, in a tale called *A Study in Scarlet,* that Holmes first made his bow. The story appeared in *Beeton's Christmas Annual,* and later the same year in book form, giving us our first glimpse of that suave and unemotional English gentleman, carelessly elegant in Inverness cape and deerstalker hat, and now forever associated in our minds with a curly stemmed brier and long-handled magnifying-glass. Holmes was backed by the stubborn, head-shaking obedience of his devoted friend Dr Watson, a personality in his own right and with as firm a place in the annals of detective fiction as the master himself.

Their creator, Conan Doyle (1859–1930) was born in Edinburgh and educated at the University there, qualifying as a doctor of medicine. But he is remembered among novelists for the rare distinction of breathing life into an extraordinary figure. The fictional Holmes was gifted with an intuitive insight into criminal psychology as well as a computer-like ability for assessing in scientific fashion the well-hidden clues to the identity of the perpetrator of the crimes he was set to solve. He is still revered by his numerous devotees; the flourishing Holmes societies and the literature regarding Baker Street's most intriguing personality which increases in amount annually, seem to ensure that his place at the pinnacle of the hierarchy of fictional detectives is as secure as it was 70 years ago.

Any collector who invested a few years ago in first editions of Conan Doyle's stories must be congratulating himself on possessing books that have trebled in value during less than five years and will almost surely go on doing so. A good copy of *The Adventures of Sherlock Holmes,* if a first edition in original cloth, will cost a present day purchaser over £50 ($120). Fine copies are almost impossible to come by, for this tall and imposing octavo is too often found in a sadly soiled and foxed condition, a tribute to the number of times the book has been read. *The Memoirs* has never been a difficult 'first', but a clean copy will now cost £25 ($60), and *The Hound of the Baskervilles,* 1902, fetches about the same price. *The Sign of Four,* 1890, another Holmes story, is moderately priced at £20 ($48). The last copy to reach the auction rooms of the 1887 edition of *Beeton's Christmas Annual* fetched no less than £480 ($1,132), despite the fact that it lacked its wrappers and most of the advertisement leaves. A sobering thought for those seeking the first appearance in print of Mr Sherlock Holmes.

Some of the high-spots in my own collection of detective fiction include *My Adventure in the Flying Scotsman,* 1888, which is Eden Phillpotts' (1862–1960) first book (he wrote well over 150 before his death at the age of 98), *The Memoirs of Constantine Dix,* 1905, by Barry Pain (1864–1928), *The Lost Stradivarius,* 1895, and *The Nebuly Coat,* 1903, both by John Meade Falkner

(1858–1932), *The Case of Miss Elliott*, 1905, and *Lady Molly of Scotland Yard*, 1910, both by Baroness Orczy (Mrs Montagu Barstow, 1865–1947) who will always be remembered for her romantic novel *The Scarlet Pimpernel*, 1905. Other writers featured in the collection include Edgar Wallace, R. Austin Freeman, whose stories of Dr Thorndyke are said to have helped the professionals at Scotland Yard, the American writer Anna Katherine Green, one of the first women writers of detective fiction and often termed the 'mother of the detective story', E. C. Bentley, whose *Trent's Last Case* (1913), had a profound influence on the art of fictional crime and detection, Agatha Christie, creator of the Belgian detective Hercule Poirot, Arthur Morrison, with his *Martin Hewitt, Investigator*, 1894 (first American edition appeared the same year in New York), and a string of others too numerous to mention in detail.

The most useful books to a collector of detective fiction I nominate as being *Murder for Pleasure*, 1942, by Howard Haycraft, *Queen's Quorum*, 1953, by Ellery Queen, and *Victorian Detective Fiction*, 1966, being a catalogue of the collection of detective fiction made by Dorothy Glover and Graham Greene. The excellent introduction to this latter work is by John Carter, the bibliographer to whose authoritative works the uninitiated in the art of book-collecting would do well to turn.

Below left
The frontispiece of the first edition of *The Memoirs of Sherlock Holmes*, 1894, by Conan Doyle, showing the struggle leading to Holmes's death. The author was forced to resurrect his hero.

Size of engraved surface: 19cm × 12.5cm.

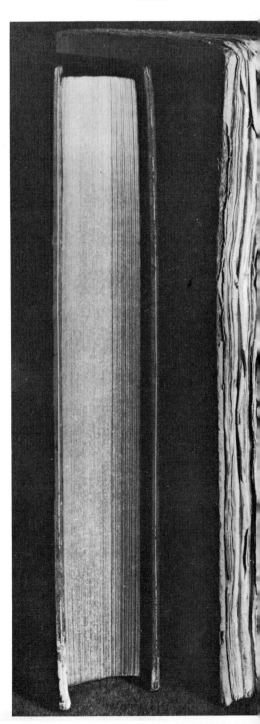

Bindings & Binding Styles

Types of fore-edges: reading left to right: (1) cut; (2) uncut; (3) trimmed.
Height of book in middle of picture: 23cm.

Bookbinding commenced when books became books as we know them today. The method of making books out of strips of parchment wound round wooden or bone rollers was eventually superseded by fastening the leaves of paper or vellum together by securing them at their inner margins. The book was then placed between protective covers, usually of wood. Between the 10th and 14th centuries, European monks, especially those in England, improved the format of books in many practical ways. Leather was stretched over the wooden boards, making flexible hinges, and this was decorated by being impressed with stamps of various designs.

The invention of printing in the 15th century boosted the craft of bookbinding to an extent that saw the separation of the art from that of the printer. Gold leaf, first used in Venice, quickly spread as a means of embellishment for the previously blind-stamped leather covers, tools of brass and other metals being cut in all shapes and designs to impress the precious metal. The end of the 15th and the beginning of the 16th centuries witnessed a quality of craftsmanship and artistic design rarely equalled in the decades that followed. Morocco leather was used for the first time, and, with tools of the utmost intricacy, craftsmen built up exquisite designs, that traced their way in gold across the polished surface of the leather. The French school of binders was pre-eminent, due to the work of Nicolas and Clovis Eve in the 16th century, Le Gascon and du Seuil in the 17th, and Padeloup and Derôme in the 18th.

In England it was Samuel Mearne, bookbinder to Charles II, who led the way, devising the 'cottage' style of adornment. The great Kalthoeber, who re-discovered the ornamentation of painted edges, and Roger Payne, who hand-tinted his endpapers, and devised bindings to harmonise with the subject of the text, while busily drinking himself into an early grave, were both innovators, followed by Gosden, Lewis, Hayday and Zaehnsdorf. Edwards of Halifax specialised in Etruscan-style bindings, and such fancies as portrait-miniatures let into the covers under transparent vellum panels. Fore-edge paintings, revealed when the edges of the leaves are splayed (although any painted decoration on the fore-edges of a book can be referred to by this term), were revived by Edwards in the third quarter of the 18th century. The gold leaf conceals the picture until the leaves are fanned out, and it disappears again when the book is closed. Examples offered today have usually been executed within the last few years. Most genuine early fore-edge paintings have the binder's imprint stamped in gilt on the extreme outer edge of the front board, thus giving a clue to the hidden picture.

Starting about 1740, books began to be issued by publishers in bindings that were merely paper-covered boards. The earliest usually had leather spines in the manner of quarter-bound books, the boards being covered with marbled paper, the outer edges of the leaves always being left uncut. Books were expensive things to buy, and were far beyond the means of the average man-in-the-street. The gentlemen in the upper income-group who purchased volumes for their libraries in most cases had them bound in leather to suit their

individual taste. The paper-covered boards and uncut edges in which the volumes were issued were therefore only meant to protect the book in its early life, the expectation being that it would shortly be sent by the purchaser to his own particular binder for dressing in the style that pleased him. There the edges would be cut and the volume bound in leather, the finish reflecting the taste of the owner and the craftsmanship of the professional binder he employed. Between 1780 and 1830 the vast majority of books were issued in paper-covered boards with uncut edges, paper labels on the spines giving details of the title and the author's name. Books of the period that originally appeared in this format are sought by collectors in preference to re-bound copies. The next best style in which to find the volume is in a binding contemporary with the period in which the book was issued, the work having perhaps been read while cased in its original boards, then sent for binding soon afterwards. Auction prices prove that a work in its original binding, be it boards, leather, or cloth, will always fetch very much more than a re-bound copy. A late re-bind, for example a volume originally issued in paper-covered boards in about 1800, then bound, say, in half-calf a few years later, but re-bound again in the period 1890–1920 (the earlier half-calf having finally disintegrated), may well be priced at only a quarter of the value of the original boarded book. Perhaps even less; and rightly so, for the outward appearance of a book should reflect in some measure the age in which it was produced, and collectors are correct to seek works in the form in which they originally appeared. From the 1830s onwards this ought to be a cardinal rule, any volume which transgresses being only allowed temporarily on one's shelves.

The first cloth bindings that were issued by printers and publishers appeared as early as the 1760s, one of which is shown as an illustration. That school-books and text-books were actually issued in this format can be proved by the number of contemporary dated inscriptions found on the pasted-down endpapers. These volumes, usually for use in schools, were bound in a coarsely woven hessian cloth, almost like fine sacking in appearance, whose durability is proved by the number of copies that have come down to us with the hinges sound and uncracked after 200 years' wear. M. Pote and E. Williams, who

Types of leather bindings. Reading left to right: (1) quarter-calf with marbled paper-covered boards; (2) sprinkled-calf; (3) diced-calf; (4) tree-calf.

Size of book on right: 22cm × 14 cm.

printed and published books for use in Eton College and other schools, often issued their text-books bound in this way. So did J. Dodsley of Pall Mall, J. Johnson, St. Paul's Church-yard, E. Newbery, Ludgate Street, and many others. Most of the little volumes issued in trade bindings of this type were priced at between one and two shillings. The cloth was too roughly textured to take a label, but sometimes youthful scholars supplied their own titles in ink. Books were therefore issued bound in a type of material akin to cloth as much as 60 years before publisher's cloth-bound volumes came into general use.

The 'earliest' cloth-bound book to bear a date upon its printed cover is *Ancient Mysteries Described,* by William Hone, as seen in the illustration. This is quite clearly and precisely dated '1823'. Nevertheless, I have no hesitation in declaring, despite the evidence of one's eyes, that the binding dates from the early 1830s. In all probability this is a 'remainder' binding, made use of to clear sets of sheets left from the original 1823 edition (the title-page is also dated 1823), as cloth with this watered-silk effect, although of an early date, did not come into use until five years later. This copy is a freak, and can be disregarded in the story of cloth binding. It is an interesting example, giving warning that the bibliographical world is full of pitfalls into which the unwary can easily slip.

Right
The earliest cloth binding to bear a publisher's date.

Size of cover: 22.5 cm × 14cm.

Left
The earliest type of publisher's cloth binding. Sometimes used for school-books and text-books from the 1760s onwards, the hessian cloth was tough and durable enough to withstand classroom use, but was not otherwise used commercially for book-binding.

Size of book: 17.5 cm × 11cm.

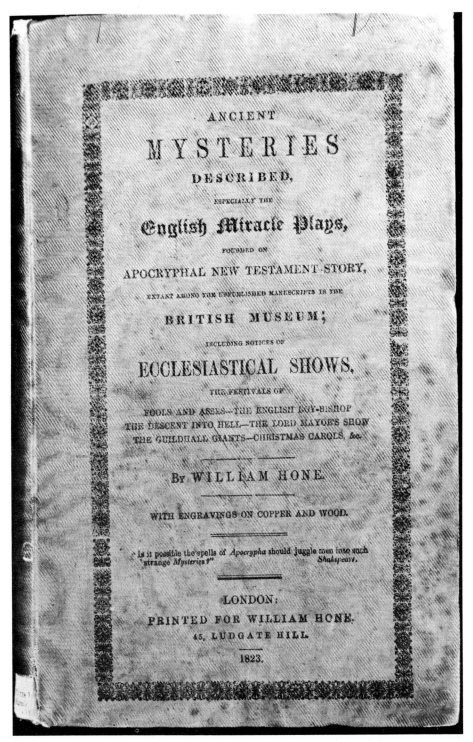

ANCIENT

MYSTERIES

DESCRIBED,

ESPECIALLY THE

English Miracle Plays,

FOUNDED ON

APOCRYPHAL NEW TESTAMENT STORY,

EXTANT AMONG THE UNPUBLISHED MANUSCRIPTS IN THE

BRITISH MUSEUM;

INCLUDING NOTICES OF

ECCLESIASTICAL SHOWS,

THE FESTIVALS OF

FOOLS AND ASSES—THE ENGLISH BOY-BISHOP
THE DESCENT INTO HELL—THE LORD MAYOR'S SHOW
THE GUILDHALL GIANTS—CHRISTMAS CAROLS, &c.

By WILLIAM HONE.

WITH ENGRAVINGS ON COPPER AND WOOD.

"Is it possible the spells of *Apocrypha* should juggle men into such
"strange *Mysteries?*"   *Shakspeare.*

LONDON:

PRINTED FOR WILLIAM HONE,
45, LUDGATE HILL.

1823.

The earliest work to exhibit a publisher's full-cloth binding was, in fact, an annual. Between the early 1820s and the late 1850s there appeared, in a multitude of guises, a number of yearly volumes, published in a variety of decorative bindings, that came to be known collectively as the 'annuals'. The first to be published in England was the *Forget Me Not,* which appeared in 1823, being issued in a slip-case in a binding of green paper-covered boards, printed and ornamented in black. But it was not until the publication of the third annual volume of *The Amulet* in 1828, that a full-cloth binding made its appearance for the first time. In the preface to this issue, the editor, Samuel Carter Hall, had this to say about the new innovation:

To the changes in the exterior of the publication, the Editor begs to direct the attention of his readers. It was the wish of many that the volume should be contained in a case, and that advantage is now given to it. But the great defect of works of this description – a defect that was almost immediately felt by every purchaser – was the perishable nature of the binding. To remedy such defect, as well as to give the volume a more tasteful and elegant appearance, it is bound in rich watered silk – an improvement on which it is unnecessary to comment.

It was not many months before the rivals to *The Amulet* started to follow suit. The first to change its format was *The Bijou,* published by William Pickering. The first annual volume, dated 1828, had been issued in a binding of printed paper-covered boards with a morocco spine. The following year the issue for 1829 appeared in a binding of red watered-silk, lettered on the spine in gilt, in almost exactly the style of the previous year's *The Amulet.* Before long there were a number of imitators, although the *Forget Me Not* remained faithful to its paper-covered boards until as late as the issue of 1831, after which it changed to cloth.

All these little volumes were bound in a type of silk cloth that had been originally manufactured as dress material. Without their slip-cases a few months' wear and tear would have been sufficient to spoil their appearance to an extent that would have made either discarding or re-binding a necessity. It was not long before cloth specially manufactured for the purpose of binding books was available to the publishing houses, and, by the mid-1830s, there was hardly a volume issued to the public that did not have an up-to-the-minute outward appearance. Cloth bindings had arrived, and had come to stay. But the transition period, between the years 1830 and 1840, is full of interest to any student of publisher's binding styles.

Many of the old traditional stigmata lingered long after the more progressive publishing houses had re-styled their bindings to suit the modern outlook. Books appeared bound in what was then an ultra-sophisticated type of glazed-cloth binding, but which stubbornly retained a spine on which was firmly glued the traditional paper label. The publishers of *The Amulet* had seen to it that the spine of their annual proclaimed in gilt-stamped lettering the title, the date, and the town of origin, to say nothing of the first use on cloth of an ornamental embellishment in the form of a musical instrument. But this was too much for the old established publishing houses. They discarded their boarded books with seeming regret, holding tightly to what they regarded as dignified forms of appeal, and only with reluctance embracing the full-cloth binding, complete with its gold-lettered spine and other marks of identification.

By 1834 the battle was won, and it was then that the first fully cloth-bound book appeared which featured pictorial covers. This was a landmark in book design, and must have caused a considerable stir in the publishing world. The idea seems to have been the brain-child of the author, the eccentric Sir Francis Bond Head, Bart. (1793–1875). *Bubbles from the Brunnens of Nassau, by an Old Man,* was published by John Murray in 1834, an illustration of which is shown. The tipped-in plates of the first edition were described as having been drawn by 'Burges's patent Paneidolon'. A second edition in an identical binding appeared the same year, but the type had been reset and all the plates, except a variant frontispiece, had disappeared. As in any new model, there had been teething troubles.

Eighteen-thirty-four was the year that also saw the first use of Baxter prints as book illustrations. Volumes I and II of *The Feathered Tribes of the British*

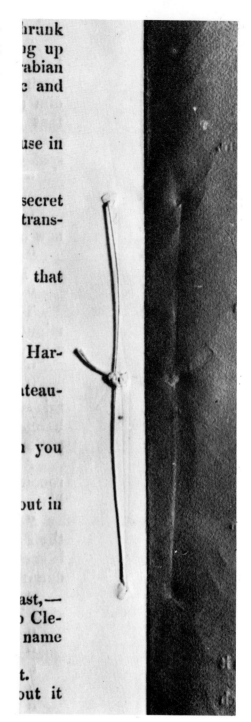

The stab-holes in works originally issued in paper-covered parts were made in the inside margins. Books bound up from the parts still exhibit these stab-holes, although the stitching and the paper-covers have been removed before binding.

Length of cotton stitching in centre of picture: 7cm.

An important landmark in publisher's binding styles. *Bubbles from the Brunnens of Nassau,* 1834, by Sir Francis Bond Head, was the first fully cloth-bound book to feature pictorial covers.

Size – right across the entire width of the two covers: 28 cm.

Islands, by Robert Mudie, both contain title-page vignettes engraved on wood and printed in colours by George Baxter. No intaglio plate was used, and the pictures look little different from the hand-coloured plates of the period. Both volumes were issued in full-cloth bindings in an all-over design of trailing flowers and leaves, the gilt lettering on the spines exhibiting one of the first uses of a surrounding ornamental design stamped in gold, this being an owl with outstretched wings. Mudie pays tribute to Baxter's new method of 'Polychromatic Printing' in the preface to the work.

Publisher's bindings in the Victorian period were continually evolving, changing, and being made the subject of often extravagant experimentation by houses anxious to make a point-of-sale impact on potential customers in the bookshops. They changed their style almost as often as ladies changed their fashions in dress. By the early 1840s the spines and front boards of the now almost universal cloth-bound books were ablaze with lettering and ornamental designs stamped in gold. By the late 1840s the gilt embellishments had spread in some cases across the entire book; spine, front board and back board glittering with artistic designs and intricate motifs, all woven in 22 car. gold. One of the most dramatic examples is the three-volume *Episodes of Insect Life,* 1849–51 by 'Acheta Domestica' (Miss L. M. Budgen) see illustration on p. 110: the entire book is covered with a Tenniel-like design of insects and plants from the pen of the authoress.

Books of the 1860s, 'sixties books' or, 'coffee-table books', as collectors term them, are sought as much for their binding styles as for the high quality of their woodcut illustrations. This decade was the last great period of hand craftsmanship in book production. The era of photographic reproduction of the plates, mechanical type-engraving, and semi-automatic bookbinding techniques was well on the way, and the 1890s would introduce an epoch of cheap mass-production and standardised methods that finished the extravagant fancies of more leisurely days. The sixties books, extending in time from the 1840s to the mid-1870s, were a high-watermark in 19th-century binding styles, condemned as vulgar and ostentatious showpieces by the age that followed, and despised and neglected by book-collectors until a generation or so ago. The word 'sixties' described a movement rather than a decade; the often lavishly ornate volumes being produced to fulfil a social need that was anything but literary. They were books produced for laying on the coffee-table in the morning-room, there to tempt the visitor whose card had been taken by the uniformed servant to the host or hostess, and who could while away the idle minutes by admiring the pictures or perhaps reading a verse or two. Very few indeed contain any original literary work, but they more than make up for the re-printing of words that had appeared many times before by the care and attention given to their bindings and the woodcut illustrations that accompanied the text. The coloured plate of *A Round of Days,* 1866, epitomises its many hundreds of differing rivals in the field. In demy quarto size, these books when new cost at least £1.05 ($2.52) a copy; double that amount if bound in morocco, and usually both styles were available. The bright colours on the cloth bindings were obtained by inlays of coloured paper, overlaid with blocking in black and gold.

Brief mention must be made of the many short-lived attempts to amuse book-buyers with a variety of weird and exotic trade-bindings, a shelf of which now makes a most interesting display of 19th-century ingenuity and inventive design. To the layman one of the most intriguing styles appears to be the deeply-incised papier-mâché bindings, contrived to look like carved ebony, the spines being of leather to retain flexibility. They are classical examples of Victorian Gothic at its most brittle, all having been originally issued in cardboard slip-cases to prevent their sides harming their soft-skinned neighbours on the shelves. Patented by Jackson & Sons, London, they were

An elaborate gilt-blocked cloth binding of 1849.

Width across entire binding: 29cm × 20.7cm.

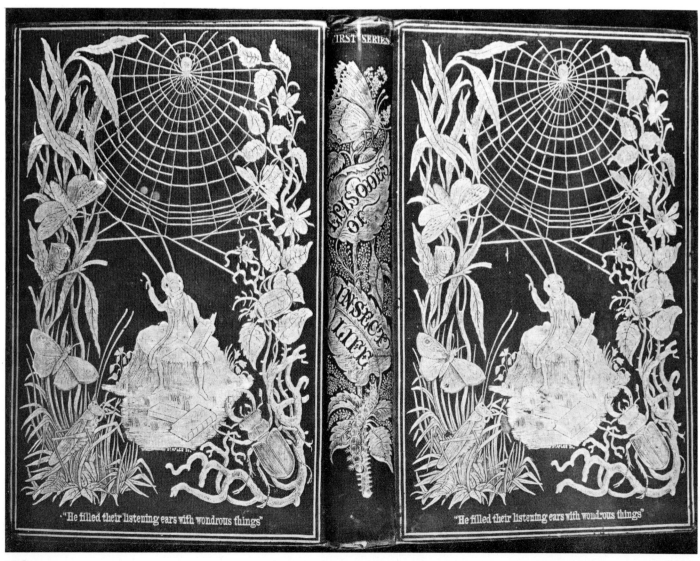

used for only about ten different titles, *The School of the Heart*, 1845, by Francis Quarles, being the first to appear. I have eight examples in the collection, and they have a fascination for visitors that their leather-bound companions seldom exert. The London firm of Remnant & Edmonds specialised in unusual bindings. Books from their bindery appeared with sides of decorated vellum, velvet, art-silk inlaid with gold, porcelain, tortoiseshell, flock, coloured paper, and brightly-stained roan. Their *pièce de résistance* was *The Preacher*, 1849, by Owen Jones, illustrated here. They invented a method whereby they were able accurately to imitate carved wood in almost Grinling Gibbons fashion. The pattern was burnt into the wood under considerable pressure, but few copies have managed to survive to the present day. A man-made plastic called Parkesite, named after one of its discoverers, was also pressed into service for the decoration of the sides of books, but its inflammability (we know it now as celluloid) has ensured that examples are rarely met with. Extravagantly decorated publisher's bindings of this period are symptomatic of the opulence, the desire to possess the brightly-beautiful regardless of expense, that characterised so much of the late 19th century. Texts were encased in *chapelle*

The Preacher, 1848, by Owen Jones, was issued in a wooden binding, which gave the appearance of having been carved by hand. The text was illuminated, and printed in gold and colours.

Size of cover: 29cm × 20cm.

ardente, more to be admired from afar than actually to be picked up and read. After well over a hundred years of mellowing, books of the sixties period and earlier still insist on being noticed if left lying within sight. How their colours must have shouted and shrilled in the days when our great-grandfathers hesitated before the counter in the bookseller's shop that displayed them fresh from the binder's hands.

Colour-printed illustrations on paper-covered boards, which had been a feature of children's books since the early 1840s, became common after the introduction of railway literature in the form of 'yellowbacks' in 1853. Sold on station bookstalls and elsewhere, these rapidly became the normal and accepted form of binding for cheap fiction, the volumes costing anything from sixpence to two shillings (6 cents to 24 cents) a copy. Cloth was however pre-eminent as a binding for books with any pretensions to quality of format, although it was possible for gentlemen with private libraries to purchase, at a reduced rate, their books in sheets for binding up in leather, styled to suit their own particular taste. The cloth itself was produced in an amazing profusion of textures and designs. Machines for embossing and graining cloth were in use from the 1830s onwards. Swatches of samples were available to publishers, displaying an almost bewildering choice of qualities and colours. Not all the early dyes used were even semi-fast to light, blues and purples if sunned for any length of time fading to a dirty-looking off-white. But in the cloistered half-light of study walls, with their backs to the south, they were quite happy; only a comparison of the hidden sides with the unprotected spine revealing the pale reflection of a once bright exterior.

To protect the cloth-bindings of books, dust-wrappers were invented in the 1860s. I must qualify that statement by the added information that I mean publisher's printed dust-wrappers. I have books here that have home-made brown-paper dust-wrappers (or the pale drab shade common in the early 1800s), carefully folded and labelled and dated in ink, that proclaim that their original owners prized them sufficiently to shield them from harm. Children's books, published in flimsy wrappers, are very occasionally found in almost mint condition due to careful protection from the time they left their shop in the late Georgian period. The parents or fond uncles who paid the bill probably insisted that their present should be so protected. The common complaint of fading cloth-covers may have prompted the incurring of the extra cost involved in issuing books in wrappers, the first known example, dated 1865, being shown on page 114. I have others dating from the 1870s, and by the 1880s they were commonplace. Even today they are still undergoing evolutionary changes, both in design and in format. A thin transparent plastic skin now protects the wrapper that protects the book, a feature not found until a few years ago.

Book cloths were decorated by blocking in gold and blind from hand-cut brass blocks. Designs were also printed directly onto the cloth, the earliest example being quoted above. Some were printed from wooden blocks, but blocking in gold needed heat for which brass or other metal dies were essential. The earliest pictorial design blocked in gold is the lyre found on the spine of *The Amulet,* 1828. The practice of including dates in the blocked design reached its height in 1842, a large proportion of books published that year having this date on their spines. Those that remained on the shelves of bookseller's shops, loudly proclaiming that they were old stock, soon persuaded the publishing houses of the folly of exhibiting a volume's age to the public eye and the idea was abandoned.

As the quantity of books published each year multiplied, so did the call for artists, to supply designs for the brass- and woodblock-cutters to shape and finish, increase in volume. Designers began to sign their work, and many have been identified by their initials hidden in decorative sprays or entwined in ornamental borders. The most prolific was undoubtedly John Leighton (1822–1912), who sometimes used the pseudonym of 'Luke Limner'. He was one of the earliest commercial artists that the revolution in binding styles produced, but Harry Rogers, Robert Dudley, Albert Warren, and Charles Bennett of shadow and silhouette fame, also derived a large part of their income from the same craft. Dante Gabriel Rossetti (1828–82) one of the founder members of the Pre-Raphaelite Brotherhood, a poet as well as a painter, took pleasure in designing the covers for his sister Christina's books. *Goblin Market,* 1862, had an austere motif of straight lines and small circles blocked in gold, an effective

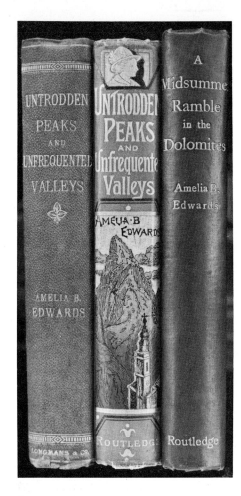

The same book over a period of 25 years. The left-hand spine is the first edition of 1873, in the middle the second edition, 1890, right is the third edition, *c.* 1898. By this time the peaks were no longer untrodden, with the result that the title of the book had to be changed, although the text is identical with those that had gone before.

Size of right-hand spine: 23.5cm × 4 cm.

Right
Macmillan's 'Cranford' series of octavo reprints of well-known texts started with *Bracebridge Hall,* 1890, by Washington Irving, and, with the re-issue of Mrs Gaskell's *Cranford* the following year, proved an immediate and lasting success. The covers of smooth blue-cloth were all heavily blocked in gold in elaborate pictorial designs, and were protected by dust-wrappers carrying the same designs.

Size of bottom right-hand book: 19cm × 12.5cm.

CRANFORD BY Mrs Gaskell Illustrated by Hugh Thomson

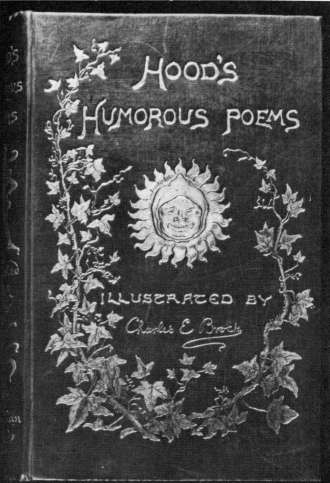

HOOD'S HUMOROUS POEMS

ILLUSTRATED BY Charles E Brock

Coridon's Song and Other Verses

Illustrations by Hugh Thomson

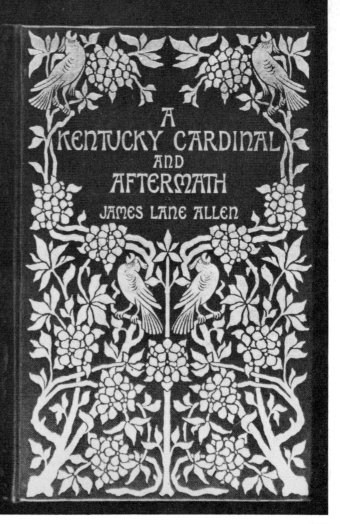

A KENTUCKY CARDINAL AND AFTERMATH JAMES LANE ALLEN

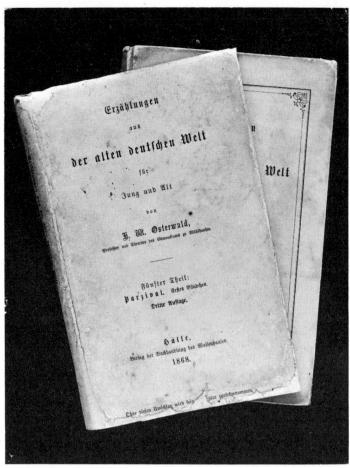

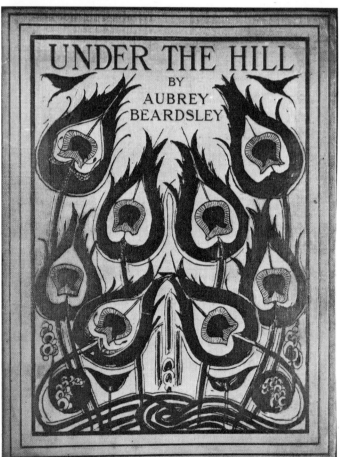

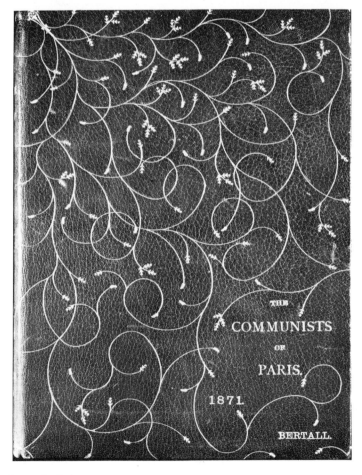

treatment but in complete contrast to all that had gone before. Swinburne's
rare first edition of *Atalanta in Calydon*, 1865, was another of his designs, white
cloth being bound over bevelled-boards, the front plain except for four golden
discs geometrically arranged. It was simple but effective, and Rossetti's designs
exerted considerable influence on those who followed.

Bindings shared in the revival of interest in typography, fine printing, and book design, that was taking place during the period when William Morris (1834–96) founded the Kelmscott Press. Although he drew almost exclusively on the past for inspiration, his influence on the future design of books cannot easily be exaggerated. He issued his first book from the Kelmscott Press in 1891, and, by the time the enterprise was wound up after his death in 1896, 53 titles had been produced. The presswork was superb, the *Chaucer* (see p. 125) having been described by many competent judges as the finest printed book ever to be published. Kelmscott bindings were all uniform in style, being a full natural vellum, blocked in gold on the spines, the fore-edges being held closed by silk ties. They are lovely volumes to handle, and one is dazzled by the technical brilliance and originality of design displayed upon their crisp white pages. But their delicacy makes them as impracticable for general reading as gold plate for household use.

Books of the nineties had a style peculiarly their own, perhaps epitomised by the format of *Silverpoints,* 1893, by John Gray. This appeared as a tall thin octavo of some 40 pages. The flowing design of leaves in a river of gold lines, blocked on the front and back covers, was designed by Charles Ricketts, who also contributed original and striking binding styles to several of Oscar Wilde's first editions. *A House of Pomegranates,* 1891, with its front cover ornamented with peacocks and fountains, set the seal on a style of ornamentation that is seen at its best in the cover design of Aubrey Beardsley's *Under the Hill,* 1904.

The 20 years immediately before the start of World War I saw the almost universal introduction of the pictorial dust-wrapper, an example of which is seen in the illustration of *The History of Mr. Polly,* 1910 by H. G. Wells. This meant that the elaborate pictorial and printed blocking on the covers of the volumes could be largely dispensed with, since the protective dust-wrapper was what now caught the prospective purchaser's eye. An exception were the novels and adventure stories produced for young adolescents. Books for boys and girls continued to display most eye-catching designs, blocked in brightly contrasting oil-colours, yet these volumes, too, were issued in dust-wrappers, the protective cover nearly always displaying an entirely different picture to that found on the cloth binding of the book itself.

The story of the evolution of publisher's binding styles is most easily appreciated by looking through the illustrations given in this present work. I have always made a point of adding to my collection only books still in their original bindings, whether this meant paper-covered boards, the glazed cloth of the early 1830s, or the gilt magnificence of the middle years of Victoria's reign. The subject is a study on its own, and a fully representative collection of the binding styles of the 19th century has yet to be assembled in anything like a complete state. Publishers 100 years ago were just as determined to catch the public's eye, and as design-conscious and *avant-courier* in respect to their rivals in the trade, as their present day counterparts in the world of book production. Perhaps in the year 2052 collectors will be searching for the early post-war paper-backs, equating them with the 'yellowbacks' and railway literature our grandparents bought. They are as symptomatic of the 1950s as were the paper-covered board-bindings Edmund Evans designed and printed so effectively a century before. There is a moral in the fact that fine copies are already as hard to find as their 19th-century counterparts. That is as it will always be, for no one bothers to keep the commonplace. Time acts as an effective sieve, but there are always a few survivors; a sufficiency but not a superfluity.

Subscribers to " CLEMENT LORIMER " may have their copies bound in cloth, with emblematic designs in gold, on application to their respective Booksellers.

Cloth cases, price One Shilling each, may be had on application.

Miscellanea

Many of the key books of English literature, and of the arts and sciences, do not fit easily into any of the chapter headings I have selected. My catholicity of taste has led me to compile a library of books that cover nearly the entire spectrum of the printed word, and without such a wide-ranging interest it would have been impossible to have written this present work. Nevertheless, book-collecting is a hobby for specialists. The horizon is so wide, that with a time-scale extending over a period of more than five hundred years, it is inevitable that interests should vary widely. Each of the chapter headings I have given could be sub-divided many times. The collector of, say, poetry, may well limit his collecting to books printed in the 18th century, or to those of the 'imagist' poets of the first quarter of the 20th century. Those who buy early printed books may be interested only in theological works before the turn of the 16th century; while in the field of natural history there are collectors of entymology who would hardly look at an early work dealing with the birds of Egypt, or a fine copy of *Vegetable Mould and Earth-Worms*, 1881, by Charles Darwin. In this chapter I hope to deal briefly with the many classes of book-collecting I have so far ignored, and with many of the key books of English literature not yet mentioned.

Old bibles and prayer books are a constant source of enquiry and speculation by the uninitiated who possess them. Many have been fondly cherished, in the form of ponderous leather-bound folio Victorian bibles, carried breathlessly from the boot of the family car, that I have had to reveal as worth scarcely anything. Old bibles have to be really old to be of interest to collectors; but inevitably there are exceptions to this general rule. It was the Reformation that gave us the English Bible and *The Book of Common Prayer*, although John Wycliffe (c. 1320–84), and his followers were responsible for the two 14th-century versions associated with his name. William Tyndale (d.1536), was the first to translate the New Testament into English, and the first edition appeared under a Worms imprint in 1525. In 1535 came Miles Coverdale's translation of the whole bible, extending to 570 leaves, a first edition of which now fetches anything up to £20,000 ($48,000). Complete copies are seldom met with. In 1537 appeared 'Thomas Mathew's' Bible, printed at Antwerp, and extending to 556 leaves, which is now catalogued at about £2,000 ($4,800). The first edition of the 'Taverner's Bible' is dated 1539; followed by 'The Great Bible', revised by Coverdale, and later officially sponsored by Cranmer, dated the same year. The Geneva Bible (often called the 'Breeches Bible' from the translation of Gen. iii : 7) the work of Protestant exiles who had fled from Mary's tyranny, is dated 1560, complete copies of which now make about £300 ($720). In 1568 appeared the 'Bishop's Bible', an official version, sponsored by a committee of English bishops, now priced at about £150 ($360), followed by the first editions of the Roman Catholic versions in English, the New Testament being printed at Reims, 1582, and the Old Testament, Douai, 2 vols. 1609–10, the complete set valued at £400 ($960) or more. With the appearance of the first *Authorized Version* in 1611 (some copies of which have the word 'he' in Ruth iii : 15, and some 'she'), the price for a complete copy soars to the £2,000 ($4,800) mark. Nearly all these early versions are found incomplete, and should only a single printed leaf be missing, the prices quoted above can be drastically reduced. Later 17th-century versions seldom make over £100 ($240), with the 18th century about a third of this amount. From then onwards we have to await the appearance of the five volume Doves Press edition, 1903–5, issued in a binding of limp vellum, for a highly prized version, now catalogued at

Right
Scrapbooks were a favourite form of entertainment in the 19th century, and are now sought by collectors, especially if they contain original paintings and drawings (as here) or verses by well-known poets. This series of pen sketches is by Harrison Weir, who is remembered for his animal portraits used extensively in book illustration.

Size of page: 28cm × 19.5cm.

116

£600 ($1,440). The Nonesuch Press edition, 5 vols. 1924–7, on japon vellum, is priced at about £100 ($240); the limited edition of 75 copies, bound in niger morocco, selling at £350 ($840). One result of the use of the English tongue in worship in the 16th century was the necessity of compiling hymns for common use, as against the Latin offices previously used. It was Thomas Sternhold, a Hampshire squire, who composed hymns taken from the Book of Psalms, which John Hopkins, a Suffolk gentleman, later published with some of his own work in the same field. *Certayne Psalmes* appeared undated in 1549; and in 1562 *The Whole Booke of Psalmes,* by Sternhold, Hopkins, Thomas Norton, and others, was added to the *Prayer Book,* a work that had itself first been published in 1549. As an example of English prose *The Book of Common Prayer* remains almost as Thomas Cranmer left it, editions before 1700, especially in contemporary bindings, often making high prices at auction.

Despite the development of printing in America since 1639, with the consequent establishment of hundreds of newspapers and scores of (usually short-lived) periodicals in the manner of the London *Tatler* or *Spectator,* little that was distinctly American in fictional prose or *belles-lettres* appeared before the start of the War of Independence. The Puritan strain in literature was the predominant influence and a leading place was given to works of theology and religious controversy. Notable amongst the protagonists were Roger Williams (*c.* 1602–83), and Cotton Mather (1663–1782). Williams, a Welshman, left England with his wife aboard the *Lyon* in 1629, only to be banished from Salem, where he had settled, for his opposition to the Puritan system of government. In 1639 he established the first Baptist church in America and proceeded to pour out a spate of books condemning religious intolerance. Best known among his writings are *A Key into the Language of America,* 1643, *The Bloudy Tenent of Persecution for a Cause of Conscience,* 1644, his most famous work, now valued at over £5,000 ($12,000), and its sequel *The Bloudy Tenent yet more Bloudy,* 1652. Cotton Mather – so named after his grandfather John Cotton, the arch-enemy of Roger Williams – was the son of Increase Mather, president of Harvard University, who wrote more than a hundred books and

Right
One of the full-page illustrations from the massive two-volume folio catalogue of Silber & Fielding Ltd., London. Issued *c.* 1885, this 'country-gentleman's catalogue' was run on present-day mail-order lines, the illustrations being printed in colour and black-and-white. Such items are now collector's pieces and change hands at high prices.

Size of page: 36.5cm × 27cm.

The first full-length book on the bicycle. The earliest known reference to a bicycle-race was of one in Paris, France, in May 1868. The famous penny-farthing was a late invention that was not due to appear for a decade or more. Bound in gilt-tooled cloth over bevelled boards, this present book has 25 full-page illustrations, and was by Joseph Firth Bottomley.

Size of title-page to bottom of paper: 17cm × 12cm.

FIG. 7 THE MODERN BICYCLE.

See Page 30

THE

VELOCIPEDE,

ITS PAST, ITS PRESENT & ITS FUTURE.

BY

J. F. B.

HOW TO RIDE A VELOCIPEDE.
"Straddle a Saddle,
then
Paddle and Skedaddle"

WITH 25 ILLUSTRATIONS.

LONDON.
SIMPKIN, MARSHALL & CO.
1869.

BICYCLES AND TRICYCLES.

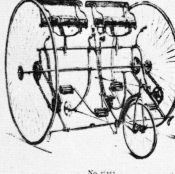

No. 16151.

"The Club Racer" Bicycle.

SPECIFICATION.—Enamelled plain black, plain hollow steel front and back forks, elliptical steel backbone, neat Stanley head with improved long centres and breeched, improved adjustable single ball bearings to front and back wheels, improved new section hollow felloe, ⅞-inch best red rubber tyres, steel hubs with direct spokes, 24-inch to 26-inch hollow handle bar, head, hubs, handle bar, and cranks plated; adjustable rat-trap ball pedals. Weight of 55-inch machine, 23 lbs. complete.

No. 16152.

The "Club" Tandem.

The advantages of the "Club" Tandem over all others are:—
1st. The front rider steers, and thus has an uninterrupted view of the road.
2nd. The steering being the same as in an ordinary front steerer, it is as easy to steer two riders as one.
3rd. Perfect safety. It is as safe as a sociable. Impossible to tilt.

4th. More space between the two riders than is usual with other machines.
In its single form this Tricycle is a central-geared front steerer.
To convert into a tandem it is merely necessary to fix three bolts. The attachment is jointed, so as to allow for inequalities of the road. Can be made to steer from the back if required.

No. 16153.

"The Club Sociable" Tricycle.

"The Club Sociable" will be found, both in design and material, to be of one usual standard quality. It is specially adapted to ladies' use, as the Patent "Cheylesmore" gear can be fitted to one of the cranks.

SPECIFICATION.—Steel tube frame, front steerer, double spoon brake, all bright parts plated, ball bearings to driving wheels and cranks, painted in two colours. Width 4 feet 11 inches.

No. 16154.

The "Rover."

Specially constructed for gentlemen requiring a light machine with vertical or bicycle position, very easy, comfortable, perfectly safe, and the best hill-climber yet made.
Open front, fitted with Stanley's patent automatic double-driving gear, ball bearings to all wheels, adjustable handles and seat, safe yet effective band brake, plated parts, hubs, handles, brackets, seat, and steering rod, &c.

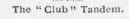

No. 16155.

The Lady's "Cheylesmore" Tricycle.

SPECIFICATION.—Open fronted, double driver patent automatic clutch action, finest steel tube frame, ball bearings to driving wheels, steering wheel and crank shaft; steel hubs with direct butt-ended spokes, all the bright parts nickel plated and polished, improved patent swing lever double spoon brake applied simultaneously to both driving wheels, painted in three colours. ⅞-inch or ⅝-inch best moulded tyres. Width of 44-inch machine, 3 feet 2 inches; 38-inch machine, 3 feet 4 inches.

No. 16156.

The "Imperial Club" Tricycle No. 1.

SPECIFICATION.—Finest steel tube frame, improved patent balance gearing, band brake, ball bearings to all wheels and cranks, all the bright parts plated, patent noiseless steering, painted in three colours. Width 3 feet 3 inches. Standard size 48 inches.
For ordinary roads we recommend this machine geared level, but we can supply it geared up to 54 inches where great speed is required, or down to 42 inches for very hilly country.
For Ladies' use 30-inch driving wheels, geared down to 42-inch, are advised.

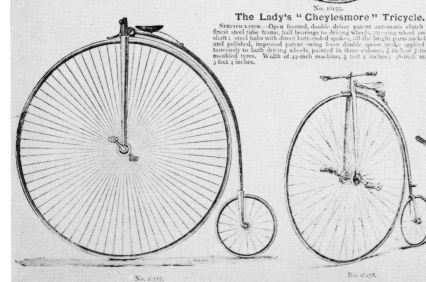

No. 16157.

The "Club" Semi-Racer.

SPECIFICATION.—Plain hollow front and back forks, elliptical steel backbone, Stanley head, and improved long centres, improved adjustable single-ball bearings to front and back wheels, steel hubs with direct spokes, 24-inch and 26-inch handle bars.

CAUTION. Any person infringing the Copyright of this Book will be prosecuted under the Act.

No. 16158.

The "Club" Bicycle.

SPECIFICATION.—Very easy sliding spring with rubber cushions in front, plain hollow forks, elliptical backbone, adjustable ball centres, ball bearings to back wheel, ⅞-inch or ⅝-inch best rubber tyres, 24-inch to 26-inch handle bar with horn ends.

Page 710

No. 16159.

The "Coolie" Cycle.

This machine is of quite a novel construction, and is built specially for use in India and other warm climates; it is made for four persons, two of whom sit at rest in front in a comfortable seat, while two coolies, perched on saddles behind, drive the machine by means of endless chains connecting the crank shafts and the driving wheel. The Cheylesmore clutch gear is used, so that the cranks remain stationary while descending hills. The machine is so arranged that the steering as well as the brake can be managed by the front as well as by the back riders.

SPECIFICATION.—It is a double driver, patent Cheylesmore automatic clutch action being used, hollow steel tube frame, ball bearings to driving wheels and crank shafts, steel nuts with patent lock-nutted spokes, all the bright parts nickel plated, and double spoon brake applied simultaneously to both wheels.

119

The Effigies of Mr George Herbert:
Author of those Sacred Poems called
The Temple.

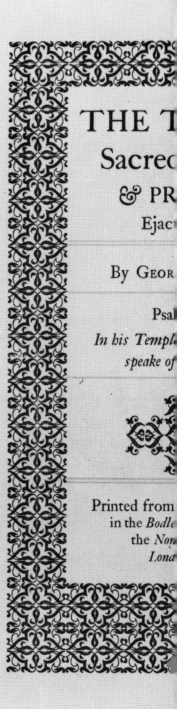

THE T
Sacrec
& PR
Ejac

By GEOR

Psa
In his Templ
speake of

Printed from
in the Bodl
the No
Lond

pamphlets, including a *History of the War with the Indians*, 1676. His *Discourse Proving that the Christian Religion is the only True Religion*, 1702, was first published in Boston. Cotton Mather's notoriety stems from his urging the persecutors to greater efforts before and during the Salem witchcraft hunt in 1692–3. A narrow, self-righteous minister and voluminous writer, his best known work is probably *Magnalia Christi Americana*, 1702, in which he outlines the history of New England Puritanism during the first century of its existence. *Hades Look'd into*, 1717, *A Midnight Cry*, 1692, and *Wonders of the Invisible World*, 1693, are others of his many literary productions.

Works of reference should always be sought in the latest possible edition: their value lies in the facts they have to impart, and these must be up to date

Limited and signed editions of specially produced books, and those volumes published by private presses, form an aspect of book-collecting that many find an absorbing hobby. The example given is from the Nonesuch Press, issued in a limited edition of 1,500 copies, and bound in woven tapestry cloth.

Size of title-page:
24.5cm × 15cm.

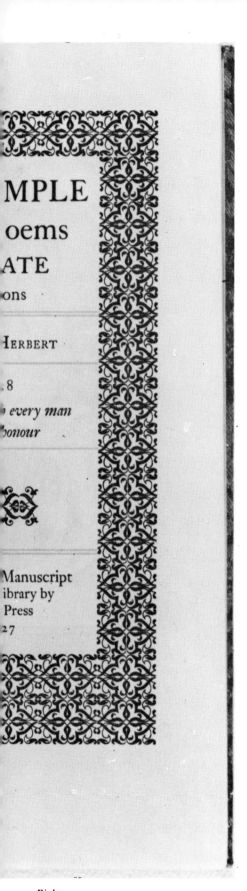

Theodore Gardelle having murder'd M.ʳˢ King, burns some of her Body & hides the rest.

Right

A copperplate engraving from *The Annals of Newgate*, 4 vols. 1776, by Revd. Villette, who acted as prison chaplain. The work became an 18th-century best-seller, and is as readable today as it was then; factual accounts of the trials, sentences, and acquittals being set out as they were taken down in writing in the courts. There are 37 full-page plates of varying degrees of horror.

Size of engraved surface: 17cm × 11cm.

and reflect modern scholarship and opinions if they are to be of use to the student. The exception to this rule lies in works whose age gives them a historical or antiquarian interest, despite the fact that the information they offer is centuries out of date and possibly totally inaccurate. The first edition of the *Encyclopaedia Britannica*, 3 vols. 1771, published by A. Bell and C. Macfarquhar, could now be expected to make about £1,000 ($2,400) at auction. The first London edition, 3 vols. 1773, with its 160 engraved plates, is also a highly valued work, being catalogued at around £400 ($960). From then onwards there is a rapid slide in value, despite the extra volumes added to the set with each succeeding edition. Sets published in the 20th century, with the exception of the latest editions, fetch very little. *Cyclopedia, or an Universal*

Dictionary of the Arts and Science, 2 vols. 1728, by Ephraim Chambers, had no connection with William and Robert Chambers, whose *Chambers's Encyclopaedia* first appeared in 1859, and still continues to add to its lustre in the present day. The first named work is now priced at about £75 ($180), and is said to have influenced the style of Samuel Johnson's *A Dictionary of the English Language,* 2 vols. 1755. This prodigious task for one man to perform, with its preface ranking amongst the finest of his prose, was a work at which Johnson laboured for eight years. The inclusion of quotations was Johnson's most notable innovation in English lexicography, and in this he revealed his unequalled talent for defining the finer shades of meaning. Copies in contemporary bindings are now catalogued at anything up to £800 ($1,920). James Boswell (1740–95) owes his immortality to Samuel Johnson, and I keep his works on the same shelf as those of his great contemporary who inspired the achievement of his life – Boswell's *The Life of Samuel Johnson LL.D,* 2 vols. 1791. It is without doubt the greatest biography in the English language, perhaps in any language. The two quarto volumes run to a total of over 1,100 pages, and my copy is in the original boards with uncut leaf edges. A copy complete with the engraved portrait, and the two engraved facsimile plates, and in a contemporary binding, would be cheap at less than £300 ($720). Of Boswell's other works I have *An Account of Corsica,* 1768, and *Journal of a Tour to the Hebrides,* 1785.

First editions and first illustrated editions of the sporting novels of R. S. Surtees (1803–64). Most were first issued in monthly parts, and all have hand-coloured full-page illustrations. Dates: reading left to right: 1853, 1854, 1858, 1860, 1865, 1888.

Height: 23cm.

No comprehensive work dealing with English literature as a whole could omit reference to the ever readable *Memoirs of Samuel Pepys*, 2 vols. 1825. *The Journal of Sir Walter Scott*, 1825–32 (best read in the revised edition by J. G. Tait, 3 vols. 1939–46), exerts the same fascination. It was after reading Pepys's *Memoirs* in 1825 that Scott determined to start keeping his journal, no doubt with posterity firmly in mind. It is certainly the greatest of his prose works, and had he written nothing else he would have gained a niche in the annals of English literature for this intimate and revealing picture of the Edinburgh of his last unhappy years. The *Journal* can be bought complete for two or three pounds; but a first edition of Pepys's *Memoirs*, complete with its often missing half-titles, is usually catalogued at about £150 ($360). With the appearance of the five-volume edition of 1848–9, the title was changed to 'Diary', and so it has remained ever since. As a reading copy I use the 10 volumes of the 1893–9 edition (Volume X being 'Pepsiana, or Additional Notes'), copies in the original blue cloth being priced at around £20 ($48). The diary of Samuel Pepys (1633–1703), is a personal self-revelation of the most intimate and frank description; while that of John Evelyn (1620–1706) was more a personal record of events as they happened around him. Evelyn's *Memoirs*, 2 vols. 1818, edited by William Bray, can be purchased for less than £75 ($180). It has continued in print to the present day.

The first of the 'sixties' books; a woodcut illustration by D. Maclise for Thomas Moore's *Irish Melodies*, 1846.

Size of the engraved surface of the plate: 19cm × 13cm.

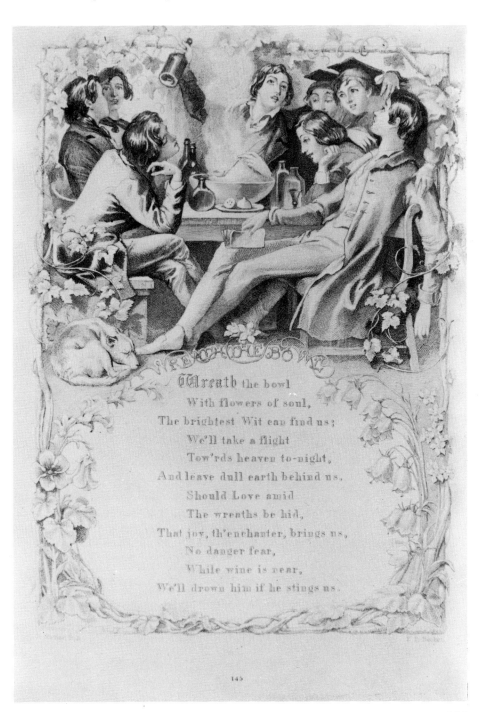

"Bring me before a court."

Maria Monk

AWFUL DISCLOSURES

OF

MARIA MONK,

AS EXHIBITED IN A NARRATIVE OF HER SUFFERINGS DURING
A RESIDENCE OF FIVE YEARS AS A NOVICE, AND TWO
YEARS AS A BLACK NUN, IN THE HOTEL DIEU
NUNNERY AT MONTREAL.

"Come out of her, my people, that ye be not partakers of her
sins, and that ye receive not of her plagues."—*Rev.* xviii. 4.

NEW-YORK:
PUBLISHED BY HOWE & BATES,
NO. 68 CHATHAM-ST.
———
1836.

All these works, and most of the important works of English literature, have been reprinted at one time or another in limited editions, usually by private presses, and issued in expensive format on hand-made paper and in luxurious bindings of vellum, straight-grained morocco, or hand-tooled calf. Private press books, signed and limited editions, and finely printed volumes of the classics, have attracted collectors since before the days of William Morris. Private presses are distinguished by aims that are aesthetic rather than commercial, and one of the first of importance was that of Horace Walpole at Strawberry-Hill (1757–97). Mention has already been made of the Kelmscott Press, all the productions of which now make high prices at auction; although it would be true to say that private press books have not advanced so steeply in value as other classes of bibliology. Yet a great many make considerably more than the original first editions of the works they are reprinting. Those seeking more detailed information can consult *A Select Bibliography of the Principal Modern Presses,* 1928, by G. S. Tompkinson, as I can give only a few examples. Many of the products of the Kelmscott Press fetch well over £100 ($240), and I give the number printed in parentheses. *Life and Death of Jason* (200), 1895, about £170 ($408); *Love is Enough* (300), 1897, about £150 ($360); *Story of the Glittering Plain* (200), about £180 ($432); *Water of the Wondrous Isles* (250), 1897, about £160 ($384). C. H. St. John Hornby set up the Ashendene Press in 1895, and even its own *Descriptive Bibliography,* a folio limited to 390 copies, 1935, now fetches well over £200 ($480). *Don Quixote,* 2 vols. (225), £350 ($840); *Lo Paradiso,* by Dante Alighieri, published by the Ashendene Press in a limited edition of 150 copies in 1905, £750 ($1,800); while his *Tutte le Opera,* 1909 (105), has been priced at over £1,000 ($2,400). Charles Ricketts started the Vale Press in 1896; and T. J. Cobden-Sanderson and Emery Walker, the Doves Press, 1899, whose five volume edition of the Bible has already been mentioned. Possibly the most famous production of the Nonesuch Press was

A one-time shocking tale of sex and murder, the story of the orgies taking place in the Hotel Dieu Nunnery, Montreal, Canada, having been invented by the Revd. J. J. Slocum. He was a right-wing dissenting minister, with a consuming hatred of the Roman Catholic church. The book had an immense sale and is still in print today; but this first edition is believed to be the only complete copy, in the original cloth binding, to have survived.

Size of title-page:
15cm × 9.5cm.

their issue of the works of Charles Dickens, 24 vols. 1937–8, now valued at about £750 ($1,800). One of the volumes is hollow, and concealed in the space is an original metal printing-plate used for the illustration of the earliest editions of his works. Chaucer's works are favourite texts for the craftsmen of the private presses to reproduce; the Golden Cockerel Press printed *Troilus and Criseyde* in a limited editon of 219 copies, small folio size, with Eric Gill supplying the illustrations. It is now a £300 ($720) book. The greatest of all private press books was William Morris's Kelmscott Press *Chaucer,* possibly the finest book ever printed, and now valued at £3,500 ($8,400). The binding of white pigskin over wooden boards was executed by the Doves Bindery. There are many other finely printed books from distinguished presses, issued in strictly limited editions, that the collector can purchase for as little as £5 ($12) upwards. The Press founded by Edwin and Robert Grabhorn at San Francisco in the early 1920s continues in being and maintains the tradition of its predecessors. The founts of type and most of the matrices designed for and used by the Kelmscott, Doves, Ashendene, Eragny and Cranach presses are now at the University Press, Cambridge.

In complete contrast to my shelf of private press books, is the one devoted to early cookery books. At the head of these must stand Mrs Isabella Mary Beeton's own copy of that classic amongst cookery books *The Book of Household Management,* 1861, illustrated facing page 24. This colossal manual of cookery and household economy took young Mrs Beeton over four years to complete, and was first issued during 1859–61 in *The Englishwoman's Domestic Magazine.* The work was then published in book-form in 1861, as a thick and dumpy

A rarity amongst books on art; the first work to deal with surrealism. Dated 1934, the work was edited by Georges Hugnet, and was issued in printed paper-wrappers as shown here.

Size: 19.3cm × 14.4 cm.

octavo of 1,112 pages, bound in purple cloth blocked in gold and blind. Of all books of the period this is the first edition most difficult to find in anything approaching original condition. The work was far too heavy for the cloth binding in which it was cased: dropped once in the kitchen and it would inevitably split its hinges and spring sections of text. Greasy fingers and a plethora of markings ensured that the leaves became soiled and dog-eared after a few years of use. No one imagined that a copy of 'Mrs Beeton's Cookery Book' as it came to be called, would be sought by collectors, or that the first edition would ever be worth more than its face value. So the book was used as it was meant to be used – in the kitchen; and when it finally fell to pieces the housewife purchased a new copy of the latest issue for her cook to ponder over. But one copy remained inviolate. The publisher, S. O. Beeton, had a velvet-lined drop-sided leather box specially made to house a copy of the cloth-bound first edition of his wife's book. This he presented to Isabella Beeton in 1861, and there it has remained ever since, complete with its coloured frontis-piece, lithographed title, and 12 coloured full-page plates. It is difficult to say what such a copy would be worth today. Complete copies rebound in half-calf are now catalogued at about £100 ($240). Poor Mrs Beeton did not have long to enjoy the success of her now world-famous book. Four years after its publication, while still in her twenties, she died of puerperal fever.

The most popular 18th-century treatise on cookery was *The Art of Cookery Made Plain and Easy*, 1747, by Mrs Hannah Glasse, although only the words 'By a Lady' were allowed to appear on the title-page. This slim folio now regularly makes well over £400 ($960) at auction. The fourth edition, the first in octavo size, appeared in 1751. *The London Art of Cookery*, 1783, by John Farley, who described himself as 'Principal Cook at the London Tavern', quickly went through several editions, the tenth appearing in 1804. The earliest manual of household management with any pretensions to completeness was *A New System of Domestic Cookery*, 1806, by Mrs Maria Eliza Rundell (1745–1828), copies in the original board bindings now being catalogued at £200 ($480) or

An important work on one of the greatest of modern artists, shown as a first edition, 1938, in printed paper-covers; and the first English edition published the same year in hard-covers with a pictorial dust-wrapper. All Gertrude Stein's works have collectors on their trail, and her *Picasso* has never been easy to procure in first-edition form.

Size of cover of right-hand book: 22.5cm × 14.5cm.

more. She followed this with *The New Family Receipt-Book,* 1810, of which I have only been able to find the second edition dated the following year. Along the shelf are *Modern Cookery,* 1845, by the poetess Eliza Acton, and her much rarer *The English Bread-Book,* 1857. *The Lady's own Cookery Book,* of which I have only the third edition of 1844, is much the rarest of the works of the novelist Lady Charlotte Bury (1775–1861), and is described by her as being 'adapted to the use of persons living in the highest style, as well as those of moderate fortune'. *The Modern Housewife, or Ménagère,* by Alexis Soyer, is dated 1850, and described as being by the author of *The Gastronomic Regenerator,* a work I would love to read.

A handful of books on wines that I have collected in recent years comprises *A History and Description of Modern Wines,* 1836, by Cyrus Redding, this being the second edition of a work that first appeared in 1833. The 1836 edition is enlarged and contains the first classification of the port-wine trade. His *French Wines and Vineyards,* 1860, became a standard work. Next to this stands *Facts About Champagne,* 1879, by Henry Vizetelly, although I lack his *History of Champagne,* 1882. One of the key books on this wine is *History of the Champagne Trade in England,* 1905, by André L. Simon, a volume remarkably difficult to find in fine condition. No collection of books on food and drink is complete without a few examples of the many hand-written recipe books in which most cooks and housewives, from before the time of Elizabeth I, kept notes of their favourite dishes. Many became commonplace-books, recording not only recipes, but the notable sayings of the famous, passages from plays, observations on the weather, the garden, the affairs of the day, and with pages reserved for medical recipes and the well-tried remedies for an assortment of ills; 18th- and 19th-century examples are still easy to acquire, but those compiled in the days of Shakespeare and Ben Jonson, or even earlier, have an historical interest that ensures a high value being placed on their sale. Previously unknown poems, passages of prose, and unrecorded sayings and doings of those who now fill pages in the *Dictionary of National Biography,* are sometimes discovered next to recipes for jugged hare or a remedy for banishing warts. Manuscript recipe books can always be read with interest, and a full transcription sometimes yields surprising results.

There are collectors whose interest in books does not extend beyond that of field-sports, angling, the game of chess, fencing, football or cricket. To deal briefly with only the first and last of the few I have named will give an indication of the wealth of specialist activities into which quite a narrow sub-division of the world of books can be endlessly divided; in this case, sports and pastimes. A collection of books devoted to the various field-sports could quite easily extend to several thousand volumes, dating in time from *The Boke of Saint Albans,* 1486, a treatise on hawking, hunting, and heraldry, compiled by several hands, the section devoted to hunting being attributed to Dame Juliana Berners. A modern facsimile is the only copy of this work I ever expect to own; and the same observation applies to the first of the two small books that form the *omnia opera* of Izaak Walton (1593–1683). *The Compleat Angler, or The Contemplative Man's Recreation,* 1653, is a 'piscatorial classic' that has been read and loved by countless people who have never had a fishing-rod in their hands. It gives us a vivid picture of a way of life that has long since gone; the characters eating, drinking, arguing, and sometimes angling; the whole permeated with the Englishman's love of the countryside, and its rivers and streams, in a manner that landscapes the imagination like the smell of new-mown hay. A first edition, complete and uncropped, would today be priced at over £1,000 ($2,400). After the appearances of the second edition, 1655, third edition, 1661, and the fourth edition, 1668, reprints embellished with a variety of copperplate-engravings become legion; many calling for the attention of Thomas Gosden, a binder who specialised in sporting books and had an armoury of brasses in the shape of creels, landing-nets, rods, flies, foxes' heads, hunting-horns, and long-barrelled guns, with which to tool in gold his morocco spines and covers. The first collected edition of Walton's *Lives,* giving us portraits of John Donne, Henry Wotton, Richard Hooker, George Herbert, and Robert Sanderson, in a manner that never fails to charm, was published in 1670, and is usually catalogued at about £50 ($120). John Major's edition of 1825 is the most pleasing of the many reprints.

Memoirs of the Life of the late John Mytton, Esq. 1835, by 'Nimrod' (i.e. C. J.

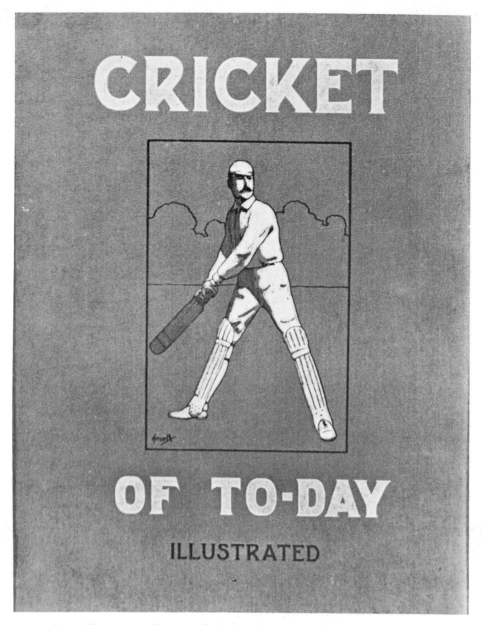

Apperley), allows us a glimpse of the huntin', shootin', and fishin' fraternity of the early 1800s; with the hero rapidly dissipating a considerable fortune, while, with equal speed, he drinks himself to death. The second edition of 1837, with its 18 hand-coloured plates (the first edition has only 12), is the better issue to possess, and is now valued at £80 ($192). *Life of a Sportsman*, 1842, by the same author, with the 36 coloured engravings once again by H. Alken, is catalogued at about £200 ($480). But it was the great Thomas Rowlandson (1756–1827) who supplied the series of hand-coloured copperplate-engravings to illustrate the three tours of the famed 'Doctor Syntax'; the poetical text being from the pen of William Combe (1741–1823). The first of these works, *The Tour of Doctor Syntax in Search of the Picturesque,* a parody on the travel books so popular at that time, appeared in the *Poetical Magazine* in 1809, and was issued as a book in 1812. *The Second Tour of Doctor Syntax, in Search of Consolation,* appeared in 1820; and the final volume, *The Third Tour of Doctor Syntax, in Search of a Wife,* in 1821. All three works enjoyed an immense success, Rowlandson's caricatures of the country parson, and of his aged horse Grizzle, matching the ribald verses of Combe in delightful fashion. A set of first issues of the three volumes is now valued at well over £150 ($360).

The first printed mention of the game of cricket is found on page 172 of Volume II of *Wit and Mirth: or Pills to Purge Melancholy,* 1719, a six-volume set of earthy songs and ballads compiled by Thomas D'Urfey.

> Fair Winnies eyes bright shining,
> And lilly breasts alluring;
> Poor Jenkins heart with fatal Dart,
> Have wounded past all curing.

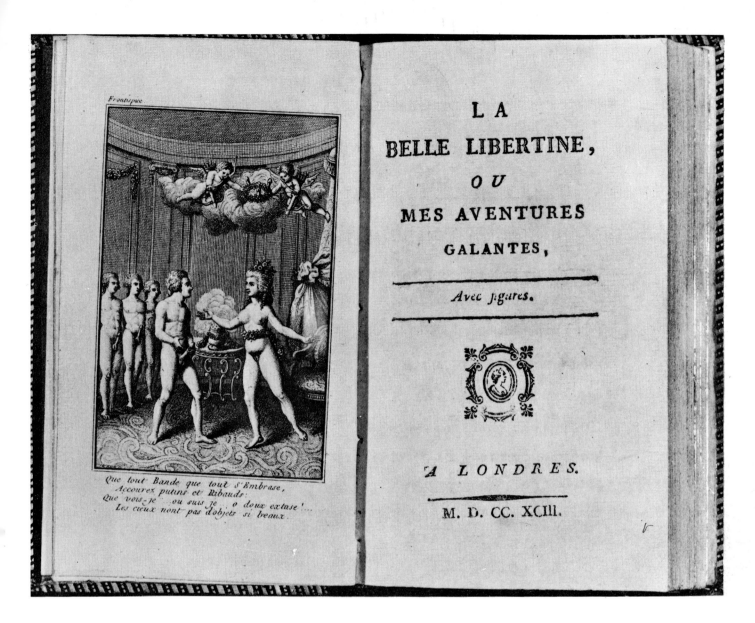

Frontispiece

Que tout Bande que tout S'Embrase,
Accourex putins et Ribauds:
Que vous-je... ou suis je... o doux extase!...
Les cieux nont pas d'objets si beaux.

LA
BELLE LIBERTINE,
O U
MES AVENTURES
GALANTES,

Avec figures.

A LONDRES.

M. D. CC. XCIII.

Illustrated pornographic works of the 18th century are now extremely rare, their mortality rate, for obvious reasons, being considerably higher than average. Despite the legend on the title-page, this little volume of some 168 pages was printed in Paris, 1793, and regales us with the amorous adventures of a lady of inexhaustible qualities. There are a further five plates in which the unknown artist has allowed his imagination full play.

Size of title-page:
12.5cm × 7.5cm.

Her was the prettiest fellow,
At Foot-ball or at Cricket;
At Hunting chace, or nimble Race,
Cots-plut how she cou'd prick it.

Amongst the few early books I have on the national sport of England are *The Young Cricketer's Tutor,* 1833, by Charles Cowden Clarke; *The Cricket Match,* 1859, by Copthall Chambers; *Cricket, c.* 1868, by Edmund Routledge, with its stricture that one is *not* to take 'a hearty dinner in the middle of a match'; and *Willow & Leather,* 1898, by E. V. Lucas; a scant offering besides the loaded shelves of the enthusiasts who have devoted years to the task. *Felix on the Bat,* 1845, by Nicholas Wanostrocht, eluded me at auction only a while ago.

From outdoor-sports to indoor-pastimes gives me a chance to make brief mention of erotica; or curiosa, as the longer-established antiquarian booksellers persist in calling these once locked and hidden books. I have contented myself with showing a single example of late 18th-century erotica, the frontispiece of which does less than justice to the copperplate-engravings that intersperse the text. As Logan Pearsall Smith once observed, 'A dirty mind is a continual feast.' *Index Librorum Prohibitorum,* 1877, by 'Pisanus Fraxus' (Henry S. Ashbee), reprinted as *A Bibliography of Prohibited Books,* 3 vols. 1962, reveals the tip of the iceberg. This is the one field of literature in which the 29th edition of the text is quite likely to command as much again as the first, especially if smoothed and streamlined into modern punchy prose. But this observation applies only to 19th- and 20th-century versions of sure-fire best-sellers. What happened in Shakespeare's day is any literary historian's guess. 'Early examples', and I quote from a bookseller's catalogue, 'are difficult to come by.'

129

Glossary

Terms commonly used in the catalogues of booksellers and auctioneers

all edges gilt (or gilded)   All three outer edges of the leaves of the book have been cut smooth and gilded with burnished gold-leaf.

Americana   Books dealing in some way with America, or printed in America.

annuals   Books issued serially at yearly intervals, and applied especially to those issued in the vogue period of 1823 to about 1855. *The Amulet, The Bijou, The Keepsake, Friendship's Offering,* the *Forget Me Not,* and *The Winter's Wreath,* are typical examples. The Christmas annuals, produced not only for children, but for adults as well, followed later. Both types contained much original work, were profusely illustrated, and exhibit a variety of novel binding-styles.

antique binding   A misnomer, usually meaning the very opposite to what the phrase conveys. The term is used by booksellers to denote a book bound in 'antique style', i.e. a book in a modern leather binding that has been made to look period in style, rather in the way reproduction furniture is artificially 'distressed' to give it an old look.

armorial binding   A leather binding stamped with a coat-of-arms, either in blind or gilt. Also used with reference to bookplates that incorporate a coat-of-arms.

as issued   In the state in which the printed work originally appeared, i.e. stitched in wrappers; in glazed paper-covered boards, etc.

association copy   A book which once belonged to an owner associated with the author of the work, or to the author himself. The proof of this is usually derived from a written inscription, or notes in the hand of the associatee.

authorised edition   A term employed to make clear that the edition offered is not a piracy. The first authorised edition is sometimes not the first time the work has appeared in print, one or more piracies of the book having already been issued, either at home or abroad.

backstrip   The spine of the book.

bestiary   A medieval treatise, often richly illustrated, containing symbolic stories about animals and other phenomena of natural history.

bevelled boards (or edges)   A refinement in binding technique whereby thick boards have their edges chamfered to give a sloping outside edge.

bibliophile   A lover of books.

binding copy   A book in the last stages of disrepair, fit only for the removal of the text prior to a complete rebind.

blank leaves (or blanks)   'Lacks its final blank . . .' means that the last leaf in the book, unprinted but nevertheless an integral part of the book, is missing. Blank leaves are usually at the beginning or end of a volume, but can occur in any part of the book. In collation a missing blank leaf at the beginning or the end of a book is possibly the least harmful fault one can discover, especially if it is a binder's blank and not a printer's. Blank leaves at the beginning of a book are often torn out to remove a previous ownership inscription.

block book   Picture books printed from wooden blocks and thought to have preceded the invention of printing from movable metal type.

blocked in blind (or gilt)   An impression made in the leather or cloth binding of a book as an embellishment. If gold is used that part of the work has been blocked in gilt.

blind stamp   An impression made by a die in the paper, often used for such words as 'Review Copy' or to denote the ownership of the book.

blurb   A publisher's puff or 'write-up' extolling the merits of the author or the book.

boards   Usually used to denote the original issued publisher's binding in which new books were encased in the period *c.* 1750–1830. This is known as the 'boards and paper-label' period. As an example: all of Sir Walter Scott's novels originally appeared in this format and are far more valuable in this condition than when rebound in leather. The edges of the leaves were either left entirely uncut or only lightly trimmed.

book-plate   A label, usually pasted on the inside of the front cover of a book, bearing indication of its ownership. Also referred to as '*ex libris*'.

breaker   A book more valuable for its plates or maps, and often destroyed to obtain these as separate entities. These plates are then sold for framing, the text which accompanied them being discarded.

broadside (or broadsheet)   A sheet of paper, usually of large size, printed on one side only. Often used for declarations, acts, or ballads and songs.

calf   The most common type of leather used for book-binding and made from the hide of a calf. Smooth in texture and can be dyed any shade.

cancel   A leaf of a book substituted for one originally printed and tipped in to its place. More rarely, a pasted scrap of paper covering words first printed but later found to be incorrect.

cartouche   An ornament, usually in the form of an elaborate scroll, on which a title or other wording appears. Found on early maps.

case   In a cased book, as opposed to one which has been bound, the boards and the cloth or other material to cover them has been fabricated in quantity ready to receive the stitched quires. The text is inserted into the ready-made case and glued in. A quicker and cheaper method than individual binding.

catchword   The first word of the following page duplicated by printing it again at the lower right-hand corner of the page immediately preceding. This may sound a tortuous way of explaining the term – it is the word you read at the bottom of the page then immediately read again at the top of the next. It helps with the collation, especially in the prelims.

cathedral binding   Leather bindings with pictures of churches blocked on them, usually in blind. The style is nearly always Gothic and was common in the period 1800–50.

chain lines   Watermarks of widely-spaced lines visible in laid paper due to the pressure of the wire mesh of the tray in which it was made. The fine, closely-set lines running at right angles to the chain lines were formed in the same way. They often prove useful when collating a book.

chapbooks Pamphlets sold by chapmen in the street and at the door. Usually sensational, poorly printed, and luridly illustrated by crude woodcuts.

China paper See *India Paper.*

coffee-table books See *'sixties' books.*

collation The verification that a book is complete. The term is also used to denote a description of the volume under scrutiny, this being given in physical terms so that the number of leaves, the register of the signatures, and a description of the book's format and binding are set out. An accurate collation is essential for any book which a collector acquires and values, for a missing half-title or an absent plate can lower the worth of the volume dramatically. To know the original make-up of a book and whether in fact a half-title is called for, a blank leaf should be present, the number of plates, etc., calls for the study of works of reference and the knowledge that comes with experience.

collotype The process of printing by means of a thin sheet of gelatine, the sensitised surface of which has been etched by actinic rays. The most accurate (and most expensive) facsimile productions are produced by the collotype process.

colophon A printer's reference at the end of a book which usually gives the place of printing and the date. Other information is also often incorporated including the printer's ornamental device or mark.

conjugate leaves Leaves joined to one another to form a single sheet.

contemporary Applied to bindings it means that the cloth, leather or other binding dates approximately from the date of the book itself. It is also used by cataloguers to denote the date of colouring of plates in a book, and ownership or other inscriptions.

courtesy book A volume containing rules of polite behaviour.

cover The front (upper cover) or back (lower cover) of a binding.

cropped A book whose margins have been heavily cut into by the binder. Sometimes the text itself is cut into, but more often the headlines or side and bottom notes suffer.

curiosa Books with an erotic interest.

cuts Illustrations printed with the text.

deckle edges Uncut edges of leaves of hand-made paper.

dedication copy The copy inscribed by the author to the dedicatee.

dentelle A French term meaning a lacy border. This is nearly always found in gilt on the inside edge where this method of decoration is employed.

device A printer's mark usually found on the title-page or at the end of a book.

diaper Cross-hatching effect used on bindings.

diced A ruled pattern in the form of diamond shaped squares used on leather and cloth bindings.

disbound A book or pamphlet lacking its original or later binding.

doublure Decorated leather inside-lining to the covers of a book. Used in place of the conventional 'paste-down'.

drop-title A title placed at the head of the first page of text rather than on a separate title-page.

dropped letter A letter missing from a page of printed type.

duodecimo A small size of book, commonly known as a twelvemo (or 12mo).

dust-wrapper The paper wrapper or jacket enclosing the book to protect the covers from dirt. An illustration of the earliest dated copy is given, but dust-wrappers are believed to date from the time of the first cloth bindings in the late 1820s.

editio princeps Latin for 'first edition'.

edition de luxe A specially printed edition of a book first issued in a cheaper format. Sometimes produced to tempt collectors to purchase a copy of a limited and highly priced edition of a text available in cheaper form.

embroidered binding Needlework bindings produced in the 17th century and earlier. A favourite occupation of ladies of the period, although some are obviously the work of professionals.

endpapers Double leaves at the front and end of a book, the outer of which are pasted down inside the covers. They may be either white or coloured, printed or glazed, marbled or patterned. One leaf, for obvious reasons, is called the paste-down, the other being known as the free endpaper. In the more sumptuous leather bindings they may be of silk, and are then known as liners.

engraving An illustration or decorative device printed from a metal plate or from the end-grain of a wood-block.

errata Errors and misprints in the printed text. If these are not discovered until after the book is completed they are sometimes listed on a pasted-in slip of paper known as an errata-slip.

etruscan style Bindings decorated with a Greek key pattern by means of staining. This style of decorated leather binding was a speciality of Edwards of Halifax. The acid staining employed was usually of a deep terra-cotta colour combined with black and gold tooling, and was most popular during the period 1790–1825.

ex-library Used to excuse the state of a book that has once been the property of a lending library. Often the cloth covers are disfigured by stains and fading where paper library labels have been pasted.

ex-libris Book-plate.

extra-illustrated A book which has had extra plates added to those originally issued. If the size of the book is large these may have to be inlaid in larger paper so as to match the size of the original pages. The practice seems to have started with the craze to add portraits, etc., to James Granger's *A Biographical History of England,* issued in two volumes, each in two parts, in 1769, followed by a supplement in 1774. Hence *Grangerising.*

facetae Curiosa; but including, besides erotica, such items as the more vulgar chapbooks, humorous sayings, books of jokes, and various other pleasantries.

facsimile The part of an imperfect book that has been added to repair the omission. A type-facsimile is a reprint that endeavours to copy the original as closely as possible. Sometimes this is done with the intention of deceiving the would-be purchaser; but in most cases the fact that the book is a facsimile of the original is clearly stated on the title-page or elsewhere.

filleting A revolving tool in the form of a wheel used by book-binders is called a fillet. Pushed along a leather binding it impresses a line or lines which are usually gilded.

first American edition The first edition published in the United States of America of a book that has previously appeared abroad.

first edition The first appearance of a work in book-form, or between its own covers.

first English edition The first edition published in Britain of a book that has previously appeared abroad.

first published edition The first edition of a book published commercially, distinguishing it from a previous edition (or editions) published privately and not offered for sale to the public.

first separate edition The first edition of a book or pamphlet, etc., published between its own covers. This distinguishes it from a previous printing incorporated with other matter.

fly-leaf The front free endpaper.

fly-title A second printing of the half-title, usually found after the last page of the preliminary leaves and before the first page of the text.

folio A book of folio size. The sheets of the book have been folded only once after printing, but as the original sheets used vary considerably in size the book itself will vary accordingly. Elephant folio is the largest form, but no definitive measurements can be given. A small folio can be topped by a large quarto, while some of the very largest folios used for art books and atlases can tax the strength of the strongest.

fore-edge painting A painted water-colour decoration on the fanned-out fore-edge of a book: this disappears beneath the gilt when the book is closed. Most fore-edge paintings are of modern production despite the fact that they appear on old books. Genuine early examples usually have the binder's name blocked in gold on the extreme outer edge of the leather binding.

format The shape, size and style of a book and that of its binding.

forme The body of type after being locked in its frame ready for printing.

foxed or foxing Brownish-yellow spots (i.e. fox-coloured) which discolour the plates and leaves of a book. Foxing is usually due to faulty bleaching during the manufacture of the paper.

frontispiece An illustration placed before the preliminary leaves of a book, usually facing the title-page.

galleys The earliest proofs taken before the type has been locked in the forme. Unlike page proofs, galleys are printed on long continuous strips.

gathering A quire or section of leaves. A *gathering* is the term used by binders for the folded printed sheets laid ready in groups of leaves for combining in the correct order to make the book.

gauffred edges The gilt edges of the leaves of a book that have been impressed with a design by the use of heated tools.

gilt edges The edges of a book after they have been cut smooth and gilded.

gothic letter *Black letter* type-face, such as used in the earliest printed books.

Grangerised Books that have been extra-illustrated.

guarded A plate or leaf of text which has been glued by its inside edge to a stub. Often used for illustrations that have been printed separately from the text.

gutta-percha An early type of rubber solution sometimes termed *caoutchouc*. Extensively used in the 1860s for the coffee-table books. Examples that have survived in near perfect state have to be carefully handled as the gutta-percha has nearly always perished and the leaves easily become loose and detached.

half-title The leaf preceding the title-page which has on its recto the title of the work (often in abbreviated form). Half-titles are not called for in all books. In rebound books where they should be present they have often been removed during the binding.

Halkett & Laing The affectionate title for the *Dictionary of Anonymous and Pseudonymous English Literature,* originally edited by Samuel Halkett and John Laing. The work has now been extended to 9 volumes in a new and enlarged edition, 1926–62.

headband A silk or cotton band of decorative appearance found fastened inside the top of the spine of a book as part of the binding process.

head-piece A vignette or type-ornament appearing at the start of a section of a book.

high-spot A fashionable first or important edition.

hinge An inside or outside joint of the binding of a book.

historiated Decorated capital letters and borders in early books and manuscripts, usually by means of painted figures of men and animals depicting scenes from history.

hollow-back Few things mar a binding as much as a once hollow-backed book that has had the spine glued down. The term is self-descriptive, and this process of binding has been in general use since the early 19th century.

horae Books of Hours. These are manuscripts or printed collections of prayers made for private use by Roman Catholics. Most were produced in Paris, but during the 14th and 15th centuries these often lavishly decorated horae appeared with many designations.

horn-book A tablet of wood, leather, metal or other material, shaped rather like an old-fashioned butter-pat, containing in a recess a sheet of printed or written paper protected from dirt and grubby fingers by a transparent sheet of thin horn. The alphabet, the Lord's Prayer, and perhaps the ten digits, appeared on the sheet for the children to read and were kept clean by the sheet of horn. The illustration on page 87 shows the first printed example of a horn-book in use. They were popular with the children who delighted to use them as bats in playground games. Dating from the middle of the 16th century they were still in common use in the early 1700s.

illuminated Initial letters, etc., hand decorated in gold, silver, and water-colours. Most often found on vellum manuscripts. Whole pages were sometimes illuminated in magnificent style.

impression The number of copies of an edition printed at any one time.

imprimatur The licence to print. The *imprimatur leaf* or *licence leaf* was usually the first leaf in the book and was common in the 16th and 17th centuries.

imprint A note telling of those responsible for the production of the book in which it is printed.

incunabula A book printed during the infancy of printing from movable metal type. See the chapter on incunabula, p.22ff.

India paper Thin paper used for printing proofs of engravings. Sometimes called *China paper*.

inlaid Coloured leathers recessed into cut-outs in the main skin of a binding. When applied to paper the term means the insertion of a plate (or a leaf of text) in a cut-out made in a larger leaf so as to bring it up to the size of the book.

inscribed copy A written inscription in a book, etc., made by the author himself.

inscription A written name, phrase or comment made in a book, etc., but *not* (unless so described) made by the author of the work.

inserted leaves Advertisements, etc., tipped into a book during or after the binding process.

interleaved A book bound with blanks specially placed

between the printed leaves so that they can be used for hand-written notes, etc.

integral leaf A leaf which is part of the gathering in which it appears.

issue A printing impression which may contain 'points' which narrow the dating of the copies then published. Copies of the same edition of a book may exhibit variations in the text, etc., where corrections or additions have been made or excisions have been carried out. These constitute differing *states* or *issues* of that particular edition and may possibly accord priority of publication or the reverse.

japon vellum A smooth glossy paper rather like vellum in appearance and often used for special *editions de luxe*. Unlike real vellum, it cannot be cleaned and to attempt to rub out even a pencil mark is to court disaster.

key book A milestone denoting a particular phase of human endeavour. Usually the earliest (or most important) work in its own particular field. Darwin's *On the Origin of Species,* 1859, provides a classic example.

label Labels may be made of leather or paper. Leather labels (or lettering pieces) were glued to the spines of books as early as the latter half of the 17th century. They were nearly always morocco leather even though the main body of the book was bound in calf or russia.

Paper labels were sometimes engraved but usually printed in type. They were pasted on the spines of boarded books from the 1760s onwards. Cloth bindings gradually displaced them from the 1830s onwards, but they were still appearing on cloth spines as late as the 1850s. Esoteric revivals of the paper-label style have taken place at intervals since that date, notably in the 1890s and mid-1920s.

laid paper Paper that has been made in a wire frame or mould. This consisted of parallel wires and the marks of these can be distinguished. *Wove paper* is made on a mesh of wire and the parallel lines are therefore not present.

large paper copy A book in which the leaves are of a larger size than that of the rest of the edition. Usually commanding a higher price and sometimes having the plates (where present) in two differing states.

lettering piece A leather label.

levant A highly polished morocco leather displaying a loose-grained surface. Originally produced in the Levant, it now mostly comes from South Africa.

limited edition An edition which is limited to a warranted number of copies. This can vary (in my own experience) from 5 copies to 1,000 or more. The copies are often numbered by hand and signed by the author and/or other interested parties.

longitudinal title Found in books in the latter half of the 17th century, these titles were printed in large type on a blank leaf at the beginning or end of the book. They were apparently for cutting out and pasting on the spine of the book when bound, but many still remain in their original positions.

loose 'Loose in case' means that the interior of the volume is in danger of parting company with its cloth binding. This can be simply corrected by a binder, invisibly and without destroying any of the original characteristics of the book.

Lowndes A reference work given in the bibliography (see p. 14).

made-up copy A sophisticated copy of a book that, without additions, would have been imperfect. This usually takes the form of missing leaves or plates being inserted from another copy of the same work.

marbled paper Marbled papers were used in England from the middle of the 17th century, mostly for end-papers. Vividly coloured, they were manufactured by lowering sheets of prepared paper on to trays containing sticky size, on the surface of which wide-toothed combs had stirred varying patterns in the dyes. They were a favourite material for boards of half-bound books in the Victorian era and earlier.

margin A collector will prefer a book with wide margins to one of the same edition that has been cropped during binding. 'Meadows of margin' is a delightfully descriptive phrase culled from a 19th-century antiquarian bookseller's catalogue. 'Margins thumbed' is as off-putting as 'dog-eared'.

mint copy A book indistinguishable from new.

misbound Used to denote a plate that has found its way into the wrong place, or an entire gathering that has been wrongly folded or bound in other than its proper position. If no part of the book is missing, a misbound plate or gathering is a fault to be forgiven and has little effect on the value of a work.

misprint An error made during the printing. Issue 'points' and states are born of such human failings. But it is often very difficult to draw firm bibliographical conclusions from such errata without other supporting evidence.

morocco A leather made from goat-skin that can be readily dyed to almost any colour. Hard-wearing, supple and pleasant to the eye, it has been a favourite with bookbinders from the earliest days. There are many differing types of morocco leathers, of which *levant, hard-grain, straight-grain,* and *niger* are the most commonly met with.

mottled calf Calf leather that has been flicked over with copperas acid, thus giving it a mottled effect.

mounted Damaged leaves which have been strengthened by backing with paper or gauze of some sort. The word is also used to denote an illustration that has been pasted down or lightly tipped on to a blank leaf, or into a space left in the text of the book.

octavo The most usual size of book. The average modern novel is almost always in octavo size. Denoted as 8vo in catalogues, the leaves collate in eights – with special exceptions.

offprint A section of a larger publication extracted and sometimes given its own pagination. Offprints sometimes have their own individual wrappers or other binding, and are usually run off from the original setting of type in which the larger work appeared.

offset The shadowy image of ink from an adjoining printed page or plate transferred accidentally due to damp or pressure.

olivine edges Varnished leaf edges of a shiny grey/green colour common on children's books from 1883 onwards.

pagination The consecutive sequence of numerals by which pages in a book are numbered. *Irregular pagination* can mean a mistake on the part of the printer of the work (a common error) or that a gathering has either been misbound or is missing.

pallet The binder's name on a signed leather binding, or the tool used for doing this.

panelled Ruled lines forming squares, oblongs, etc., on bindings, whether gilt or blind, cause the work to be described as panelled.

paper boards Boards used for binding the sides of a book, usually covered with plain paper. *Original boards* has come to mean the same thing in bookseller's catalogues.

parchment Split sheepskin like thin vellum; used for binding as well as for deeds and special manuscript work.

parts; part issues Novels have appeared in weekly or monthly parts since about 1830, with such best-sellers as Charles Dickens's *Pickwick Papers*, 1836–7, setting the pace which others were quick to follow. At the end of a paper-wrappered parts issue the work was usually issued as a single volume in publisher's cloth. But those who had read the story as a periodical often had the complete set of parts bound up at the end of the issue. Half-calf or half-morocco was a favourite method of binding for the part issues of the novels of the period, and the original stab-holes can usually be detected in the inside margins of the leaves where the (now discarded) wrappers were sewn. The late 1870s saw the last of them.

paste-down The outer half of the end-paper pasted on the inside of the front and back covers of a book.

pictorial cloth Pictures printed direct on to cloth bindings started in the 1830s. I give an illustration of the first fully pictorial cloth cover, issued in 1834 (see p. 109).

pictorial paper covers In December, 1852, Ingram, Cooke & Co., issued Horace Mayhew's *Letters left at the Pastrycook's* (dated 1853); followed in April, 1853 by *Money: How to Get, How to Keep, and How to Use It*. These two books started the 'yellow-back' era, being the forerunners of those multi-coloured eye-catching publications designed as cheap reading for the masses. *Money*, printed predominantly in yellow, probably gave the name to the series. The first issues were in paper wrappers, later to appear in paper-covered boards which almost immediately became the format for all 'yellow-backs'.

pigskin A tough leather binding sometimes decorated in blind. Inclined to become brittle with age.

pirated edition An unauthorised edition marketed (often abroad) without payment to the author.

plate mark The indented mark made in the leaf on which an engraving has been printed by use of a metal plate.

plates Full-page illustrations printed separately from the text.

pointille Gilt dots applied to leather bindings.

points Facts regarding the physical make-up of a book. These sometimes help to establish priority of issue.

prelims Short for *preliminary leaves,* being those leaves which precede the text of a book. They are nearly always the last to be printed.

presentation copy A volume that contains an inscription showing it to be a gift from the author, publisher, etc.

press book A book issued by a private press.

press-mark A mark denoting where the book is kept in a library, usually written or stamped on the spine.

pristine condition Original condition. Applied to an un-sophisticated copy of a book.

private press A printing house not beholden to publishers. The owner may conduct the press himself, or employ printers to do the work for him. But he chooses the works to be published and sets out how they are to be printed and bound. The editions issued are usually strictly limited in size.

privately printed A work produced at the expense of the author or other private persons. It is not distributed through commercial channels. Often the refuge of the egotist.

proofs Trial impressions taken from type to which corrections may be made by the author and/or others. *Proofs before letters* are impressions taken of engravings at the beginning of the run and before the crispness has worn off the plate. They contain no caption or other printed matter.

provenance The history of a book's previous ownership. Book-plates, signatures, coats-of-arms, secret marks, etc., may give us evidence that enable us to trace the hands through which it has passed and the shelves upon which it has stood.

publisher's cloth Conceived as a temporary binding in the 1820s before the volume should be leather bound, the use of cloth for edition-binding had become general in both Britain and the U.S.A. by the mid-1830s. A type of watered-silk derived from dress material was amongst the first style of publisher's cloth to be used and appeared on the annuals of the period. A tough and hard-wearing hessian cloth had been used since the 1760s for the binding of school text-books, etc.

quarter-bound A volume with a leather spine, the sides covered with paper or cloth, and without leather protective corners, is *quarter-bound.*

quarto A book between folio and octavo in size. The leaves collate in fours (with certain exceptions). Sometimes written '4to'.

quire A gathering or collection of printed sheets. One-twentieth of a ream.

raised bands Ridges on the spine of a book, containing cords of sewing used in the binding.

reading copy The text of a book still in readable condition. The binding is usually soiled and/or tattered.

re-backed The hinges of a leather-bound book are the first to wear. If these become badly cracked the spine may be lost or need renewing. A book given a new spine is said to have been *re-backed.*

re-cased A book removed from its covers and then replaced, usually with the addition of new end-papers. With care this method of saving the life of a book can restore it almost (but never quite) to its original condition.

recto The front, or obverse, side of a leaf. Its opposite is called the *verso.*

register A guide for the binder in the form of a list of signature letters, usually at the end of a book.

re-issue Any issue but the first.

remainder binding When a book is no longer a commercial proposition, the publisher may dispose of the unsold sheets to a wholesaler or other interested dealer. This is called *remaindering,* and the new owner of the printed sheets has them bound up and sold at a cheaper price than the book previously commanded. This *remainder binding* will usually differ considerably from the original. In the 19th century, three-volume novels were often *remaindered* as a single volume.

re-margined A frayed copy of a leaf of text or (more often) a frontispiece may have to have one or more of its original margins renewed. It is then said to have been *re-margined.*

remboîtage The use of a leather binding for a book other than that for which it was originally intended. A valuable text may be removed from an indifferent binding and recased in a more elegant or better-looking binding. This binding, taken from another book, will have had its original labels removed and new ones substituted.

reprint A new impression from the same setting of type. Also used for an entirely new edition.

re-set A new setting of type. A leaf or plate that has become loose in a book is *re-set* by the use of paste or glue.

review copy A copy of a book sent out in the hope of attracting a review of the work. Review slips and review stamps are sometimes found in these copies, usually giving evidence that it is of the earliest issue of that particular edition.

rings at auction Dealers who take part in the criminal practice of defrauding the owner of a work of art, etc., of its market price at auction. They agree not to bid against each other, then re-auction the work privately at a settlement or knock-out, sharing amongst themselves the difference in the article's true value and the price they depressed it to at public auction. The practice is all but unknown in the U.S.A. but is common in Britain and in Europe.

roan A cheap type of leather that easily peels off a book in strips.

romantique binding Brightly coloured block-bindings examples of which are given in the illustrations. *Cartonnages Romantiques* on cloth and paper covered boards were extensively used in France during the period 1845–80, especially as an attractive binding for children's books.

rough or reversed calf Unpolished suède-like leather used for works of reference since the latter half of the 18th century. Johnson's *Dictionary* was issued in a publisher's binding of reversed calf in two volumes in 1755.

Roxburghe binding A distinctive style of binding devised by the Roxburghe Club. It was a quarter-binding with a flat leather spine lettered in gilt, usually a dull red or green, with paper-covered boards. The Roxburghe Club dates from the time of the sale of the Duke of Roxburghe's books in 1812.

rubbed A binding that has been scuffed by friction of some sort.

rubric The heading of a chapter written or printed in red. Initial letters were also often rubricated by being hand-painted in red.

russia leather A rich dark leather having a characteristic smell due to the introduction of birch-bark oil into the dye. Made from cowhide, it was in vogue for bookbinding in the late 18th and early 19th centuries.

secondary binding Not a remainder binding, but the issue of the printed sheets that were not bound up for immediate publication when the book first appeared. A slow-selling book may be bound up a few hundred at a time during the period of several years as copies are called for by the booksellers. The bindings vary on each occasion, often only slightly, but usually sufficient to make detection easy.

section A gathering of printed sheets in a book.

serialisation Fiction is sometimes reprinted after its appearance as a book, or first appears in serial form in a newspaper or magazine before being issued in book form. Both are *serialisations*. Defoe's *Robinson Crusoe* appeared as a serial in *The London Post* as long ago as 1719.

sewed and stitched Gatherings of printed sheets are sewn vertically, and sometimes a particularly slender volume may be issued sewn in this naked state, without as much as a wrapper to clothe it. 'Stitched as issued' would be the bookseller's description.

shaken A cloth book that is loose in its covers, or one that has gatherings loose, is said to be *shaken* or *shaky*.

shaved Cropped close by the binder so that some of the wording or numerals have been *shaved* by the knife.

sheep A cheap leather often used for binding early children's books. Like roan, it is inclined to peel off in long strips.

sheet The unfolded sheet as used by the printer.

shelf-mark A press-mark.

short-title Often used for hand-lists and indexes, a short-title gives just sufficient words for the work to be recognised.

shoulder-notes Notes printed at the top of a page in the outer margin.

side-notes Notes printed in the outer margin alongside the text.

signatures Numerals or letters of the alphabet printed in the tail-margin of the first leaf of each gathering of a book. They enable the binder to collect up and bind the gatherings in the correct order. Preliminary leaves, being printed after the rest of the book is made up, often do not have a *signature* letter or other mark.

silked Fragile leaves are sometimes strengthened by a transparent material to extend their life and are then said to be *silked*. The modern method is to spray a fine mist of plastic material on to the leaf.

singleton A single leaf, not conjugate with any other.

'sixties' books Lavishly illustrated and finely produced cloth-bound books of the period *c*. 1845–70. Most popular in the 1860s their woodcut illustrations attracted the talents of the most eminent artists. Also known as *coffee-table books*.

skiver A cheap type of thinly split leather that has been tanned in sumach. Used for lining hats, but sometimes used for cheap bookbinding.

slip case A box into which a book can be slipped and which shows the spine.

solander case A type of box for preserving the bindings of books. Invented by D. C. Solander (1736–82) it has a fall-down front held by a spring-catch.

sophisticated copy A made-up copy of a book, not in its original pristine state.

spine The backstrip of a book.

sprinkled A leather binding speckled with marks of a contrasting colour. Usually found on calf bindings, and also on the edges of leaves and visible when the book is closed.

stab-holes Part-issues of books were often sewn through sideways, leaving holes in the inner margins when the stitches were later removed.

stapled Wire staples are still used to hold together the leaves of magazines, but they rust with age and are unsatisfactory for bound books.

state Applied to illustrations, this means the evidence of first or later use of the engraving given by signs of re-etching, wear, re-engraving, the adding of additional matter in the form of words, etc. Normally speaking, the earlier the *state* the more desirable the plate.

stereotype A technique widely used in the U.S.A. in the 19th century, enabling numerous reprints to be made without using the original type. This enables the type to be distributed and put to other uses. A solid plate of type-metal is made from a plaster or papier-mâché mould, thus giving an impression of the original type. This is then used for printing new copies of the book.

sprung Gatherings which have become proud and displaced in a book are said to have *sprung*. They are difficult to sew or glue back invisibly and spoil the appearance of the volume.

straight-grain morocco A morocco with artificially induced grain in a pattern of straight lines giving a pleasing texture. Used since the middle of the 18th century for the more expensive styles of binding.

stub A narrow strip of paper on the inside margin of a book. Sometimes left there intentionally, but always worthy of investigation in case a leaf or plate has been cut away and removed.

sub-title An explanatory-title, used in addition to the main title of a work.

suppressed A passage or a whole book may be *suppressed* and withdrawn from circulation, or an attempt may be made to do so. Hilaire Belloc's first book, *Verses and Sonnets,* 1896, was suppressed by the author as containing 'more than one piece which I thought below the sufficient standard, so that I have long withdrawn it from publication and had the copies destroyed . . .' But a few copies always seem to escape and are enhanced in value by their rarity. The first edition of *Alice in Wonderland,* 1865, gives us a classic example.

tail   The lower edge of a leaf.

tail-piece   An ornamental device at the end of a chapter.

three-decker   A three-volume book, nearly always a novel of the 19th century.

ties   The silk tapes or ribbons threaded through the extreme outer edge of a binding (usually vellum) intended to tie the book shut when laced together.

tipped in   A plate or leaf, etc., lightly glued into a book.

tissues   Protective tissue-papers inserted opposite plates to prevent them off-setting on to the text.

title   Usually taken to mean the title-page. 'Lacks its title' spells doom to a book, at least as far as I myself am concerned.

tooling   'Tooled in gilt – or blind' are the terms used for the impressions made by binders' metal implements used in finishing a book.

tree calf   Calf leather binding stained by the action of copperas acid and pearl-ash to give it a grained effect not unlike walnut.

trimmed   The edges of leaves that have been roughly cut level by the binder. Leaf edges that are absolutely smooth are usually referred to as *cut*.

type facsimile   A reprint of a book in which the aim has been to approach as near to the appearance of the original or earlier printing as possible.

uncut   A book in which the edges of the leaves have not been cut or trimmed. *Unopened* means that the leaves have not been severed from their neighbours by a person wishing to read the book.

unopened   See *uncut*.

unpressed   A book that has not been subjected to the binder's

press. The leaves are therefore somewhat crinkled, giving the volume a greater thickness than is usual.

variant   For often unexplained reasons copies of the same edition display variations. These can be in the text, the binding, or even on the title-page. Differing cloth colours of the same edition are often met with, especially in books produced during the latter half of the 19th century. Several bolts of cloth were used by the binders at one and the same time, and they chose the colours at random. No priority of issue can be attributed to a particular copy on that score, unless other evidence can be evinced in support. The same observation applies to most other minor variations in format.

vellum   The untanned skin of a goat, sheep or calf, specially treated so that it can be written or printed on. Most old manuscripts were written on vellum, and a few copies of some of the most famous of early books have used this material instead of paper.
   Limp vellum was often used in the binding of books, and Carnan used it, stained green, for the spines of his children's books in the 1770s.

verso   The backside of a leaf, the front of which is called the *recto*.

vignette   A small pictorial design, used as a head- or tail-piece to a chapter in a book. It is not enclosed in a frame or border.

washed   The cleaning and probably the defoxing of leaves is called *washing*. Bleach is used to remove the stains, but this chemical must afterwards be scrupulously rinsed out or damage will eventually result. After washing, the leaf is resized, if it needs it (see p. 20).

watermark   An emblem incorporated in the wire of the paper-making tray, the outline of which can be seen when the finished paper is held to the light. Watermarks help in the identification of the paper in which they appear and are also useful in collating and dating a book.

wrappers   A paper-backed book is said to be in *wrappers*. The word means a book bound in paper wrappers, rather than a hard-back however it is bound.

yapp   *Yapp* is a style of binding, named after its inventor, in which the edges of the book are overlapped by the material used for binding. This is usually limp leather of a suède appearance.

yellow-back   See *pictorial paper covers*.

Illustration from the title page of the first edition of Oliver Wendell Holmes' *Over the Teacups*. The first American edition, dated 1891, did not appear until several weeks after the edition printed in England.

Opposite
A 19th-century 'dummy' book; the type having been set in preparation for the water-colour designs of the artist F. A. Lydon (1836–1917). He integrated a series of water-colour drawings with the letterpress, as shown here; but the book was not published. This unique copy is complete with 12 full-page original water-colours, the title-page being shown.

Over page, left
Typical of the elaborate gift books of the sixties period, known as 'coffee-table books' or 'sixties' books. Collected as much for their fine woodcut illustrations as for the quality of their cloth or morocco bindings; the title shown here was published in 1866 by George Routledge & Sons.

Size of front cover:
26cm × 20cm.

Over page, right
An original water-colour drawing made *c.* 1850 for the page of the Victorian album illustrated opposite page 137.

Sizes to edges of
page: 32cm × 25cm.

L'ALLEGRO

AND

IL PENSEROSO

BY JOHN MILTON.

ILLUSTRATED BY F. A. LYDON

LONDON:
GROOMBRIDGE AND SONS, 5, PATERNOSTER-ROW.

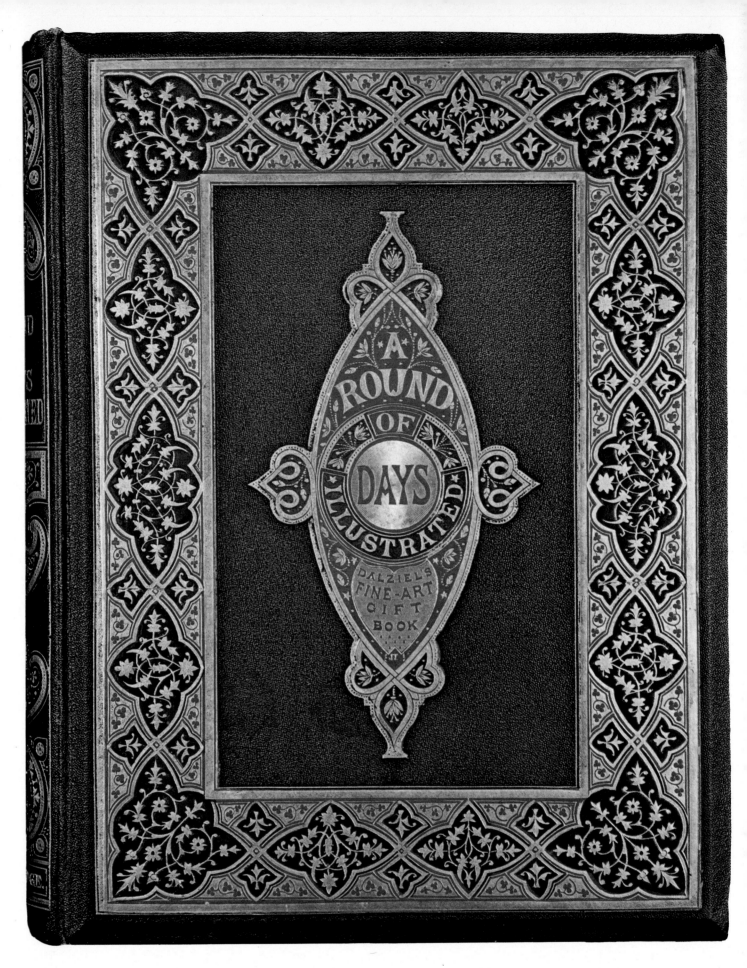

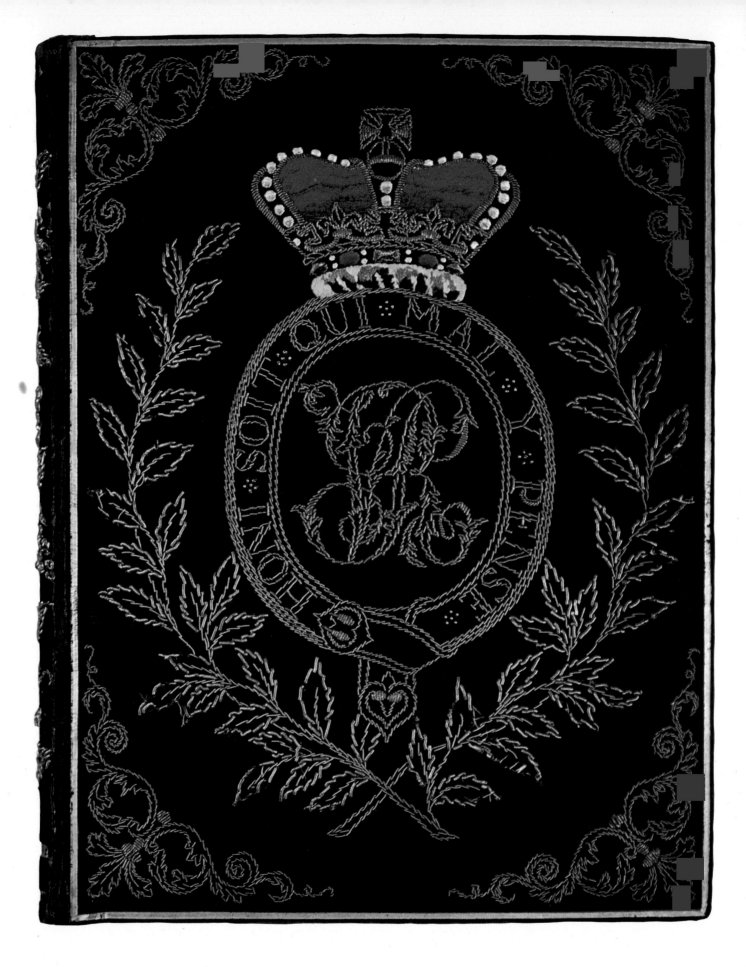